Rocking the Closet

NEW PERSPECTIVES
ON GENDER IN MUSIC

Editorial Advisors
Susan C. Cook
Beverley Diamond

*A list of books in the series appears
at the end of this book.*

Rocking the Closet

HOW LITTLE RICHARD, JOHNNIE RAY, LIBERACE, AND JOHNNY MATHIS QUEERED POP MUSIC

Vincent L. Stephens

UNIVERSITY OF
ILLINOIS PRESS
Urbana, Chicago, and Springfield

Publication of this book was supported by a grant from the AMS 75 PAYS Endowment of the American Musicological Society, funded in part by the National Endowment for the Humanities and the Andrew W. Mellon Foundation.

Manufactured in the United States of America
1 2 3 4 5 C P 5 4 3 2 1
∞ This book is printed on acid-free paper.

Library of Congress Cataloging-in-Publication Data

Names: Stephens, Vincent L. author.
Title: Rocking the closet: how Little Richard, Johnnie Ray, Liberace, and Johnny Mathis queered pop music / Vincent L. Stephens.
Description: Urbana : University of Illinois Press, [2019] | Series: New perspectives on gender in music |
Identifiers: LCCN 2019013782 (print) | LCCN 2019014569 (ebook) | ISBN 9780252051661 (ebook) | ISBN 9780252042805 (cloth : alk. paper) | ISBN 9780252084638 (pbk. : alk. paper)
Subjects: LCSH: Homosexuality and popular music—United States. | Gay musicians—United States. | Gay singers—United States. | Music and race—United States. | Little Richard, 1932- | Ray, Johnnie, 1927–1990. | Liberace, 1919–1987. | Mathis, Johnny.
Classification: LCC ML3477 (ebook) | LCC ML3477 .S75 2019 (print) | DDC 781.64086/640973—dc23
LC record available at https://lccn.loc.gov/2019013782

For Harry Bakst, Thaddeus Davis,
Paula Harwood, Alex Tizon, and Clyde Woods,
whose creative imprints endure

Contents

Preface

I OFTEN FEEL LIKE A TRAITOR to my generation, at least musically. Based on my vintage (circa, *ahem*, the mid-1970s), I was born into the era of disco and soft rock, but I quickly converted to the gospel of MTV, including dalliances with mainstream pop, college rock, rap, and new jack swing, and then graduated to hip-hop and modern rock. According to the doctrine of what Kelefa Sanneh calls "rockism," at my age I am supposed to be nostalgic for masculine "alternative music," such as Nirvana and R.E.M., and the "classic hip-hop" of Run DMC, 2Pac, and the Notorious B.I.G., and I should also be yearning for "real music" to return (Sanneh 2007, 351–52).

Alas, much of the music I *actually* listened to as a child and the music that has sustained me for most of my adult life is not necessarily the most masculine or critically *respected* music. Much of my favorite music actually harks back to a gentler era of pop music before rock 'n' roll. It is true that in college I purchased an array of cassette tapes (which eventually gave way to CDs) spanning from the soothing soft rock of Christopher Cross to the *unhip* 1980s and 1990s pop music that was my adolescent bread and butter: epic adult contemporary ballads and neo-disco dance pop as sung by Mariah Carey, Taylor Dayne, and Whitney Houston. Definitely *not* rock.

I was simultaneously becoming something of a pop-music collector and scholar, probing music history genre by genre and listening to disco artists like Donna Summer, lush Philly Soul groups like The Spinners, the idiosyncratic melodies and offbeat harmonies of singer-songwriter Laura Nyro, 1960s rock (Creedence Clearwater Revival), 1960s soul (for example, Otis Redding, Sam & Dave), classic singing groups and Motown (the Drifters, the Shirelles, the Supremes, the Temptations), and prerock pop/jazz artists like Nat "King" Cole, among many. By graduate school, I was plumbing the depths of vocal jazz divas like Sarah Vaughan and Ella Fitzgerald and exploring related genres, including cabaret.

By the standards of the rock-music critical establishments, my tastes were not entirely *respectable*. Soft rock, diva pop, disco, and cabaret are particularly suspect; they are too soft, emotive, expressive, stylized, and ultimately too feminine and too *queer* to be respected by what has long been a very masculine, heteronormative critical view of what matters in music. Anger, aggression, carnality, and rage are viewed, contemporarily, as emotions that are more meaningful. The parallels between these gendered values were not lost on me when I began my initial research in the early 2000s. Originally, I planned to conduct an ethnographic study of music listeners to explore the ways in which values of authenticity surface in their tastes and preferences. The more I studied notions of authenticity within critical writing on popular music, the more I began to understand how biased this discourse is toward the music produced and/or frequently enjoyed by certain populations, especially girls, women, and queer men.

These biases intrigued me and led me to explore the notion of *queer* music, which I narrowed down to a study of critical responses to queer musicians of the post–World War II era. As I was learning about figures as disparate as Liberace, Dusty Springfield, and Sylvester, I was also reading some relatively recent work by scholars like Wayne Koestenbaum, D. A. Miller, and Christopher Nealon. Their works, Koestenbaum's *The Queen's Throat* (1993), Miller's *Place for Us* (1998), and Nealon's *Foundlings* (2001), were notable for questioning the false assumption that queer life before the Stonewall riots of June 1969 was merely a dress rehearsal for today's more political and liberated community. Heather Love's *Feeling Backward* (2007) also complemented these observations by directly questioning the glossing over of historical shame for the more positive and affirming pride of today. Each author enlightened me intellectually to embrace the continuity of queer experiences across time and generations, rather than to settle for an easier and more digestible teleological narrative of LGBTQ history. I found this approach more honest and satisfying and therefore decided to focus the research on queer musicians who began their careers before the formal political movements sparked by the Stonewall riots.

In examining the careers of the featured artists in *Rocking the Closet*— Liberace, Johnnie Ray, Johnny Mathis, and Little Richard—I found myself appreciating their deft and occasionally sophisticated ability to navigate what could have been a very dangerous and treacherous territory. I also examined the music of Dusty Springfield, Laura Nyro, Elton John, and the women's music movement (see Stephens 2005). Homophobia, genderphobia, racism, and other forms of discrimination posed serious threats to their livelihoods not only as professional entertainers but also as citizens. Individually, they were able to circumvent certain societal prejudices through a mix of calculation, coincidence, and luck. The stories I tell about Liberace, Ray, Mathis, and Little Richard are tied together by the *queering tools* each artist used and by their ambivalent relationship to identifying sexually. But they are very much individual stories about the process of becoming, rather than the stories of a broad movement. Some artists maintained the illusion of sexual availability, while others were nearly undone when they, or their strategies, were questioned publicly.

I intentionally avoid our present-day tendency to label pre-Stonewall queers as *closeted* because this term misses the nuances of their negotiations. At the height of these artists' popularity, many people may have deduced their sexual orientations, based on their deviations from typical masculinity, and still listened to their music. Others were arguably drawn to the fact that these artists were *different* from the norm in pop music. Some people are undoubtedly still in denial. Clearly, the relationship between these performers and their audiences involved some forms of exchange and of interaction that were pleasurable enough to transcend some of the prejudices associated with the postwar era. The elusions they performed were part of this exchange and integral to the range of pleasures they offered both musically and affectively. Even after decades of political organizing around queer visibility, the pleasures of "queering tools" and sexual ambiguity endures in the careers of more contemporary performers like Adam Lambert, Ricky Martin, and Sam Smith.

Writing *Rocking the Closet* illuminated the cultural riches of the queer past, even in its fragmented, jagged form, and, more personally, it also narrowed the gap between the past and the present in my own head. Growing up as a queer-identified person, I, like my preferred music, was often *too much*. My affective excesses belied a proper boy-child and my peers marked me as "different." Like many queer people, I endured an incalculable amount of personal anguish about my place in the world for a long time. But, through sheer will, I persisted through the layers of internal and external homophobia. The momentum that has propelled me forward, through various sociopolitical victories and backlashes related to LGBTQ life, derives from a variety of movements, figures, and tactics, including but not limited to the Stonewall riots. The four stories I profile, and their relationship to the present, are significant to me because they highlight the ongoing struggles, regardless of politics, that surround our ability to render the most intimate parts of ourselves publicly, honestly, and humanely.

Acknowledgments

WRITING *ROCKING THE CLOSET* is the result of years of thinking, rethinking, writing, rewriting, debating, discussing, and constantly challenging myself to delve deeply and widely into the lives and careers of the artists I discuss and thereby expanding my intellectual outlook in numerous ways. I am grateful to a number of people who have helped me with this journey.

I am grateful to John Caughey, Bill Cohen, Sheri Parks, and the late Clyde Woods for their expert guidance. I am especially thankful to Nancy L. Struna, who has always challenged me and championed my work. I feel blessed to have worked with her.

I thank my parents Betty Brown and Ralph Stephens not only for caring about education and creativity but also for encouraging me to pursue my interests.

I am eternally grateful for the support of my dear friend and "sister" Carmen Gillespie. She always encourages me to have faith in my writing and ideas even when I do not. A person could not ask for a truer friend or for a better conversational partner. To the Gillespie ladies, Chelsea and Delaney, I love you; you too are an important part of the story.

My dear friend Koritha Mitchell is a great person, a challenging teacher, and an accomplished scholar who was there during the genesis of this project. I am in awe of her intelligence and vigor, and I deeply respect the work she does as an activist and scholar.

Special thanks to Eric and Susan (and Tim and Seth!) who have been sustaining forces in my life for so long; life would be unimaginable without you.

Many thanks to Theo Cateforis for being an inspiring scholar and true colleague.

I thank Dawn Johnson and Joelle Davis Carter for being great friends at Maryland and beyond!

A shout out to my dear friends and colleagues at the University of Maryland College Park, Syracuse University, Bucknell University, and Dickinson College who have supported, encouraged, entertained, and challenged me in incomparable ways. I am especially grateful to Gary Steiner for reading an earlier version of chapter 5; Peg Cronin for help in crafting my prospectus; Donna Bickford for listening to me work things out; Jerry Philogene for recommending several helpful books on Harry Belafonte; Helene Lee and Katie Schweighofer for being supportive writing partners; Maiko Arashiro, Say Burgin, Stacey Moultry, Naila Smith, Amaury Sosa and Eddie Tu for moral support; Riccardo Dragani for his photographic eye; and Julia Savage-Lee for vital technical support.

A special thanks to poet Abdul Ali, whose poem "In Nineteen Eighty-Four" in *Trouble Sleeping* (2015) partially inspired my preface.

This publication is possible through a publication grant awarded by the Dickinson College Research and Development Committee.

Elements of chapter 4 were published previously in 2010's "Shaking the Closet: Analyzing Johnny Mathis's Sexual Elusiveness, 1956–1982," *Popular Music and Society* 33 (5): 597–623.

Finally, I appreciate the insights of the University of Illinois Press's Laurie Mathieson and Julie Laut, and three insightful reviewers for taking a genuine interest in shaping *Rocking the Closet* into a book and for providing essential editorial advice.

Introduction

Queering Post–World War II
Masculinity through Music

THE DEATHS OF DAVID BOWIE, Prince, and George Michael in 2016 inspired a number of writers to reflect on the ways these performers challenged male gender norms of their time (Devega 2016; Morris 2016; Rosenberg 2016; Street 2016). Despite the conservative tenor of the 1970s and 1980s, they defied the zeitgeist and attracted mainstream audiences.[1] Looking back at several earlier generations of musicians reveals that audiences have enjoyed and embraced male performers who challenged the conventions of masculinity in popular music, otherwise known as "queering," since the early 1950s. The Queer Quartet, who serve as the focus of *Rocking the Closet*—Johnnie Ray, Little Richard, Johnny Mathis, and Liberace—were prominent cultural figures who achieved significant commercial success in the 1950s. These musicians employed a discernible group of queering techniques to shape their personae and build audiences. These techniques helped them navigate post–World World II male gender norms and have continued to inform the queering approaches of musicians who have followed them. Examining their careers informs my argument that queering expectations is an appealing and enduring artistic strategy in postwar popular music, not an incidental or tangential aspect of a musician's success.

The Quartet's success seemingly contradicts a common script about what was culturally permissible before the 1969 Stonewall riots. Katherine Schweighofer captures this suppressive framing of queer history by observing how

> the entire LGBT movement has been given a closet/coming out story as well: historians frequently refer to the movement's more visible moments (Stonewall and sometimes the Compton's Cafeteria riots) as coming-out

moments, with earlier decades (particularly the 1940s–1960s) as times characterized by secrecy, hiding, and loneliness. Ironically, although the closet
metaphor is usually intended to acknowledge and respect the difficulties
faced by earlier queer generations, it also forces individuals who lived beyond an in/out binary into an anachronistic closet, instead of truly reflecting the way sexuality shaped their lived identity. (Schweighofer 2016, 228)

The framing of queer history in such binary terms, between danger or visibility, elides the ways manipulations of gender propriety have informed the
careers and shaped the appeal of queer male musicians across eras and genre.

The notion of the closet, which is central to my analysis, relies on a static
public versus private boundary that obscures important nuances. There are
highly public people who thrived prior to the late 1960s who did not *come
out* as genderqueer or sexually queer but were assumed to identify outside of
heteronormative identities, based on behaviors that challenged the dominant
gender norms of the era. Not labeling themselves was not simply about cow-
ardice; rather, it provided them with mobility in certain instances, providing
them with an ambiguous appeal. It also reflected a struggle to clarify personal
identity and public expectations. Each case is different, but the popularity of
the Quartet suggests something palatable and acceptable about these musical
figures, regardless of their perceived or actual social identities. I entertain
several perceptive possibilities: their queerness, notably their diversion from
normative masculinity, may have been a *draw*; their queerness may have
given them less access, or no access, to certain cultural spaces; their queerness may have simply gone unnoticed to audiences, making certain gestures
a non-issue. This hidden history is obscured by the constant repetition of
formulaic queer historical narratives that have dominated and silenced the
range of stories. Studying queer musicians is an important mode of listening
more closely to the surfeit of elisions and slippages that made the postwar
era queerer and more dynamic than we have typically imagined.

Queering as a Popular Strategy

What is queerness and why is queerness important to my discussion? *Rocking
the Closet* employs the term *queer* to refer to "identities and practices that
foreground the instability inherent in the supposedly stable relationship
between anatomical sex, gender, and sexual desire" with an emphasis on
practices (Corber and Valocchi 2003, 1). While each man is cisgender—notably, they identify with their assigned sex at birth—the combination of their
bisexual orientations and the range of public behaviors they espoused that

fall outside of dominant masculine norms of the era places them in the queer axis. Central to studying queer practices is exposing the ideological fiction that works to stabilize heterosexuality and, by association, heteronormativity, "the set of norms that make heterosexuality seem natural or right and that organize homosexuality as its binary opposite" (4).

Queerness is an interrogative notion that allows us to question historical tropes like teleology.[2] In LGBT history the common narrative centers visibility as the hallmark of the post-Stonewall era and posts coming out as the signature act of liberation. Following this logic, contemporary musicians should no longer be hesitant about coming out because we have moved forward politically and socially as a nation, as measured by various judicial and legislative victories. Alas, this formulation is unsatisfying because it does not account for the ongoing social role of heteronormativity, homophobia, and genderphobia in twenty-first-century life, and it informs this study's concluding discussion of "queering" techniques among male musicians in a contemporary post-Stonewall society.

Gender deviance feeds speculation about sexual orientation, which compels musicians who deviate from gender expectations to convey a sexually ambiguous or elusive image. A male musician does not have to identify sexually as bisexual, gay, or omnisexual to queer the music, costuming, and performing apparatus associated with his act. But queering opens him up to speculation. Sexual elusiveness is an effect of queering behavior, and managing to convey ambiguity is an important and enduring way queer musicians have navigated their identities. The immediate benefit of elusiveness for musicians is their ability to survive commercially and socially during times when homophobia and genderphobia are socially acceptable. Though I focus on musicians who began recording nationally in the 1950s, it is essential to understand that musicians continue to employ "queering" strategies in the present as well.

When we take a closer look at popular culture after World War II, we can see that audiences were highly interested in novelty, exoticism, and difference. These interests surface in the mass consumption of popular music and are observable in popular film, literature, and other genres. For example, it is not coincidental that mainstream tabloids like *Confidential* focused on rumors of gender deviance and reached their commercial peaks in the 1950s. Throughout my discussion of the queering techniques musicians use I discuss some of the potential ways audiences may have read and interpreted the personae of the musicians.

Rocking the Closet focuses on queer public behavioral elements that challenged postwar masculinity in the artistry and personae of the musicians. Queer sexuality includes bisexuality, homosexuality, omnisexuality, and pansexuality. Each member of the Quartet is either bisexual or homosexual based on autobiographical and/or biographical accounts. As such, my critical concern is not the ontology of their sexuality. I am interested in how they managed to "queer" popular culture and simultaneously remain, or at least *attempt* to remain, sexually elusive.

For the record, Liberace claimed in his autobiography to have lost his virginity to a blues singer named "Miss Bea Haven" (Liberace 1986, 40). Many have interpreted this as a camp joke (*misbehavin'*), but this is what *he* has declared publicly. Scott Thorson, his lover from 1977 to 1982, has written about their sexual relationship and Liberace's claim that he first had sex with a man from Wisconsin in the 1940s and socialized in a network of gay men during this time (Thorson 2013, 17, 19). Johnnie Ray was arrested twice for soliciting male police officers. He also was married to Marilyn Morrison from 1952 to 1954 and had a long-term affair with columnist Dorothy Kilgallen. Little Richard discusses his identity as a former practicing homosexual in Charles White's 1984 biography. He was also married briefly to Ernestine Campbell (1959–1960). Johnny Mathis discussed his homosexuality in a 1982 interview with *Us Weekly* but said very little about his sexuality after that. A 1993 *New York Times* profile and a 2002 *London Observer* article featured one of the more public notices regarding his sexuality. In 2017 he discussed his sexuality openly on television for the first time on an episode of *CBS Sunday Morning*.[3]

Though each figure is sexually queer, I distinguish their sexual orientations from their public personae since their queer gender behavior is not dependent on their sexual orientation or self-identifications. This characteristic is equally true of other musical performers who have queered some aspect of popular music, such as Michael Jackson and Prince, but are not necessarily queer sexually. Even if the Quartet's members never identified their sexual orientation or had their orientations "outed" later, their public behavior discernibly queered the mainstream in historical terms. This study's focus is not to "out" them but instead to explore the range of strategies they used during the socially complex postwar era.

Postwar Masculinity and Popular Culture

Postwar White Masculinity

The men *Rocking the Closet* studies must be understood in the context of postwar masculine norms, which operated differently for white and African American men. These norms developed from ideas about gender solidified in the 1910s through the 1930s largely through popular culture. While many of these norms were constructed against effeminacy and homosexuality, audiences were surprisingly amenable to certain kinds of queer masculinity when they circulated in the realm of popular entertainment.

Michael Kimmel's 1996 classic study of masculinity, *Manhood in America*, identifies several dominant types of masculinity that define common understandings of the postwar era and describes the conflicting emotions they sparked among men. Organization men, sometimes referred to colloquially as "men in gray flannel suits," worked in America's booming postwar corporate sector. Many of these men were war veterans, and almost all were married men with children or were aspiring to fulfill these social roles. A core dilemma for these men was feeling emasculated and confined by corporate demands for conformity. Sloan Wilson's 1956 novel, *The Man in the Gray Flannel Suit*, captured this tension between the need to provide for their families, through adhering to corporate expectations, and the desire for greater individualism and adventure (Kimmel 2012, 185; S. Wilson 1956).

Kimmel observed the toll of pressure on men of the period to be reliable providers, good husbands, emotionally accessible fathers, and to maintain their individualism by referring to it as the "Goldilocks Dilemma." He notes, "Men had to achieve identities that weren't too conforming to the march of the empty gray flannel suits lest they lose their souls; but they couldn't be too nonconforming lest they leave family and workplace responsibilities behind in a frantic restless search for some elusive moment of ecstasy" (Kimmel 2012, 170). Kimmel's term partially derives from the archive of books and articles on postwar masculine anxiety, or the "male malaise of conformity," chronicled by multiple authors during the 1950s. C. Wright Mills, David Riesman, and William Whyte were key social "experts" who argued that modern men lacked identities in a world that defined them within corporate and familial boundaries (Coontz 2000, 37; Kimmel 2012, 173).

At the opposite end were rebels, or dangerous men who "threatened social stability, domestic harmony, and corporate responsibility." Delinquency, homosexuality, communist ties, and/or the Beatnik lifestyle were all threats constructed against normal masculinity. Countless social scientists and journalists warned parents to be leery of raising effeminate domesticated boys lest they become delinquent rebels striving to prove their masculinity in antisocial ways (Kimmel 2012, 176). Reactionary public figures like Senator Joseph McCarthy, along with his followers, also linked effeminacy with homosexuality and intellectualism, which, when viewed together, were imagined to make such men more vulnerable to communism (170–71).

The conformist masculine schema Kimmel outlines is a standard I use to assess the queerness of the study's male musicians. Notably, considering the era and the pervasiveness of expectations, I continually illustrate how the men featured in *Rocking the Closet* reflect, challenge, and complicate these standards. In summary, *normal* men in the postwar era aspired to participate in heterosexual marriage, establish and head a nuclear family, perform a vaguely defined *non-effeminate* masculinity, and adhere to a capitalist economic provider ethos.

These rigid formulations exclude many subject positions, such as hypermasculine rather than effeminate homosexual men and/or homosexual men who did not conform to the intellectual egghead stereotype. As such, these gaps also opened up room for queer masculinities to flourish especially when they elided crude, obvious stereotypes.

Post–World War II "Race Men"

Though society expected all men to conform to the notions above, missing from Kimmel's rich analysis is a thorough exploration of the relationship between American masculinity and American racial constructs after World War II. While Kimmel discusses *Native Son* and *Invisible Man* briefly (Kimmel 2012, 166, 174), I address the dual pressures for black men to serve as *race men* who demonstrated they were true *men* worthy of equal citizenship while still remaining socially respectable. This is essential to understanding the black men *Rocking the Closet* discusses.

Hazel Carby traces the roots of the race-man concept to the late nineteenth century via Alexander Crummell's formation of the American Negro Academy, an institution committed to training a new generation of intellectuals who would uplift the race by articulating "the great message we have for humanity" that was exclusively male (Carby 1998, 5). She also examines the deep influence of gendered notions of black leadership on W. E. B. Du Bois's influential vision of uplift in *The Souls of Black Folk* and intellectual descendants like Cornel West (9–41). Her larger argument analyzes the way social critics placed racial uplift primarily in the hands of men, to the exclusion of black women, but I focus on the practical functions of this construct for blacks, despite its limitations.[4] The term "race man," Mark Anthony Neal argues, "describes black men of stature and integrity who represented the best that African Americans had to offer in the face of Jim Crow segregation. It has lost some of its resonance in a post–civil rights world, but it remains an unspoken measure of commitment to uplifting the race" (Neal 2007). Similarly, Hillary Crosley cites the "earnest, dapper role model unabashedly committed to black uplift"—that is, actor, singer, and activist Harry Belafonte—as a quintessential example of a "race man" (Crosley 2013).

In the postwar era the "race man" concept gained greater prominence and significance via popular culture through athletes like Jackie Robinson and multimedia entertainers like Belafonte, Nat "King" Cole, and Sidney Poitier, among others. Gerald Early, in his *This Is Where I Came In* (2003), contextualizes the era: "From World War II on, American popular culture reflects the ever-intensifying need of the black male for self-assertion, particularly since this desire had been artificially and cruelly repressed before. Jackie Robinson represented this new urge in one realm; trumpeter Miles Davis represented it in another realm" (60–61).

Many of these "race men" successfully crossed over to white audiences and became acclaimed, respected, and popular figures. Their acceptance, however, was always tenuous. Black audiences applauded their ability to represent the race properly through their talent and dignity but also expected them to remain *authentically* black, which included conforming to culturally specific notions of respectability and normalcy dating back to the nineteenth century. Examples of this include the "easy, exterior image" Cole presented to the public, which "helped to maintain codings of black manhood that left private, sexual beings unexplored in popular culture" (McGill 2005, 38). Poitier's "cool boil" acting style, which "struck a delicate balance, revealing racial frustration, but tacitly assuring a predominantly white audience that blacks would eschew violence and preserve social order," is another example (Goudsouzian 2004, 1).

Despite internal racial pressures to represent the race respectably and white pressures for these men to convey appeal but avoid sexual titillation and/or political radicalism, there were exceptions. Exploring ripples and slippages that bordered between the novel, the permissible, and the dangerous is integral to my overall argument that queer masculinities circulated despite the seeming social conventions of the era. For example, Belafonte was definitely a "race man" who projected a dignified image of blackness and advocated for civil rights for blacks. He was equally pivotal for using his muscular, tanned body strategically to break the mold of black male figures by projecting a visceral sexual appeal that made him the first "Negro matinee idol" (Stephens 2014, 122–23; McGill 2005, 30–31).

Beyond even this breakthrough is something more unexpected. When we compare black men traditionally understood as queer, based on their gender behavior and/or sexual orientation (such as Little Richard and Johnny Mathis) with black men traditionally understood as straight (including Belafonte, Cole, and Poitier), we see a central commonality. Notably, they all equivocated in expressing black male sexuality, regardless of their orientation.[5] In many ways this made their expressions of masculinity queer insofar as they were discouraged from expressing virility or physical intimacy. If (black) postwar men were expected to marry and procreate, how could they do so if society forbade them to acknowledge they were *sexual* beings?

Belafonte was a sex symbol, but he was not sexually intimate in any of his films in which he was featured as a romantic lead opposite a white actress, including the 1957 *Island in the Sun* (McGill 71; Stephens 2014, 128–29) and the 1959 *The World, the Flesh and the Devil* (Stephens 2014, 140–44). Similar accusations of sexual neutering have plagued Poitier's career in the eyes of various film critics and scholars.[6] In popular music, black male sexuality was also controversial. A seemingly benign image of an overzealous white female fan admiring Billy Eckstine evoked irate letters and limited his career options, according to some critics.[7] Cole's short-lived NBC television variety series lost corporate sponsors in 1957 because he appeared onscreen with white female singers like Peggy Lee. These interactions were chaste, but the juxtapositions were enough for Southern television stations to avoid airing the show. Mathis, who borrowed musical and social cues from Cole and Eckstine, took these lessons to heart and learned to project a neutral, non-threatening sexuality in his vocal delivery and public image. On the opposite end of the spectrum, Little Richard drew from a tradition of "carnivalesque, comedic" black masculinity, embodied by predecessors like Louis Jordan, to present his sexuality as exaggerated and unthreatening (McGill 2005, 36–37). If black men shared the pressure to equivocate via neutering their sexuality and avoiding interracial sexual interactions, sexually queer black men had an additional level of pressure within the black cultural milieu.

The postwar black press, dominated commercially by *Ebony* and *Jet* magazines, constructed homosexuality along strict gender lines and conflated gender transgression with homosexuality. As Gregory Conerly argues, "These magazines suggest that for many blacks, male homosexuality was tolerable under certain circumstances; lesbianism was almost universally condemned" (Conerly 2001, 385). Conerly draws this conclusion after surveying both magazines' stories on homosexuality in the 1950s. Most stories published in these magazines framed homosexuality as a social problem that was a by-product of gender inversion (for example, homosexual men were men who thought they were women) that could be corrected. Thus, the magazines published numerous stories about people who were gender inverts but who became *normal* through medical treatments, religious conversions, and other methods.

The roots of this conflation of male effeminacy with homosexuality was not unique to the black press and preceded the mid-1940s by at least two decades. Reflecting on previous historical studies of sexuality, James F. Wilson notes in *Bulldaggers, Pansies, and Chocolate Babies* (2010) that in the 1920s, "the press, gossip sheets, and moralists, tended to label all so-called sexual deviants as 'sexual inverts' or members of the 'third sex,' and to them they were discernible" (7). Based on these stereotypes, in the public mind lesbians "were associated with 'manliness' and masculine clothing" and gay men "who were called 'pansies,' 'fairies,' and 'fags,' were identified by their femininity and their affinity for dresses, makeup and wigs" (7). The consistency of these stereotypes made it easier for queer people who did not conform to "experiment with same-sex trysts or establish relationships and avoid being found out" because of straight culture's ignorance of queer worlds (7). This is important because it meant extreme stereotypes failed to capture the vast range of possible gender presentations.

Pansies, Sissies, and Popular Culture

Paradoxically, despite stigmatizing homosexuality as a perversion of gender norms, audiences of the 1920s through the mid-1940s (the period that immediately precedes the era this book covers) embraced certain forms of commercial queerness. George Chauncey's 1994 *Gay New York* traces the roots and usage of the term "pansy" and its commercial manifestations in 1920s New York culture. Vito Russo's 1987 *The Celluloid Closet* illustrates the emergence of the pansy craze in pre–World War II cinema, and James Wilson explores the commercial appeal of pansy performers in black drag-ball culture (Wilson 2010). Each of these historical scenarios establishes a commercial precedent for mainstream consumption of queerness, even in a flamboyant and exaggerated form. If, for example, audiences conflated gender inversion with homosexuality, men who were more muted in their behavior could be more difficult to detect than others, making them relatively safe figures to consume.

In *Gay New York* Chauncey illustrates the rise of the so-called "pansy craze" in the nightclub scene as one built on the rise of Harlem drag balls: "Seizing on the public's fascination with this new phenomenon, Times Square entrepreneurs began to evoke the flamboyant image of the pansy to generate business. 'Pansy' acts began to appear on the stage, in the press, and in the clubs, but at this point they usually were the gay equivalent of blackface: straight actors putting on drag or stereotypical mannerisms to mimic and ridicule gay men, to the hoots and jeers of an anti-gay audience" (Chauncey 1994, 310). The height of the pansy craze in New York was 1930 and 1931. Beyond New York, magazines such as *Vanity Fair*, which depicted pansy entertainers like Jean Malin in cartoon form, and *Variety*, which reviewed pansy-themed nightclub acts, solidified pansies as a national entertainment phenomenon (314–18).

Russo notes the prominence of queer characters and pansy jokes in the films of the 1910s and 1930s. This was toned down somewhat in the 1930s through the 1950s, a period when the Motion Picture Production Code required careful coding such that "borderline gay characters fell into well-worn innuendo and reliable sissy credentials, but said the same things" (Russo 1987, 31). Among the most prominent actors to specialize in "sissy" characters was actor Frank Pangborn, wildly popular for the time in part because audiences knew he was not a "sissy" in real life (34). Audiences somehow compartmentalized these elements and embraced sissy characters. As Russo notes, "Sissies were an outlet for unspeakable ideas. Sissies were fun, too. They were a refuge for nonconformity" (32). Russo notes the dual functions of sissies. Referring to films of the 1910s and 1920s, he observes a masculine dynamic that remained at play in the 1950s—notably, that "early sissies were yardsticks for measuring the virility of the men around them. In almost all American films, from comedies to romantic dramas, working class men are portrayed as much more valuable and certainly more virile than the rich, effete dandies of Europe, who in spite of their success with women are seen as essentially weak and helpless in a real man's world" (16).

Beyond entertainment value, these images conveyed clear messages about the social utility of certain masculinities, especially when depicted in film. Because the sissy figure existed chiefly as a contrast to "real men," popular culture has long perpetuated a mythology of authentic malehood as "strong, silent and ostentatiously unemotional" (Russo 1987, 5). Though this model continued well into the postwar era, it did not prevent audiences from engaging with gender transgressions, especially if they were contained in an entertainment context.

To return to the postwar black magazines, they regularly covered urban drag-queen balls, placing male gender inversion in the "proper" realm of entertainment. In fact, "the balls were not only popular among blacks, but also received some institutional support from the police and the black church" (Conerly 2001, 387). Alongside the annual balls, female impersonators were a regular feature in many black nightclubs (389). Comparatively, the magazines and their readers viewed male impersonators as an aberration. The most famous of these was featured in a story written by Harlem Renaissance entertainer Gladys Bentley detailing her conversion from abnormal gender expression and sexual desires into a proper married woman (Bentley 1952, 92–98). Though this seems quite homophobic and genderphobic by contemporary standards, the magazines sometimes approached female gender inversion more ambivalently. For example, they presented the life of Georgia Black, a man who allegedly lived as a woman, as "bizarre" and "moving" (Conerly 2001, 392; Knadler 2002, 162). Though I explore this in greater depth herewith, it is relevant because it illustrates room for slippages. Men who desired men but were not effeminate were potentially undetectable as homosexual, as were men who were not impersonators. Similarly, the communities depicted in these stories suggested that black communities accepted female impersonators in certain contexts.

In sum, postwar standards of masculinity insisted on the need for (white) men to lead families as heads of households and thrive in the corporate sector, which required a modicum of conformity. Rigid conceptions of masculinity made it easier to stigmatize male types that refused to conform to these narrow standards. Attempts to normalize and contain masculine possibilities, however, were too narrow to encompass certain masculinities.

In contrast, black men, who had been characterized historically as hypersexual and thus "dangerous" struggled to be valued as men. Society expected a certain level of virility from white men, but black men seeking broad social acceptance were expected to mute their sexuality, including avoiding interracial desire. The black mainstream also expected them to lead their struggle for respectability, which meant asserting themselves as proper men while avoiding homosexuality or its signifiers. Ironically, the neutered sexuality they presented was queer compared to that of their white counterparts, with rare exception.

The masculine standards that haunted postwar men are an outgrowth of masculine stereotypes that emerged in the 1910s through the 1930s that conflated effeminacy, intellectualism, and weakness with homosexuality. Popular culture, including drag balls, nightclub performances, and film, constructed this stereotype. Despite social stigmas toward homosexuality and gender nonconformity, audiences were strangely tolerant of male effeminacy in entertainment contexts, consuming drag, "pansy," and "sissy" characters. These tendencies for audiences to compartmentalize attitudes about sexuality, and the ways queer men who defied stereotypes could function and flourish, inform my argument that the norms of eras do not necessarily stifle the ability of queer men to gain popularity and build mass audiences.

When we examine the personae of popular queer male musicians of the 1950s it is clear, based on their reception, that postwar audiences were primed to expect some degree of queerness in popular culture. Divergences from broad stereotypes ingrained in the public's memory allowed queer male performers to translate elements of queerness into styles and personae openly without necessarily labeling what they were doing or labeling themselves. There was no overt queer *craze* during the 1950s, but plenty of queer men made vast cultural imprints. Queer musicians were able to prod popular culture to embrace a range of masculine expression while maintaining a certain sexual ambiguity by employing tools drawn from a carefully honed toolkit.

Rifling through the "Queering" Toolkit

The toolkit the musicians employ refers to queering strategies, techniques, and considerations musicians pioneered in the postwar era that other musicians have continued to adapt and expand. The repertoire of tools has expanded over the decades. As a scholar, I feel compelled to register my ambivalence about queer heritage logics (for example, Liberace is the gay father to David Bowie and Elton John) because they tend to be too flat and linear to capture the nuances of history. Nonetheless, certain strategies, and their variations, have surfaced repeatedly in the careers of queer musicians. Integral to these elements is a conscious calibration of behavior to the norms of the era. Postwar masculine norms blended broad elements from previous notions of masculinity drawn from the 1910s through the 1930s, such as equating effeminacy with homosexuality, combined with the social technologies of the postwar era. The tensions between conformity and rebellion that defined postwar masculinity created spaces for a wider range of public masculinities than is typically acknowledged. Arguably, many of the tools musicians used were not necessarily meant to mask their sexual orientation exclusively, even if this was an effect. Still, people who were sexually queer had to modulate carefully to tap into the novelty appeal of queerness while avoiding anything that would alienate the mainstream.

Examining patterns among queer male movie stars of the 1950s offers a useful starting point. These patterns represent a kind of shorthand or formula for buffering men known to be queer sexually. Rock Hudson and Tab Hunter were both marketed as sex symbols. Their brawny physiques and handsome square jawlines implied ruggedness and virility. Because homosexuality was so firmly associated with effeminacy, their appearances assured audiences that they were men and not women. They were cast regularly in traditionally masculine roles reflecting respectable male images of the time in westerns, war movies, and heterosexual romantic films. The repetition of these roles gradually unified their public identities with attributes of the characters they played. Further, though their appearance and demeanor implied heterosexuality, arranged dates with female starlets, coordinated by film studios, ostensibly confirmed it.[8]

The brooding persona of Montgomery Clift and Anthony Perkins assured audiences of the assimilable nature of these types into masculine ideals. Though part of their popularity was the novelty of their vulnerable screen qualities, many of their roles balanced this out with gender-normative and thus sexually normative signifiers. Clift was cast in military roles (*From Here to Eternity*), and Perkins frequently played immature young men who grew up through being loved by older, more powerful women. Film studios also arranged publicity dates between them and various actresses. Their differences were a draw, not necessarily a liability, and audiences could see what they wanted to see.[9]

Lest these descriptions seem improbable or overly calculated, consider that several biographies and autobiographies have noted explicit measures to curb their queerness. For example, Hudson's acting training included erasing traces of femininity in his smile, speaking voice, wrists, and hips. Similarly, Clift censored and corrected elements of his performances when he felt he appeared too effeminate. They, or at least their handlers, were aware of the era's norms and labored to assure their conformity to expectations. In cases of the "queer studs" and the "brooding idols," their film roles and their personal lives were managed in ways that framed them as heteronormative. Though the actors have distinct careers, these studio system techniques unite the actors together under the veil of masculine normalcy.

The musicians present even more challenges given the diversity of the genres they represent, their racial diversity, and the different directions of their careers. Five queering tools continually surface throughout the careers of the Quartet in various combinations:

Self-neutering

Self-neutering describes a form of benign neglect that plays to the concept of compulsory heterosexuality.[10] In a society that equates external gender behavior with sexual orientation, the absence of certain behaviors feeds into the dominant narrative about human sexuality. To phrase this another way, it is difficult to explicitly accuse a man of being bisexual, homosexual, or pansexual if the man does not have a romantic partner and downplays his own sexuality. Several of the men featured in this study do not discuss romantic relationships with anyone of any sex publicly. Chastity has wholesome connotations that also contribute to their social acceptance.

Behaviors that conform to acceptable gender norms in other ways may buffer musicians from the lack of associations. For example, men who have a large female fan base adhere to a heteronormative script regarding sexual desire. Similarly, men who work so hard developing their careers that they do not have time to date or marry conform to expectations of men as breadwinners. Additionally, because popular culture, such as the black mainstream press and pulp novels, constructed radical gender transgressions as the primary mark of sexual deviance, men whose affects dwelled somewhere between virility and effeminacy were relatively safe from scrutiny. Because these figures lack a direct association with a specific romantic partner, queer baiting is more challenging for would-be outers. The absence of a partner could engender speculation and/or ridicule but not necessarily explicit accusations.

Simultaneously, several musicians were paired publicly with an array of women, including models or actresses. These publicity dates were a common promotional technique for celebrities and were often arranged by managers for the press. These relationships conveyed the appearance of normalcy but were ephemeral by design. There are no indications in such relationships that the male and female figures were sexually intimate, and the publicity dates did not result in long-term dating, marriage, or children. Most of the musicians who self-neutered did so effectively enough for a sufficiently long span of time that questions about their intimate lives essentially disappeared from interviews and profiles.

Self-domesticating

One of the key ways single men could signify their allegiance to heteronorms was to ground themselves in heteronormative frameworks. This surfaces in multiple ways, including identifying overtly with one's biological family and referencing the family in interviews and/or incorporating family into one's persona. An even more direct way to do this is to allude to marriage as a goal publicly or to marry a woman. The powerful iconicity of the nuclear family as the social ideal loomed throughout the careers of each of the musicians. Another related domesticating technique, which ties in with *self-neutering*, is to emphasize one's persona and performing style as wholesome, normal, and family friendly. When pushed, many of the musicians consciously de-emphasized sex and downplayed anything that might have appeared socially transgressive in their act.

Self-neutering and *self-domesticating* are distinct tools, technically. Queer musicians, however, often employ them simultaneously because both typically serve a similar function. Notably, they deflect potentially negative attention away from any potential difference from the heteronormative expectations by either downplaying the appearance of sexuality period or adhering explicitly to postwar ideals regarding gender roles, sexual orientation, and family structure.

Spectacularizing

Several queer musicians cultivated trademarks in their self-presentations, including visual trademarks in hair, makeup and clothing that distinguished them from other performers. These trademarks were also novel enough to deflect attention away from other potentially more disturbing elements of their personae or identities. For example, Little Richard feminized himself with pancake makeup and processed hair, and he exaggerated his appearance enough to standout visually from other 1950s R&B singers. This helped him cross over to a white teenaged audience because the technique neutralized the implicit cross-racial sexual threat. Liberace, who was born Wladziu Valentino, was determined to stand out from other classical musicians. He selected the name "Walter Buster Keys" as his initial showbiz moniker (which he eventually shortened to Liberace) and interspersed pop songs to appeal to his popular audience (Pyron 2000, 95). The combination of these gimmicks, alongside such classical faux pas as wearing a white tuxedo in concert, caused a minor scandal in the classical world. Collectively, these gestures distinguished him and made him unusually popular for a classical performer.

These trademarks often drew attention to the musicians for their shock value, which could deflect attention away from their sexuality and other personal elements. Style continually evolves, so by definition what appears shocking or radical in one era exists on a continuum. Little Richard adapted a more radical kind of overt "transvestism" in his 1970s stage wear, and Liberace pushed sartorial flamboyance to new heights from the mid-1960s onward (Garber 1992, 354). The combination of either of these, with the comedic elements of their personae, potentially made them less threatening. Because these figures are consciously investing time and energy in stylizing themselves, we can see how these *spectacular* qualities were often as central in reviews and profiles as their music or personal lives.

Playing the Freak: External and/or Self-enfreaking

The term "freak" has many connotations in the American lexicon. The term is typically associated with so-called "freak shows" and circus sideshows, which were mainstream entertainment from the 1840s through the early 1940s in

Europe and the United States.[11] My framing of postwar musicians draws on notions of freaks and *enfreakment* articulated by essayist and novelist James Baldwin and photographer and advocate David Hevey, respectively (Baldwin 1985, 677–90; Hevey 1992, 62).

The concept of "freak" I use refers to cultural discomfort with gender fluidity derived from Baldwin's essay "Here Be Dragons." He argues, "To be androgynous does not imply both male and female sexual equipment, which is the state, uncommon, of the hermaphrodite. However, the existence of the hermaphrodite reveals, in intimidating exaggeration, the truth concerning every human being—which is why the hermaphrodite is called a *freak*" (Baldwin 1985, 677; emphasis added). Baldwin posits the idealized version of American male sexuality as an entity inseparable from American ideals of masculinity. He lists binaries like "cowboys and Indians, good guys and bad guys, punks and studs, tough guys and softies, butch and faggot, black and white" to conclude that the "ideal" is "so paralytically infantile that it is virtually forbidden—as an unpatriotic act—that the American boy evolve into the complexity of manhood" (678). Joseph Vogel's essay on "Dragons" also ruminates on the social impact of gender anomalies: "The androgyne, similarly, evokes both fascination and fear in American culture—fascination because he/she seems exotic and different, and fear because he/she feels uncomfortably familiar. In embodying a liminal space 'in the middle,' in ambiguity, the androgyne becomes problematic for those invested in protecting established borders of identity" (Vogel 2015, 467). The tension between familiarity and difference is sensitive territory that has given unconventional men ("freaks") access to the mainstream but has troubled their abilities to navigate it smoothly.

Hevey's notion of enfreakment, the stylization of "difference," through processes of marketing and stylizing the non-normative, for consumption (Hevey 1992; Richardson 2010, 5), also informs my concept of the interplay between perceptions of difference and acts and gestures that inform, produce, and reinforce this difference. Hevey coined this term to describe the nature of subjects in Diane Arbus's photographs of people with developmental disabilities, and it has since gained critical import. He notes how "Arbus's enfreakment of disabled people, spoke to the able-bodied fear of millions," and how in terms of impact "the enfreakment in her disability images was internalised by the non-disabled viewers because the disabled subjects, while chosen for their apparent difference, manifested body language and identity traits recognisable to everyone" (Hevey 1992, 62). The perceived impact of enfreakment is typically a gap between the body being observed and the observer. Rosemarie Garland Thomson's *Extraordinary Bodies* (1997) argues that "enfreakment emerges from cultural rituals that stylize, silence, differentiate, and distance the persons whose bodies the freak-hunters or showmen colonize and commercialize" (10), and Andrea Zittlau views enfreaked images as "a construction of deformity that confirms the collective identity of its (non-disabled) audience" (Zittlau 2012, 151).

In the context of *Rocking the Closet*, the notion of *playing the freak* applies in two ways. First, regardless of the artist's intentions, it refers to the ways audiences, critics, and other observers read, interpret, and classify certain behaviors and characteristics of artists as *freakish*—notably, elements that diverge from social norms around gender, including clothing and mannerisms. Sometimes the intent is to stigmatize and marginalize, though occasionally these observations may engender empathy and compassion from audiences. These may surface in various written and verbal forms, including reviews, commentaries, and tabloid coverage, to name a few examples.

Second, performers may consciously choose to amplify their *freakishness*. The artist may be simply expressing their natural style, but in many cases they are reacting to a specific event, a critique, or other stimuli. In the latter case, they are literally playing or toying with the concept, throwing it back on the society that tries to contain them. The result is a discernible set of actions warranting interpretation. Within the relatively conservative economy of masculinity I explore, from the postwar era to the present, audiences have tolerated and even celebrated the myriad ways popular figures have defied social norms of masculinity. The fusion of performers pushing boundaries and audiences embracing these defiant acts have arguably expanded the limits of masculinity and have, perhaps in a more important sense, informed some questioning of the very idea of gender norms. The emergence of challenges to gender norms is not a historical inevitability that simply comes with the passing of time, nor is it a product of one strand of organizing, such as politics. Rather, it exemplifies an ongoing historical tug-of-war over the functions and limitations of norms (Eaklor 2001, 286, 288, 290).

Many queer musicians embody the Baldwinian notion of "freak" by presenting bodies and sounds that traverse male and female gender boundaries. This includes vocal qualities, perceptions of ability and strength, and androgynous visual style. The "freak" elements of performers could serve as a safe form of curiosity in an era of safety and conformity. For example, this quality was essential to the distinctive sound and unique appeal of jazz and R&B singer Jimmy Scott, whose stunted physical development made him sound like a female singer. Related to this is the freakish quality of male vulnerability, which was also an anomalous element of public male figures of the postwar period. Vulnerability can make a male seem more empathic, like someone who needs to be taken care of, a role that provides value and utility for those doing the caretaking, even symbolically. Marked physical differences as well as the implication of vulnerability applies to the careers of several musicians in this study.

Playing the Race Card (or Not)

The racialized nature of American masculinity means each man performs masculinity in a racial context, though with different implications. As I have noted earlier, various historical forces and racial anxieties led many black male celebrities, regardless of sexual orientation, to embrace either comic imagery or sexual neutrality to avoid offending mainstream audiences. These forces shape the calculated personas of the black musicians within the quartet. The ways black musicians attempted to navigate race was sometimes a fusion of hoping their participation in styles associated with white performers would draw less attention to their race, or banking on novelty and spectacle.

Appealing to white cultural sensibilities was an aspiration, though unspoken, for white performers as well. White performers had greater mobility in navigating the racial color line in popular music. Transcending expected white postwar musical norms was a novel move that laid the foundation for rock 'n' roll and its immediate precedents. This has important overtones for Ray's initial career. Comparatively, hewing to familiar European American genres and their implied prestige, ranging from neoclassical music to pop crooning, meant white musicians could extend familiar musical traditions and pretend racial difference was not a social issue. The tensions between addressing race, or pretending to be oblivious to it, informs the careers of members of the Quartet.

* * *

Each of these queering "tools" operates in relation to each other and are best understood in relation to the musician's social identities. For example, Mathis aimed to draw attention *away* from his personal life. Chapter 4 describes how he self-neutered by having no public intimate relationships on record and by avoiding controversies. Though he projected a contemporary dandy image, his low-key style inverted the kind of attention that *spectacularizing* and *self-enfreaking* might engender. In this instance, he aspired to an *anti*-style and *anti*-spectacular approach in service of achieving discretion. The tools are also multigenerational strategies and techniques singers in other generations and genres have adapted to coincide with the gender dynamics of their time. Throughout the book I discuss the ways that other queer male musicians have employed these tools and note the emergence of newer tools, including conscious efforts by gender normative musicians to attract queer audiences and their relation to what often appears to be a more relaxed climate regarding gender. The toolkit always operates in the space between what is visible, what is implied, as well as what is disclosed, and what is accepted. In this vein, I now turn to the enduring metaphor of the closet and the way it shapes how we understand queer history.

Before and beyond Stonewall: Conceptualizing Queering and Sexual Elusiveness

The Stonewall riots did not start the lesbian, gay, bisexual, transgender, and queer (LGBTQ) rights movement. Rather, they are the culmination of decades of community building and resistance among queer people. Understanding that distinction is essential to engaging with *Rocking the Closet*'s argument that LGBTQ people developed a variety of subcultures, cultural sensibilities, and cultural strategies that paralleled the birth of its political movements. Queer culture always operates in tandem with queer politics. In the 1950s the existing constellation of queer cultures yielded one of the most enduring strategies for queer people: sexual elusiveness.

Projecting sexual elusiveness was a central strategy that popular figures of the 1950s, especially musicians, employed to balance personal authenticity with their desire to connect with audiences. Members of the Quartet defy much of what we thought we knew about the 1950s. They were all commercially popular male musicians who projected ambiguous masculinities in various combinations that endeared them to the public. All four cultivated sexually ambiguous personas that provide them with an almost novel appeal. Examining Mathis's ability to "self-neuter" or the ways Johnnie Ray "played the freak" moves us beyond focusing exclusively on their sexual object-choice, which is the focus of sexual orientation, to locate gendered practices that are queer in relation to expectations of cisgender males of their generation.

Though many critics could interpret their acts of elusiveness along the usual critical fault lines—as politically subversive, heroic gestures or as cowardly symbols of a repressive era—neither explanation is especially nuanced or satisfying. When understood in the proper historical context, sexual elusiveness reflects specific musical, commercial, racial, and gendered realities that defy easy applications. How and why did "queering" masculinity emerge as a successful strategy, and why has it endured?

Two scholars who inform my thinking about "queering" and the ongoing appeal of sexual elusiveness are Christopher Nealon, in *Foundlings: Lesbian and Gay Historical Emotion before Stonewall* (2001), and Heather Love, in *Feeling Backward: Loss and the Politics of Queer History* (2007). First, I was seeking a language to think about the way queer people formed cultures and communities before the development of formal political movements. I also wanted to avoid reducing them to mere "closet cases" with false consciousness. As Eve Sedgwick, in her *Epistemology of the Closet* (1990), has noted, the closet is far more nuanced than its parameters might suggest, notably we remain compelled by "that most intriguing of all genres, the coming-out story that doesn't come out" (248). By today's progressive standards the pop figures of the 1950s seem sad, closeted, and pitiful. All the codes and veils they used defy more than forty-five years of liberationist philosophy.

Taking a closer look reveals the intricacy of queering tools and that these tendencies were not relegated to some imagined past. Nealon's discussion of connections between 1950s physique magazines and the thinly veiled erotics of contemporary muscle magazines illuminates this phenomenon. The contrast he draws between the supposedly closeted nature of the magazines in the 1950s, which "can serve, if we let them, as sketches for the movements of a sexuality that, because it is never isolable in persons, is also open to a hopeful earliness *in* history, not before it," and more recent iterations of muscle magazines from the 1980s onward, illustrates the ongoing function of ambiguously queer artifacts (Nealon 2001, 139). He notes how "the 1980s brought a wide variety of thinly closeted 'workout' magazines to newsstands—a stepping-stone to homosexuality for a whole new generation of gay men" (136) and how magazines like *Burn!*, *Men's Fitness*, and *Men's Workout* "still do mask their homoeroticism by alibis that faintly imply a collective identity—if only the shared consumer demographic of hip, in-shape young guys who are in the know about the latest protein shakes and club music (who are, that is, not so much Greeks as Dudes)" (179). By doing so, he draws our attention to the artificial boundary between the pre-political and overtly political, or the pre- and post-historical eras of modern queer history.

Queer men did not stop buying muscle magazines simply because they had political movements available to them after the 1970s. They are not mutually exclusive entities. Similarly, just as audiences had to read between the lines and interpret the sexualities of queer pop musicians of the 1950s, a closeted pleasure may have been part of the thrill; today's queer pop stars do not necessarily feel immediately compelled to reveal themselves even if there are more social and political supports. The jouissance (enjoyment) of veils, the appeal of open secrets, as well as anxieties about being found out in a (still) heteronormative society continues to impact queer identified men, as well as those perceived as queer. The political movement did not erase the continuum of pleasures and safeguards *open secrets* represent. Nor did they eliminate the ambiguity and uncertainty about translating personal desire into public affiliations and identities. Nealon's reasoning informs my conception of the Quartet as proto-queer figures whose toolkits have endured across generations of musicians and changed forms over time. They did not employ these strategies for an explicit "political" outcome, but the culmination of these gestures was a nod toward more flexible gender norms in popular culture.

Second, I was seeking a method/technique to sift through artifacts that point us in directions beyond the unsatisfying binary of the closet and politics. Too often queer writers perform a kind of intellectual dodge where they dismiss people and practices as sad, miserable, closeted, and other adjectives of defeat. This tends to affirm outness and other kinds of visibility as markers of moral and political authenticity. This continually surfaces, for example, among critics who resented Liberace's refusal to formally come out as gay in a prescribed fashion.

Comparatively, some critics and writers have reevaluated queer artifacts and reclaimed them for various critical purposes. These recoveries/rescues are often well-intentioned ways to make peace with the past in an empathetic and understanding fashion for historical context and limitations. The limit of such practices is a kind of critical obfuscation that relegates the dark emotions—shame, self-loathing, disdain—to the distant past so we can tell uplifting, triumphant stories affirming the queer pride narrative. Love's critical focus on "the negative affects—the need, the aversion, and the longing—that characterize the relation between past and present" in relation to queer history constitutes an approach I frame as *looking backward* and provides a useful frame for investigating queer texts in their time and context (Love 2007, 32). The axis of her analytical lens is not just to disparage the past uncritically. She draws important attention to the way writers scrub darkness from the history of queerness in favor of more positive, digestible stories of progress. Her argument is worth quoting at length:

> In attempting to construct a positive genealogy of gay identity, queer critics and historians have often found themselves at a loss about what to do with the sad old queens and long-suffering dykes who haunt the historical record. They have disavowed the difficulties of the queer past, arguing that our true history has not been written. If critics do admit the difficulties of the queer past, it is most often in order to redeem them. By including queer figures from the past in a positive genealogy of gay identity, we make good on their suffering, transforming their shame into pride after the fact. (32)

This reasoning has helped me open my mind to address the "difficulties" beyond historical reclamation. The growth of LGBTQ political movements and academic tools are examples of developments that have made it easy to presume that the present is fundamentally better for musicians who employ queer techniques or for queer people in general. The book's chapters highlight ambivalences to make room for emotions outside of pride and affirmation. When artists from the queer past express indifference or even hostility toward queerness as a social identity, we must account for their experiences as valid parts of the historic narrative of queering. Love's argument provides a way to look beyond lionizing these figures or ridiculing them toward interpreting their experiences with historical and contextual nuance. The combination of biographical information and the "queering" tools helps us capture some of these layers.

Queerness and Sexual Elusiveness in Popular Music

Since I am using a method informed by two literary theories to queer history and the medium of popular music, I necessarily ground my analysis in a few key musical concepts. *Rocking the Closet* is an intimate history centered on personae. Personae is an essential part of how audiences access performers whom they can never really know intimately. Simon Frith's 1996 *Performing Rites* offers a useful working definition of personae essential to my discussion.

Rocking the Closet embraces Frith's concept of performance as "a social—or communicative—process" dependent on audiences and their interpretations. Interpretation depends on "the audience's ability to understand it [the body] both as an object (an erotic object, an attractive object, a repulsive object, a social object) and as a subject, that is, as a willed or shaped object, an object with meaning" (Frith 1996, 205). Voices, bodily images and movements, and biographical information all contribute to audiences' consumption of musicians, which is not defined by consuming stars "but their performances" (211). Since pop musicians are continually constructing and reinforcing the presence of their personae in recorded performances, concerts, visual representations (television, film, the internet, posters), and press coverage, understanding how audiences respond to various aspects of star personalities and the range of pleasure they derive is essential, especially with regard to audiences of musicians who are insinuating rather than overtly disclosing aspects of their intimate lives.

Within Frith's discussion, we can see the way sexuality informs our engagement with performers' personae. Seduction is an integral part of the relationship between the performer and the audience because, as Frith argues,

> we realize that the singer is making us an offer ("Know me!") that is essentially false, yet is true to our fantasy of what the offer might be, that it might be just for us ("To know me is to love me"). The listening fantasy, to put this another way, is that we control the music (the sexual exchange) when, in fact, the performer does. . . . The presence of even a recorded sound is the presence of the implied performer—*the performer called forth by the listener*—and this is clearly a sensual/sexual presence, not just a meeting of minds. (215, original emphasis)

There is an inherent sensuality to the listening fantasy that pop singers offer their audiences, and it makes critical attention to audiences' engagement with performers' roles as sexual objects of desire and identification key sites for understanding the pleasure audiences derive from sexual ambiguity. In a postliberation era, ambiguity could be easily dismissed as coy, dishonest, apolitical, and/or frustrating. We must also consider the *pleasure within ambiguity* as a central component of the fantasies queer musicians enact. Perhaps we listen more intently and look more closely when we cannot quite discern whom and what we are experiencing musically.

An example of how personae informs perception is Barbara Bradby's ethnographic study of a community of Irish lesbians who actively projected their perceptions of sexual orientation onto performers. Bradby's interviewees used a combination of "myth-making, fantasizing and rumor circulation" via sharing musical tapes and informally gossiping in small networks to categorize performers as lesbian (Bradby 1995, 42–43). These three communicative modes illustrate how audiences construct truth about performers. Beyond the specific circumstances of her study there is a broader social import to examining audiences, especially those of queer musicians, which is providing a window into how to be queer and what queerness might look like. In *I Wanna Be Me* (2001), Theodore Gracyk's observation that "the real contribution of popular music may be its power to expose listeners to a vast arsenal of possible identities" and that "in allowing a listener to 'inhabit' new positions . . . mass art can suggest life options that were previously unthinkable" (215) speaks directly to the unique social value of popular music for audiences drawn to the personae of queer musicians.

Thinking about queer sexualities specifically requires tools for thinking about how oppression/suppression shapes personae and responses to them.

Musicologists popularized the unique role of music as a filter for homosexual subjectivity and desire produced in the context of homophobic oppression. Phillip Brett connects the emotional ambiguity of musical performance to queer emotional affects by arguing that "it is performance that attracts and entices most people to become musicians in the first instance. . . . Music is a perfect field for the display of emotion. It is particularly accommodating to those who have difficulty in expressing feelings in day-to-day life, because the emotion is unspecified and unattached" (Brett 1994, 15). Such emotionalism could apply to anyone attracted to music, regardless of sexuality, but Brett provides the example of gay children to illustrate homophobia's impact on artistic production by noting that, "to gay children, who often experience a shutdown of all feelings as the result of sensing their parents' and society's disapproval of a basic part of their sentient life, music appears to be a veritable lifeline" (15). Nadine Hubbs's *The Queer Composition of America's Sound* (2004) advances this further: "Adults too, including queer adults, found refuge from social rejection and alienation in nonverbal, embodied, intimate engagements with music" (99). Beyond these examples, Hubbs offers a compelling argument for addressing the relationship of queer audiences to queer performers' personae and why music has served as an important expressive form for queers by noting that "music, being nonverbal and experienced as deeply embodied and unmediated by social structures, affords alternative modes of emotional and erotic intimacy that may have (a) provided critical succor for persons, including queer subjects, who felt excluded by and alienated from social structures, and (b) (not only evaded but) weakened the tyranny of the gender and sexual classifications in which twentieth-century queer persons found themselves invidiously caught (100–101). Hubbs draws her point from a study on the social networks of white gay male classical composers of the twentieth century, but nonetheless it offers more broadly applicable critical possibilities for understanding popular music and queer affectivity.

Both Brett and Hubbs allude to alienation, exclusion, and stigma as particularly relevant to queer people at the same time they identify music as a space of transcendence. Illuminating the context of this oppression and the conditions that enabled queer people to persist is important for readers to connect queer codes to larger historical realities. The postwar gender economy generated new social norms around gender that created social obstacles for independent women, queer people, single adults, and other nonconformists. A recurring theme in *Rocking the Closet* are the malleable boundaries of gender norms shaped by audiences' ignorance, curiosity, and fascination that allow for some seemingly paradoxical occurrences in the mainstream. Even within the era's political and cultural confines, there were opportunities for multiple forms of rebellion and transgression, and audiences were willing "accomplices." These openings made it possible for queer people to build a clandestine social culture with political implications. The proliferation of different forms of queer culture in the public sphere, including the popularity of sexually elusive figures in a heteronormative culture, characterizes the paradoxes of the era. Chapter 1 explores these paradoxes in greater depth as well as the surfeit of resistance that surfaced culturally. The tension between the push for a new normalcy and the culture's craving for alternatives fueled the positive reception to many of the more anomalous elements characterizing the Quartet.

A Look Ahead

Chapter 1, "Visibly Hidden: Postwar Disorientation, Queer Community, and Queer Ambivalence," frames the postwar experiment as a concentrated effort to regulate the social sphere that actually resulted in disorientation. This disorientation opened up space for a variety of challenges, including the gradual rise of queerness as a cultural sensibility. Despite conscious efforts to link gender deviance with sexual *perversion*, and to stigmatize them, this coverage also made queer culture visible. The chapter articulates the tension between the pre- and post-Stonewall eras and explores ambivalence as an important part of the queer experience that informs the way artists navigate individual and group identity. A unifying thread of chapters 2 through 5 is a discussion of the question of "How did he do it?" Notably, the chapters describe the "queering" tools musicians employed and their impact on various audiences, including consumers, cultural critics, and journalists. Each chapter also highlights the ways queer ambivalence about personal and communal identity informed their navigations.

Chapter 2, "A Freak Deferred: Johnnie Ray Navigates Innovation and Convention," explores the unique paradox of early 1950s superstar Johnnie Ray's career. Deaf, effeminate, and inspired by black popular music, he was an anomaly, and this was part of his appeal. Audiences embraced him for bringing a new level of emotional expression and vulnerability to crooner pop, but critics enfreaked him. They thought he was inauthentic, unmusical, and a poor influence on the young. Though his fans continued to find him appealing, and he enjoyed his enfreaked image to an extent, he grew increasingly nervous, especially because of an arrest record for soliciting male sex. He attempted to domesticate and neuter himself personally and musically to appear more conventional. For example, he was married for two years and tried to record bloodless novelty songs and sentimental pop. Ironically, these gestures made him increasingly irrelevant during the rise of rock 'n' roll where the musical, sexual, and racial transgressions he offered initially became positive commercial attributes. He was a progenitor of rock 'n' roll who was surpassed by it. Ray had legitimate reasons to fear a backlash for his queerness, but he seemed to have underestimated his audience's capacity and willingness to embrace his vulnerable masculinity.

A beneficiary of the postwar audience's burgeoning attention to music made by cultural outsiders was Little Richard. Chapter 3, "Spectacular Vacillations: Little Richard Charms and Disarms America," showcases the broad range of queering tools Little Richard employed. He spectacularized just enough visually and musically to be recognizable as a black male R&B performer and to stand out. In doing so, he played the race card from multiple angles, fitting in just enough with black music to be authentic and appearing as sexually nonthreatening to a white audience. This had the effect of neutering him sexually, which was intentional. After his initial fame, he domesticated himself, retreating from the spotlight, subduing his image, attending a religious college, getting married, and abandoning secular music for gospel.

He returned to secular music in the mid-1960s and amplified his status as the original self-enfreaking rock 'n' roller, including more overtly blurring gender visually and spectacularizing in concerts and on television. He redefined himself as a headliner in rock 'n' roll nostalgia shows. From the late 1970s through the mid-1980s he vacillated between domesticating and neutering himself in the name of religion and seeking a secular audience. Even when he domesticates himself, there is a discernible spark that appeals to audiences. Through examining reviews, his visual image, and television appearances, I illustrate how he has reached relative equilibrium between his faith and his freakishness.

The pressure to resonate with black audiences and appeal to white audiences led Johnny Mathis to play the dandy rather than the freak. Chapter 4, "Fine and Dandy: Mapping Johnny Mathis's Negotiations of Race, Sexuality, and Affect," details the way he built his persona around being a nonthreatening, sexually ambiguous figure who relayed a polished, respectable "race man" image. Vocally, his tenor signified queerness to some listeners, but his appearance and affect were too mild to raise serious suspicions around his sexuality. Though he was part of an emerging black male celebrity culture of the 1950s, his intentionally neutered and domesticated dandy image insulated him from controversies related to dating, marriage, and racism that had an effect on his peers. He has crafted a black dandy image that has allowed him to maintain a cool distance from controversy. Even when he began speaking more overtly about his connection to gay culture and his own identity, he attracted limited fanfare, indicating a deft mastery of "queering" unobtrusively.

Chapter 5, "Building an Empire of Illusion: Liberace and the Art of Queering," examines the array of tools Liberace employed from the early 1950s through his death in 1986. Liberace established himself through spectacularizing in subtle ways, such as branding his namesake, adding unusual details to his performances, integrating pop melodies with classical music and intentionally ignoring traditional classical dress codes. He expanded his reach through television, enchanting audiences, especially women, with his spectacular but sexually neutral white, middle-class, family appeal. Music and television critics rejected his image, essentially enfreaking him for his genteel masculinity, which tabloids exploited through queer baiting. He responded by counterdomesticating via elaborate efforts to convince audiences that he was dating Hollywood starlets and pursuing marriage, and by creating a more masculine version of his television image. His audiences enjoyed him as is and ignored these peripheral efforts, but he grew concerned when a newspaper column attempted to frame his masculinity in sexualized terms. He triumphed through using sexual neutrality and his domesticated image as the antidote to insinuations that his act was sexual. The effect was a newfound freedom to enfreak himself further via sartorial and performative spectacularizing that cemented his image as an icon of tacky, campy, but expensive glamour. Even toward the end of his life, when a former lover attempted to "out" him in a palimony suit and as he was suffering from HIV/AIDS, he domesticated himself in an attempt to maintain certain illusions with his audience. He mastered a variety of tools in various configurations to modulate a host of expectations.

"Disquieting and Exciting: Queering Tools in Popular Music and Queer Becoming" concludes the book by examining "queering" as an ongoing process of becoming for people who challenge gender conventions in popular culture. I read these gestures as personal and social indicators of people working to understand who they are and where they belong socially. I examine contemporary examples of post-1950s musicians who employ "queering" tools and discuss an example of an emergent tool. I also ruminate on potential ways tools could be explored in a variety of other musical contexts. An endemic element of such practices is an ongoing navigation of slippages within and around normative notions of gender.

CHAPTER ONE
Visibly Hidden
Postwar Disorientation, Queer Community, and Queer Ambivalence

THE NEWNESS OF THE post–World War II culture fundamentally meant varieties of subcultures were being incubated within or in parallel to the dominant mainstream culture of the time. The postwar era is as much about Beat culture, civil rights activism, nascent second wave feminist organizing, commercial pornography, and a more visible urban homosexual culture as it is about nuclear families, suburban housing developments, and consumerism. This chapter elaborates on some of the slippages in gender norms that the Introduction alludes to by tracing their roots in a "disorientation narrative" (Breines 1992, 6). Bustling forces beneath the veneer of prosperity and uniformity mobilized some unexpected energies that countered the conformity and the monotony that colors memories of the era.

I begin by outlining the emergence of new postwar social norms and how growing discontent with these norms is inspiring various social rebellions. Next, because the policing of gender is so integral to the postwar mindset, I examine how the stigmatizing of gender deviance put gender deviants at risk. Simultaneously, such exposure also gave them the visibility that provided an ironic catalyst for community building. As queer communities formed nationally, liberation politics emerged and clashed with the homophile movement. The chapter's third section examines this generational divide. Though certain elements of the liberationist philosophy retain their social and political power today, notably the politics of visibility, one of the most overlooked aspects of pre-liberation culture was an unspoken anti-identitarian perspective about sexuality. I conclude with a discussion about how James Baldwin and Gore Vidal queered the way we understand gender and sexuality, in both their work and life, through rejecting the notion of affiliating with a sexual identity group. They parallel members of the Quartet in important ways. Both writers were popular artists who were legibly queer in their art and personae, and yet they were unconcerned with *coming out*. Many observers certainly made insinuations about their sexuality. But their conscious self-projection of sexual ambiguity, rather than explicit identifications with LGBTQ communities, gave them unique, expressive freedoms as artists unburdened by social or political loyalty to a singular sexual community. Beyond this effect, it reflected the ambivalence, uncertainty, and complexity about the meaning of their individual queer identity and the burgeoning prospect of affiliating with communities of desire.

Postwar Experimentation and Disorientation

The immediate postwar period is a national civic and cultural touchstone that was not only endorsed but was also an industrially supported solidification of the *American Way of Life*. This newly modernized, national lifestyle trumpeted a democratic government antithetical to socialism and fascism; a free-enterprise capitalist economy; social tolerance for religious and racial differences; and the emergence of the nuclear family as a social microcosm of national values (Foner 1998, 236–47). We know historically that this dream was not equally accessible to all or even most of the population. Various legal and industrial realities, such as de facto segregation and restrictive housing covenants, ensured different segments experienced newfound prosperity unequally, if at all. However, understanding the official narrative is key here.

In *The Way We Never Were* (2000), Stephanie Coontz reminds contemporary readers that the nuclear family is a modern development not a transhistorical structure: "For the first time in more than one hundred years, the age for marriage and motherhood fell, fertility increased, divorce rates declined, and women's degree of educational parity with men dropped sharply. In a period of less than ten years, the proportion of never-married persons declined by as much as it had during the entire previous half century" (25). For example, before suburban migration, extended kin were more integral to family structures, and ethnic ties among second-generation European immigrants were stronger (Del Mar 2011, 107). The excitement regarding the newness of the nuclear family outweighed these shifts and emerged in the popular responses to television programs, films, magazines, and "expert" literature that depicted the new quality of life that white couples experienced as they transitioned from cities to suburbs, the working class to the middle class, and extended families to contained nuclear families. In a sense, they were pioneers, and "not, as common wisdom tells us, the last gasp of 'traditional' family life with roots deep in the past. Rather, it was the first wholehearted effort to create a home that would fulfill virtually all its members' personal needs through an energized and expressive personal life" (May 1999, xxii).

Anxieties about sexual and gender propriety are staples of most historical and sociological investigations of the era. These created unique opportunities for outsiders to penetrate the mainstream. As Wini Breines notes in *Young, White, and Miserable* (1992), "Anxiety accumulated around other more personal issues too; sex, gender, and the family were beset with ambiguity," and she cites historian William Chafe (*The Unfinished Journey: American Since World War II* [1986]) in support: "The nature of family life, particularly in suburbia, was far more complicated and tension-filled than stereotypes of the fifties would have us believe" (8). She eloquently frames the era's contradictions and paradoxes by locating them as part of a "disorientation narrative" where "the alter image" to the image of "a white, affluent, suburbanized society compensating for the deprivations and disruptions of the Depression and World War II" is "of a people alienated, disoriented, and discontent" (6).

Women, for example, were expected to serve both as erotic companions for their husbands (D'Emilio and Freedman 1988, 308–9) as well as mothers who were primarily devoted to raising normal, well-adjusted children. After analyzing the results of the Kelly Longitudinal Study (KLS), historian Elaine Tyler May, in her 1999 study *Homeward Bound*, outlined women's sense of feeling compromised intellectually, professionally, and emotionally by their domestic roles (25–28). Michael Kimmel's *Manhood in America* (1996) also noted the impact on men when he depicted male malaise as the "Goldilocks Dilemma" (170). May concluded that despite the iconic happiness associated with heterosexual married couples of the time, "their poignant testimonies . . . reveal a strong undercurrent of discontent; their hopes for domestic happiness often remained unfulfilled" (xxiii).

Domestic discontentment culminated in a series of reactionary behaviors and rebellions. Coontz notes the rise in the use of alcohol, prescription drugs, and tranquilizers among women during the postwar period, quoting a 1949 *Life* magazine story that recalled how "suddenly and for no plain reason" women were "seized with an eerie restlessness" (Coontz 2000, 36–37). The synthesis of these symptoms surfaced most pointedly in 1963 via journalist Betty Friedan's *The Feminine Mystique*, described by historian Sara Evans as giving "a name to the malaise of housewives and the dilemma of those who did not fit the mold" as key to the book's cultural impact on women. One measure of its seminal articulations was that "thousands of letters flooded Friedan's mailbox, as women poured out the stories they had thought no one would ever understand" (Evans 2001, 195). In *The Story of American Freedom* (1998) Eric Foner recalls *The Feminine Mystique*'s pivotal role as "the public reawakening of the feminist consciousness," even if "Friedan's mailbag also contained evidence that reactions to her critique differed strongly along lines of class and religion" (295–96). Consumer culture served as major outlet for men and included *Playboy* magazine's debut in December 1953 and its influential philosophy that men should "enjoy the pleasures the female has to offer without becoming emotionally involved" (D'Emilio and Freedman 1988, 302). Other sources of rebellion included an invigorated fitness culture (for example, the popularity of fitness equipment salesman and TV star Jack LaLanne), which promised to re-create the male body as an antidote to domestic ennui, and the iconization of the Western—in fictional literature, TV "horse operas," and films, which reminded men of the "rugged individualist" archetype they had abandoned (Kimmel 1996, 181–83). "Beat" culture offered even more radical possibilities for men: "In the Beat, the two strands of male protest—one directed against the white-collar work world and the other against the suburbanized family life that work was supposed to support—come together into the first all-out critique of American consumer culture" (Ehrenreich 1983, 53).

The gay and lesbian constituents of the queer community recognized gender as a major organizing category with potential social consequences for effeminate men and masculine women. One of the best ways to gauge the burgeoning social consciousness of gays and lesbians during the postwar period is to understand the kinds of questions and tensions that emerged as queer communities developed a political culture and cultivated new relationships with popular media. At issue was how to achieve social and political liberation without sacrificing queerness. This is less a matter of competing political philosophies than the question of what constituted social progress in the context of sexuality.

Historians usually cite the founding of the Mattachine Society in 1951 and the Daughters of Bilitis in 1955 as the birth of the homophile movement. Though both of these groups disbanded eventually, their desires for homosexual men and women to be understood as social minorities, comparable to racial and religious minorities, eventually inspired smaller homophile groups. These include San Francisco's Society for Individual Rights (SIR), founded in 1966, and larger organizations, notably the East Coast Homophile Organizations (ECHO), founded in 1963, and the North American Conference of Homophile Organizations (NACHO), founded in 1966 (McGarry and Wasserman 1998, 153, 150, 156). All of these are signposts of a burgeoning awareness among gays that they had shared interests and the ability to organize and demand equal protection from harassment and discrimination under the law. The ways governmental agencies, the popular press, and other entities simultaneously stigmatized gender and sexual deviance created a hostile climate for queer people but also, ironically, mobilized some awareness that those who expressed themselves queerly had a culture and potentially an identity and a community.

Stigma + Publicity = Queer Visibility

Clearly defined gender roles and an imperative for parents to socialize children as future citizens were central features of the nuclear family, which was an essential ingredient of social normalcy. There was immense social pressure for adults to form nuclear families and settle into consumerist lifestyles. Adults who resisted this tacit expectation were socially aberrant and vulnerable to being perceived as subversives. This was especially true for known or suspected queers. David K. Johnson terms the political manifestation of these anxieties the "Lavender Scare": "a fear that homosexuals posed a threat to national security and needed to be systematically removed from the federal government" and that "permeated 1950s political culture" (Johnson 2004, 9). From February through November 1950 the U.S. government fired nearly six hundred federal civil servants suspected of homosexual activity, a number that grew into the thousands (1–2). During the postwar era this fearful behavior also led to the wide-scale firing of homosexuals in private industry and the routine policing of homosexual social spaces. These represent some of the main forms of social control intended to enforce national values. Managing the range of what was gender appropriate is integral to these forms of control.

There was a complex dynamic attached to this systematic harassment. It socially stigmatized homosexuals *and* simultaneously verified the existence of homosexuals to other homosexuals. Homophobic forms of social control, such as stigmatizing effeminacy, contributed to a growing sense among dispersed homosexual men and women that there was the potential for a homosexual culture even if it tended to be represented crudely. Michael Sherry's *Gay Artists in Modern American Culture* (2007) captures the contradictions of this postwar dynamic by noting how "Americans created modern antihomosexuality in part by examining queers and queerness in the arts. They bequeathed to us images of gay people as curiously both silly and sinister, protean and perverse, creative and corrupting, invaluable and insidious: as both outside and inside American life. Gay people contributed to these images, albeit rarely from a position of power" (2).

Michael Bronski in his *Pulp Friction* (2003) reminds us that "midcentury America was a unique historical moment for homosexuality. The Second World War had generated profound dislocations and disruptions of traditional ideas of sexuality and gender" (13–14). For example, in Allan Bérubé's 1990 study of gays and lesbians during World War II, *Coming Out under Fire*, he quotes poet Robert Duncan's 1944 essay "The Homosexual in Society," published in the magazine *Politics*, as an early example of public pleas for homosexual liberation as an extension of human liberation. Bérubé comments that "Duncan's coming out, and his critique of forming separate homosexual groups, anticipated a political discussion that began to appear in gay novels immediately after the war" (251) and lists Jo Sinclair's *The Wasteland* (1946) and John Horne Burns's *The Gallery* (1947) as representative examples (250, 251). He also briefly reviews mid-to-late-twentieth-century discourse on the notion of homosexuals as minorities, as published in *Cosmopolitan, Newsweek*, and the letters column of the *Saturday Review of Literature* (250–51).

These World War II and postwar examples of homosexual discourse clearly illustrate a transitional moment when public engagement with homosexuality was possible in mainstream media. Bronski elaborates on this transition by pointing out the tension between social expectations and social curiosities regarding sexuality. He cites the mainstream's response to Alfred Kinsey's 1948 study *Sexual Behavior in the Human Male*, especially its revelation about homosexual behavior among adult men at various stages of their adolescence and maturity, as exemplifying the country's budding postwar fascination with male homosexuality (Kinsey, Pomeroy, and Martin 1948; Bronski 2003, 13–14). According to Bronski, "the contradictions generated by and embedded within this fixation were tremendous. Here was a country obsessed with ridding its government of 'subversive' homosexuals, yet it idolized performers like Liberace and Little Richard and refused to acknowledge their—rather evident to many—homosexuality" (13–14). Queer gender behavior, not necessarily sexual object-choice, is the implicit link Bronski is making. Clearly, "homosexuality was very much in the public consciousness. If anything, it was more integrated into popular culture than it would be in the late 1960s and the early 1970s. This is not to say that public discourse about homosexuality in the 1950s was more enlightened or tolerant . . . but it was understood and discussed in very different ways" (2). This historical pause is about something present versus something more legible, which speaks to the dynamics of queer life before the rise of visibility politics.

Homosexuality figured prominently in mainstream discourse about social threats to family, normalcy, and democracy. Two popular genres that stigmatized male homosexuality for the general public were nonfiction exposé books and tabloids. Journalists Jack Lait and Lee Mortimer led this market through a series of exposés of life in major U.S. cities. They frequently, and disparagingly, reference homosexuality throughout their 1948 *New York: Confidential!: The Big City after Dark*. For example, chapter 4, "The Theatah!," warns readers: "Unfortunately, too many of the adolescents have been tinged with political radicalism and tainted with homosexuality. Yet, the New York theater is still the most vital and vibrant facet of show business, and from it comes almost everything good in its bastard offspring, radio and the movies" (Lait and Mortimer 1948, 39). Their discussion of the Fifty-Second Street jazz scene in chapter 5, "Swing Lane," notes, "Two other developments in the street—said to be natural consequences of its jazz madness—are the presence of reefer (marijuana) addicts and homosexuals, of all races" (45). In chapter 8 there is a discussion of Greenwich Village, which is titled "Where Men Wear Lace Lingerie" and is a smirking treatise on homosexuality. According to the authors, "There really are two Greenwich Villages—the one the sightseer glimpses and the less appetizing one inhabited by psychopaths dimly conscious of reality, whose hopes, dreams, and expressions are as tortuous as the crazy curves in the old streets" (66). As I noted in the introduction, the black mainstream press also constructed homosexuality in extreme gendered terms. The contrast between "freaks" who pervert gender norms draws attention to the presumed naturalness of gender normative behavior, which amplifies the normalcy of gender-conforming blacks at a historical moment when blacks were seeking civil rights and greater mainstream acceptance.

New York: Confidential! was a hit, and Lait and Mortimer continued to outline the gay presence in America's biggest cities in books such as *Chicago Confidential* (1950), *Washington Confidential* (1951), and *U.S.A. Confidential* (1952). Johnson describes how *Washington Confidential*, which featured lurid descriptions of urban homosexual culture, became a *New York Times* bestseller and was quickly reprinted in a paperback edition that sold in the millions. In terms of impact, "it spawned a veritable cottage industry of similar exposés and led one year later to the founding of the tabloid magazine *Confidential*, which carried on the tradition for the rest of the decade" (Johnson 2004, 91).

Scandal sheets, or tabloids, were one of the most important sources for understanding how the public developed an understanding of the behaviors and individuals that signified sex and gender deviance in the 1950s. They emerged when the Hollywood studio system was disbanding and studios had less control over public stars' images. A central aim of tabloid journalism was to provide alternative images to Hollywood-produced discourse from studios and press agents (Desjardins 2001, 207, 215). Former film critic and studio publicist Ezra Goodman noted in *The Fifty-Year Decline and Fall of Hollywood* (1961) how scandal sheets functioned to offset the pallid and tentative writing in mainstream journalism's celebrity coverage (53). Scandal sheets became such a phenomenon that *Time* and *Newsweek* published stories on the public's fascination with them in 1955 ("The Press in the Sewer," 90; "The Curious Craze for Confidential Magazines," 50–52). Goodman noted that scandal magazines scared and fascinated people and were a major subject in the Hollywood scene of bars, cocktail parties, and hangouts (51). The most popular and influential tabloid was *Confidential*, which began publication in 1952 (Desjardins 2001, 207). Mary Desjardins notes that scandal magazines "were considered illegitimate and were read by a smaller audience than the legitimate press (although the circulation figures claimed for *Confidential* ranged from 250,000 to 4 million, which put them in good competition with fan magazines)" (217). Though there were numerous scandal sheets, including *Q.T.* and *Hush-Hush*, *Confidential* was the most infamous, a fact attested to by the State of California's 1957 criminal libel and obscenity charges against the magazine (207). According to Goodman, *Confidential*'s primary interest was in sexual peccadilloes (Goodman 1961, 53). Along with Desjardins, David Ehrenstein's *Open Secret* also notes how *Confidential* capitalized on the scandalous nature of homosexuality via "outing" celebrities such as Marlene Dietrich and the pop performers Johnnie Ray and Liberace, whom I discuss in chapter 2 and chapter 5 (Desjardins 2001, 213; Ehrenstein 1998, 100–101).

During the 1960s, homosexuality migrated gradually from a topic of scandal in exposés and tabloids to a mainstream social issue that captivated print and broadcast journalists and intrigued audiences. For example, from 1963 to 1966 the *New York Times*, *Life*, *Time*, and *New York Times Magazine* published supposed exposés on homosexuality (Doty 1962, 1, 33; Welch 1964, 68–74; *Time* 1966, 40–41; Schott 1967, 44–72). One of the common themes in each was the notion that homosexuality was a growing "epidemic," especially in urban areas like New York and San Francisco. *Life* magazine was the only source to note that despite the *appearance* of more open expressions of homosexuality, there was no data to support the assertion that homosexual desire or culture was more prevalent (Welch 1964, 79–80). This qualification is important because homosexual themes were prominent in popular literature, and there was certainly homosexual authorship in multiple cultural fields. Most so-called exposés of the era presumed that the general population was radically unfamiliar with homosexuality as an ontological reality and cultural sensibility, which lacks historical credibility. Though the postwar black press's coverage of homosexuality was narrow, its stories on drag performance reflected a long-standing tradition of covering black drag since at least the 1920s (Wilson 1956, 79–89; Conerly 2001, 387–91; Chauncey 1994, 244–67).

The readers of gay exposés, queer-baiting tabloids, *Sexual Behavior in the Human Male* (referred to colloquially as the *Kinsey Report*), and gay and lesbian pulp novels all constitute a public highly aware of homosexuality.[1] If anything, the mainstream print media's sudden interest in homosexuality reflected *their interests* rather than a change in how homosexuals presented themselves publicly. The coverage may have also reflected an increased ability for heterosexuals to detect homosexual "codes." Throughout the 1960s, several feature writers publicly chided gay playwrights for supposedly masking homosexual motifs through heterosexual characters and attempted to provide tools and primers for audiences to "decode" plays.[2] The notion that gay creative artists were mocking heterosexual culture was central to these articles, as was a desire for gay authors to be more straightforward in presenting homosexuality. This plea could be interpreted as an attempt to contain homosexuality rather than to integrate it socially. The dominant motif of these stories that needs correcting is the notion that homosexuality was *outside* of the mainstream when homosexual authorship pervaded a wide range of *mainstream* creative genres.

The second presumption the mainstream print media perpetuated was the "homintern" hypothesis that homosexual artists were part of an exclusive secret network that had "infiltrated" women's fashion, literature, theater, and dance. As Johnson notes,

> Like the Comintern, or Communist International, homosexuals were thought to make up a worldwide network, or "homintern." First used around 1940 . . . the word *homintern* conveyed the idea of a global homosexual community, particularly in the literary and artistic world. By the 1950s, fear that American culture was increasingly dominated by this community found expression in publications from highbrow journals like *American Mercury* to scandal tabloids like *Confidential*. Some feared homosexuals had a "stranglehold" on the theater, television, and radio. Some feared this "powerful coterie" of homosexuals and their sympathizers would "lead to a gradual corruption of all aspects of American culture." (Johnson 2004, 34–35)

In addition to a conspiratorial perspective, several of the articles mentioned above proffer essentialist interpretations of homosexuals as being uniquely gifted at embroidery and disguise, and such works feature hostile dismissals of homosexual artists' abilities to create substantive, enduring art. Sherry thoroughly addresses these themes in *Gay Artists in Modern American Culture*; *Rocking the Closet* seeks to respond to the absence of attention to popular music in these attempts to *expose* homosexuality in mass culture.

Journalists' emphases on certain genres over others in their homosexual theorizing reveal the unique way popular music exposed audiences to homosexuality yet protected homosexual musicians from the kinds of conspiratorial scrutiny directed toward other creative fields. Writers could turn to supposedly veiled themes in theater to support the theory of gay artists as deceivers. They could turn to literature to depict gay authors and themes as depraved, petulant, and/or tawdry and could also cite women's fashion as a marker of gay male misogyny toward women's bodies (Time 1966, 40). Popular music, however, was strangely absent from these formulations, despite the well-established commercial careers of figures like Liberace, Little Richard, and Johnny Mathis, by the time the 1960s-era stories began appearing in mainstream publications. Arguably, popular music is a more difficult genre to employ in support of the implied gay arts mafia conspiracy. Though Sherry, Nadine Hubbs, and other scholars have noted the gendered implications of certain critiques of gay male classical composers, popular music lacks sufficient critical attention in this regard (Sherry 2007; Hubbs 2004). My approach aims to clarify how careers as popular music performers enabled queer musicians to achieve mainstream notoriety without being directly evoked in media panics on homosexuality in the arts.

From the mid-1940s throughout the mid-1960s the mainstream media, with the support of various "experts" drawn from medicine and social science, represented homosexuality as a lurking social problem. Though these depictions aimed to steer the public toward viewing homosexuality disdainfully, significant segments of the public were fascinated, intrigued, and even titillated by homosexuality, especially in veiled form. The black press also employed homosexuality as a topic of interest, featuring homosexually themed headlines on magazine covers.[3]

Queer people were certainly among those intrigued by the flood of stories. Despite the stigmas these mainstream publications imposed *on* gay men, they also, ironically, signified the existence of a palpable culture *to* gay men. John D'Emilio's *Sexual Politics, Sexual Communities* (1998) characterizes the spate of articles on homosexuality in the 1960s as "resources for homosexuals and lesbians in search of a subculture" (139). Christopher Nealon complements this in his *Foundlings: Lesbian and Gay Historical Emotion before Stonewall* (2001), noting that "print media offered gay men and lesbians the opportunity to begin to identify as part of a group" (113). These nonfiction sources were buttressed by other developments that helped gay men covertly develop a sense of identity. As noted in the introduction to this book, commercial physique art aimed at men, along with print media stories, are important examples of "pre-liberation" era sources of homosexual publicity. *Becoming Visible* argues that, "though postwar physique publications were drenched in homoerotic subtext and claimed a homosexual audience (at least some segment of a larger audience), they never proclaimed themselves to be homoerotica as such. Indeed, the success of physique art and photography lay precisely in its ability to effectively 'pass' and thus appeal to a broad public" (McGarry and Wasserman 1998, 122–23). Magazines like *Physique Pictorial, Tomorrow's Man, Vim, Trim,* and *Grecian Guild Quarterly* were among the 1950s-era magazines whose images "provided images for isolated gay men to imagine themselves as (homo)sexual beings" (118). Beyond individual consumption, Nealon argues that "acts of purchase and identification together encouraged the initial development of a gay male community" (Nealon 2001, 124). We see a similar communal effect in the mass distribution of gay male pulps and the embedded informational codes I discuss in the introduction.

As homophile organizations were exploring the political potential for an organized political movement, gays and lesbians also developed multiple cultural resources that depicted their needs and desires. The development of gay cultural artifacts and the emergence of queer "sensibilities" sometimes causes conflict within the political community for exposing subjectivities not necessarily deemed helpful for broader social acceptance. Drag performances and female impersonation, expressions of "camp," and images of homosexual sex, overt and suggestive, are among the cultural expressions nurtured within homosexual cultures that generated tensions with political movements (Bergman 1993, 4–5). This was true during the homophile era and remains an area of contention, usually articulated in terms of what images and depictions constitute images perceived as helpful or harmful for queer political progress.

Many of the queer textures listed above were criticized for framing gay men too overtly as *different* from rather than comparable to heterosexual culture during the homophile years. For example, Bob Mizer founded the Athletic Model Guild (AMG) in 1948, and men subscribed to his catalog service for years before the commercial burst of physique magazines in the early 1950s (McGarry and Wasserman 1998, 117–18). This commercial genre's emergence before homophile politics invoked little controversy among gay men. Comparatively, in 1964 when Charles Polak began publishing the physique magazine *Drum*, during a period of significant homophile organizing, he directly questioned the movement's cautiousness about certain forms of gay culture by reminding members of the community that gay desire was central to the rights movement (Loughery 1998, 283). John Loughery's *The Other Side of Silence* notes that Polak "was adamant that sex itself had been avoided for far too long by those who wanted to 'raise consciousness,' and that reticence had created another large gap between audience and activist" (283).

Drum, as well as other physique publications, outsold more politically minded publications like *ONE* and *The Mattachine Review*, an indication that gay men were interested in culture and politics—though culture had the upper hand in popularity. Polak's intervention represented how the public exposure of gay subjectivities remained a contentious issue for those who would prefer to render politics more salient. A struggle to balance these two arenas deepened during the liberation era. The scholarly issue that has arisen from the tensions the Polak example illustrates was the struggle to chronicle how desire, feeling, and affectivity preceded formal politics. Arguably, the politics of desire was a new kind of politics with multiple strands, not just direct action and legislative advocacy. Cultural politics and more traditional forms of activism such as direct-action protests and legislative advocacy can both function as modes for accessing freedom. Trouble emerges when we frame these as polar opposites rather than understanding and appreciating them for their distinct qualities and reconsidering them as potentially complementary modes. Between these lies ambivalence among queer people about articulating personal identity, finding community, and engaging with the personal as a communal and political identity. The Stonewall divide is a key turning point in the artificial tensions between cultural expression and politics.

Challenging the Stonewall Divide

As I have noted previously, the preeminent moment defining modern queer history are the riots that began on June 28, 1969, and continued for six days. I wrestle with the weight of the history of the riots throughout *Rocking the Closet*. Though there were important precedents to Stonewall, including a 1959 riot at Cooper's Donuts in Philadelphia, ECHO's 1965 protest at the White House, and the 1966 riot at Compton's Cafeteria in San Francisco, Stonewall garnered an unprecedented level of sustained national attention. Tonally, it represented a new shift away from fears of police violence and the assertion of masculine violence toward a direct, unapologetic confrontation with such forces. As Allen Ginsberg famously stated in *Newsweek*'s article

"Policing the Third Sex," "the guys that night were so beautiful. They'd lost that wounded look that fags all had ten years ago" (Newsweek 1969, 76).

As the defining benchmark of gay liberation ideology Stonewall carries a great deal of mythology and cachet, yet the riotous spirit of Stonewall never represented how *most* queer people were responding to homophobia then or how they respond contemporarily. Though coming out, and the politics of visibility, emerged as the primary gesture of social and political liberation for queer people, there has always been a range of expressions and embodiments of queerness. Liberation provided an ideology and fueled a movement, but movements rarely encompass the majority of a particular population or subgroup. More often than not, elements of movements filter down into populations in some form.

We must remember that political tensions always existed within the homophile groups who were increasingly torn between defining themselves as a minority group who were essentially the same as heterosexuals and thus deserving of equal treatment, and as a separate culture who should be accepted on their own terms. Returning to the men of the Mattachine Society, they initially defined their purpose as unifying homosexuals and educating homosexuals and heterosexuals about the distinctive nature of homosexual culture (McGarry and Wasserman 1998, 142–43). In 1953, however, a more conservative leadership redefined the society's mission by arguing that homosexuals deserved tolerance *despite* their differences (D'Emilio 1998, 77–80). The core belief of this assimilationist approach, which dominated the philosophy of homophile groups until the mid-1960s was: "Homosexuals were the same as everyone else and simply needed help adjusting to mainstream society" (McGarry and Wasserman 1998, 145). The liberation era was comparatively focused on motivating society to *accept and value* homosexual difference rather than emphasizing their social conformity (D'Emilio 1998, 150–214, 224–39; Loughery 1998, 303–55; McGarry and Wasserman 1998, 140–252; Faderman 1991, 180–270).

Even among these groups, diverse perspectives emerged. For example, the political tactics and anarchist structure of the New Left–oriented Gay Liberation Front (GLF) differed greatly from their offshoot the Gay Activists Alliance (GAA), which gained fame for "zapping" famous homophobes publicly, and often illegally. The most prominent gay rights group of today, the Human Rights Campaign, has a more conservative agenda (for example, marriage), a more structured and well-funded organizational approach, and less confrontational strategies (Bronski 2011, 210–12; Hirshman 2012, 107–11). While these groups differ in mission and tone, they share an investment in the political utility of gay visibility; thus, they exemplify the liberation-era ideology, even if they use different tactics toward different ends.

Somewhat distanced from these grand tensions were the quotidian lives of queer people who navigated closet pressures in relation to their social contexts. For queer creative and performing artists, particularly those who had developed large audiences, there was not a magical dividing line between their liberated and post-liberated selves. Considering the generally formulaic nature of commercial art, whatever aesthetic aspects drew audiences initially is what artists maintain usually. More important, from a historical perspective the pressure to conform within certain ideals and norms of gender that occurred prior to June 1969 did not suddenly fade in July 1969 or during the 2010s as I write this study.

If we allow ourselves to look back at the 1970s, when the Gay Liberation era began, we see that many queers dismissed pre-liberation textures as antiquated, apolitical examples of self-loathing that fueled homosexual prejudice toward homosexuals. The elaborate veils and codes homosexuals previously used to communicate with one another were viewed as the antithesis of the coming-out philosophy since it defined disclosure as the most important tool for gays to express their authentic selves and to engender empathy and understanding. Contested notions of authenticity defined the discourse in the 1960s and persists into the present. Battles over authenticity have shifted partially because scholars have shown the wealth of expressions that circulated before the traditional political movement became more dominant and valued than cultural politics.

Bronski argues that gay liberation was a youth movement: "One of the great projects of the Gay Liberation Movement was to create a new gay culture that was both to replace the older oppressive gay culture and to salve the wounds and scars that had been inflicted on homosexuals" (Bronski 2003, 12). The price of this intention to forge a new distinct gay culture apart from the heterosexual mainstream and a previous generation of homosexual authors was, ironically, "the dismissal of past 'innovation,'"—notably, the complex ways gay authors had managed to integrate their work into mainstream culture without necessarily isolating it as "gay culture." Sherry refers to an emergent trend in 1960s mainstream media that diminished the cultural production of gays in the creative arts as superficial works that reflected the pathologies of their authors. As he notes, "The repudiation of mid-century queer creativity was done in part by a new cohort of activists, unwittingly in league with those who had disparaged that creativity for decades" (Sherry 2007, 207). He illustrates the denigrated role of gay artists by noting how the 1972 anthology *Out of the Closets* "said little about creativity," because "the daily mores, rituals, and stereotypes of culture were a concern, but not formal cultural production" (206).

In the 1978 *Lavender Culture*, co-editor Allen Young criticizes contemporary gay men in the arts who "often prefer to climb the ladder of success in the established institutions of culture (the literary world, the ballet, the theater, etc.) rather than engage in the often frustrating and financially dubious struggle for an independent gay-oriented cultural expression" and views the "display [of] heterosexual imagery" in their productions as "self-destructive" (Young 1994, 24). Elsewhere in the essay, Young defined the camp sensibility as "the most significant gay contribution to contemporary culture" but viewed much of the camp slang used among gay men as reflecting "many levels of prejudice and self-contempt" (31). Finally, he was leery about the gay creativity myth: "Even the worst homophobes will usually agree that gay people are especially creative" (33). He was responding specifically to the myth that gays must suffer in order to produce and the mainstream contempt toward liberation since "all of that creative energy would be lost once people come out of the closet and became comfortable with their homosexuality" (34). By viewing the topic of gay creativity as an external myth even gays believed about themselves, he failed to give sufficient attention to one of the main reasons gay artists were able to appeal to the mainstream audiences prior to Liberation. Notably, as Sherry argues in his defense of pre-liberation male artists, they "had seen themselves as in the mainstream and indeed had constituted it, rather than merely observing it" (Sherry 2007, 231). Their perceptions are important because elusiveness and ambiguity were accepted ways for queers to integrate themselves into the mainstream.

These brief examples illustrate a tendency by writers and critics influenced by liberation politics to dismiss pre-Stonewall culture because it is not traditionally political. Doing so reduces its authors to mere closet cases, minimizes the quiet power of "open secrets," and embraces a "minority" identity at the expense of recognizing gay artists' roles in defining and not merely reacting to the mainstream. A more nuanced consideration of the pre-political generation's complex negotiations of gender propriety becomes more apparent when we closely examine popular culture of the era.

The liberation era's break from the cultural past has artificially condensed public attention to the range of homosexual affectivities prior to Stonewall by reducing the value of culture to politically and culturally unsatisfying "acceptable" and "unacceptable" categories. In the 1994 reissue of *Lavender Culture*, Cindy Patton's foreword pinpoints new challenges for those seeking to illuminate gay and lesbian history:

> After a decade of academic research and fragmenting politics, we are more
> sanguine about the absolute value of narrativizing gay and lesbian experi-
> ence. There is a tension between two ways of telling "our" story. One presses
> a broad claim about the pervasiveness and continuity of homosexual *culture*,
> while the other privileges lesbian and gay *politics* but relies less completely
> on the meta-narratives of liberation's forward march or of liberal pluralism's
> capacity to muddle through. (Patton 1994, xiii)

She posits the historical pre- and post-Stonewall divide to pinpoint the culture and politics tension: "Here, Stonewall divides a timeless time of oppression from the entry into the Time of History. *Before 1969*: we could only
chafe and give up our fullest possibilities. *After 1969*: we could say who we
are and in the unifying power of our speech, fight back" (xiv). This pre- and
post-Stonewall paradigm views "the riot" as one that "provided the 'real'
event necessary to claim our first break into history's eye. There would be
no retreat, no 'going back into the closet'" (xv). Prior to the "riot," multiple
events were already happening on the cultural front. These served as a basis
for queers to have culture and community; arguably, the interplay between
culture and politics continues to define contemporary movements for gender
and sexual equity.

We must remember that "coming out" can be as confusing as it is clarify-
ing, since as an act of disclosure it only reveals a fact about sexual identity
but says little about desire or behavior itself. Judith Butler's insights on the
way queer sexual declarations can feel unsatisfying and incomplete despite
the political import accorded to outness is especially useful to my discussion.
Butler's questions regarding disclosure, "Is the 'subject' who is 'out' free of its
subjection and finally in the clear? . . . What or who is it that is 'out,' made
manifest and fully disclosed, when and if I reveal myself as a lesbian? What
is it that is now known, anything? . . . Can sexuality even remain sexuality
once it submits to a criterion of transparency and disclosure, or does it perhaps cease to be sexuality precisely when the semblance of full explicitness
is achieved?" are particularly relevant to queer artists (Butler 1993, 308–9).

Being "out" implies being understood as something discernible, yet there
are infinite varieties of sexual expression, including murky, ambiguous, fragmented versions that operate between the light and the shadows. These forms
are more difficult to acknowledge when certain forms of recognition are
prized over others. As Butler notes, the dilemma of "outness" lies in defining
what is being exposed to whom and understanding how the "what" can easily
become something static and finite. A related question raised by the politics
of visibility is, "Which version of lesbian or gay ought to be rendered visible,
and which internal exclusions will that rendering visible institute?" (311).

Part of my motivation for examining the Quartet is the friction between the perception of them as pre-political and the sophisticated layers of queerness in their rhetoric. They managed to "queer" the cultural landscape without declaring their sexual identification (at least initially) and simultaneously resist stable versions of sexual identity. In many ways, they also challenged the idea of being "known" sexually by illustrating how reductionist sexual identity can be for an artist. A brief look at two key literary figures illustrates this and can help us transition our attention to the ambivalences about identity and belonging evident among the Quartet.

Writers without Borders: Pre-political Queer Ambivalence and Anti-identitarianism

In addition to challenging teleological argument, *Foundlings* also informs my attention to an anti-identitarian element among the Quartet. Both critical projects seek to capture the tension between being an individual and potentially choosing to affiliate with a discernible group. I am responding specifically to Nealon's observation that the "pre-political" queer texts he examines reflect "an overwhelming desire" among their authors "to *feel historical*, to convert the harrowing privacy of the inversion model into some more encompassing narrative of collective life. This is why I think of my materials as 'foundling': the word allegorizes a movement between solitary exile and collective experience—one that is surely still a part of contemporary queer culture" (Nealon 2001, 8).

In our haste to historicize figures as representatives of queer cultures we often bypass the time and space individuals need to understand things about themselves *before* recognizing themselves as members of a community. Even after they "become" members their process of becoming continues. There is a potentially wide range of emotions and sensations—isolation, uncertainty, shame, joy, discovery, and beyond—a queer person experiences privately before ever coming into a conscious identification or affiliation with an identity community. Rather than dismissing these as shameful, negative, closeted, and other moralistic adjectives, we must engage with them as valid reflections of human subjectivity and understandable social responses to homophobic and genderphobic cultural messages.

As detailed in this book's introduction, the handlers of film stars, and the stars themselves, tried to cover up their sexuality under forced heteronormative gestures, which parallels some of the strategies queer musicians employed. Queer artists in other genres conveyed a range of strategies with useful insights for understanding the ways musicians navigated queerness.

Poet Allen Ginsberg and novelist Truman Capote embraced their location on the edge of gender and sexual normativity and wove this boldly into their art and personae.[4] Comparatively, Gore Vidal and James Baldwin rejected sexual labels and modeled a proto-anti-identitarianism that defies conventional readings of them and, more important, public expressions of queerness.

When compared to Capote and Ginsberg, Baldwin's and Vidal's navigations and disavowals of sexual identity teeter on a boundary between the discernible and the unknowable, a theme especially close to the heart of my discussion. In this respect they offer the clearest parallel to the way some members of the Quartet defined their personae. Both writers attempted to manage queer sexualities in the 1950s onward, publicly disavowed the notion of sexual desire as an "identity," and yet were too intelligible as queer thinkers to evade perceptions of them as sexually queer. The work they produced as writers and intellectuals, including fiction and essays, was difficult for audiences and critics to distinguish from them as people.

Vidal's *The City and the Pillar* (1948) was one of the first popular novels focused on a homosexual relationship. Vidal wrote prolifically and boldly over six decades about a range of sociopolitical topics, including sexuality. Conservative writer William F. Buckley Jr. infamously threatened him and called him a "queer" on live television in 1968, and Vidal lived with male companion Howard Austen for more than fifty years (Gordon 2015). Yet he never identified as homosexual, gay, or queer. In fact, he largely rejected the notion of sexual identities. In his 1979 "Sex is Politics," he argues: "Actually, there is no such thing as a homosexual person, any more than there is such a thing as a heterosexual person. The words are adjectives describing sexual acts, not people. These sexual acts are entirely natural; if they were not, no one would perform them" (Vidal 1993, 550). He finds the premise of sexual labeling futile. "The human race is divided into male and female. Many human beings enjoy sexual relationships with their own sex; many don't; many respond to both. This plurality is the fact of our nature and not worth fretting about" (550). His confidence on the page belied his private struggle and a dogged management of his sexuality.

Vidal's novelistic depiction of a homosexual relationship *The City and the Pillar* offended the critical establishment deeply. As he recalls in *Palimpsest*, "One Orville Prescott, the daily reviewer for *The New York Times*, told my editor that he would never read much less review another book by me. *Time* and *Newsweek* followed suit. Seven novels went unnoticed in their pages" (Vidal 1995, 122). He then turned to making a living writing for "television, movies, theater, and the essay" (122). Biographer and Vidal acquaintance Jay Parini tells a slightly different story, noting that Vidal's novels were ignored in the daily *Times* but not the Sunday *Book Review*, "the most important publication at the time. The real problem was reviewers didn't especially like the novels that followed *The City and the Pillar*" until *Julian* in 1964 (Parini 2015, 73).

Regardless of Vidal's public disavowals of sexuality as a category, he struggled with his homosexuality privately, attempting therapy briefly and clinging to the potential notion of his bisexuality, "an idea he held on to dearly," as his longtime companion Austen noted (Parini 2015, 71). Gore's queer sexuality was intelligible to many, especially after *City* was published, and privately he worried that his lack of access to a traditional family life would stifle his political ambitions. Parini claimed Gore despised the term "gay" to the extent of calling himself a degenerate, "with a certain degree of self-loathing irony," and shied away from public alignments with gay rights, including the AIDS-era protests of the 1980s and 1990s, "afraid to find himself implicated in some way" (64).

Even though Baldwin is widely heralded as the "father" of black gay literature and as a key progenitor of black queer theory, he is difficult to appropriate for gay or queer theoretical or political projects (Brim 2014, 27–28). Baldwin never *identified* as homosexual, bisexual, or heterosexual and was also averse to the term gay (Leeming 1994, 358). His first published discussion of his own sexuality came in "Here Be Dragons," where he describes sexual encounters with males and females, as well as homophobic and genderphobic violence he experienced growing up (Baldwin 1985, 681–86). Baldwin's disinterest in identifying sexually does not mean people did not *perceive* him as queer but that he was uninterested in helping them label him. Challenging labels and addressing intersections and "impossible desires"—described by Matthew Brim as "working with and beyond prescribed identity categories," "those illegitimized desires, often between men and often between races that have been pushed to the very edge of thinkable"—was integral to his creative life (Brim 2014, 2).

Though his social circle knew he had same-sex relationships and had somewhat haughty, effeminate mannerisms interpretable as stereotypically queer behavior, he was not "out" in the way this term is traditionally understood. *Time*'s May 1963 Baldwin cover story, which characterized him as "a nervous, slight, almost fragile figure, filled with frets and fears . . . effeminate in manner," was one of the first public suggestions that Baldwin, who authored novels with queer characters, was potentially gay (*Time* 1963, 26). Eldridge Cleaver's incendiary attack on Baldwin's masculinity and sexuality in *Soul on Ice* solidified the notion that Baldwin was one of *them*. Baldwin was shocked by Cleaver's attack and devastated by intraracial criticism in general. By most critical accounts, he never quite recovered and was ambivalent about portraying queer sexualities in his work for a long time (Field 2011, 48; Field 2015, 72).

Despite the *Time* story and Cleaver's attack, Baldwin insisted that *Giovanni's Room* was not primarily *about* homosexuality, even if it was depicted there and in other works, and he never affiliated with the gay political movement (Field 2011, 45). Insistent that he was an artist, not a representative, he felt compelled to join the civil rights movement but was less convinced about the urgency of sexual politics (47). Though this seems hypocritical or contradictory today, Matt Brim in his *James Baldwin and the Queer Imagination* (2014) has effectively framed Baldwin as a paradox (5, 11, 32). His same-sex desires and social location in queer circles did not translate into sympathetic depictions of male effeminacy or transvestism. He has also engendered criticism for his masculinist attitudes about male-female relationships and failure to represent lesbianism (Field 2011, 48–49; Field 2015, 9). Baldwin remains a compelling critical figure for literary studies, queer studies, gender studies, and similar endeavors for his ability to trouble the category of "black gay male" writer. Brim recognizes the "specificity of one's intersectional identity" but reminds us that "identity for Baldwin is less a marker of static sameness and difference than of unrecognized, painfully assimilable otherness within the self," which informs his critical project of exploring the queer imagination, "a way of registering the alchemic dynamic by which 'a person' emerges, fails to emerge, or refuses to emerge amidst socially prescribed identity categories" (Brim 2014, 12).

In sum, Vidal rejected the way sexual practices morphed into identities on a philosophical level. He also had legitimate concerns about how his sexual identity would limit his access to fulfill certain political ambitions. Baldwin emerged as a writer of note during the flowering of the civil rights movement, which was a dangerous and controversial affiliation. When we consider the country's segregated landscape, we have little reason to believe he identified with the mostly white male homophile movement, a single-issue movement that focused on sexual orientation, not racial or gender equity. Further, if *he* had drawn attention to his apparent effeminacy, with its implied associations of "queerness," this would have distracted many from taking him seriously as an artist or activist. His career predates contemporary awareness of intersecting oppressions, so adapting the compound identity of black-queer would have limited him.

As I show throughout, the desire to claim figures as heroes is an understandable source of pride for queer history that distorts the struggles musicians had simply being themselves. For example, we can easily can applaud Little Richard's bold, brazen rock 'n' roll persona as the antidote to 1950s blandness. Rarely, however, do we consider how he reconciled becoming famous for the kind of over-the-top genderplay that led his family to eject him from his home as an adolescent. Little Richard embraced his exoticism for strategic racial reasons: "I started wearin' makeup, so that they wouldn't feel threatened when I was in clubs, around the white girls, 'cause they think you're comin 'round to get them, when your mind ain't nowhere like that. Their mind is sex, y'know" (Gill 2004, 3), but he struggled to form a stable public identity beyond this initial reactionary flamboyant persona. Liberace is a frequent critical target for never "coming out" as gay and, by association, embracing his sexuality as an identity with political implications. Chiding him for not conforming to identity politics allows us to neglect the notion that beneath the costumes, the wink, and the quips he may have *struggled* with the meaning and social implications of his sexuality. Optimally, we can shift our focus from merely historicizing or memorializing toward humanizing these figures.

The pride paradigm has made it difficult for contemporary scholars to reconcile a desire to minimize the pathologizing tendencies of homophobia and genderphobia rhetoric with the critical imperative to tell a fuller story about how people navigate queer identities. As such, there is an urgent need to address the lack of a "critical vocabulary for describing the destitutions and embarrassments of queer existence" (Love 2007, 107). Simply stated, it is hard to embrace figures that seem to disavow queerness, whether it is their sexuality and/or the queering gestures they perform publicly. This requires us to recognize embarrassment, shame, and/or uncertainty as legitimate feelings of the pre-political era that endure.

Heather Love's reading of Radclyffe Hall's classic lesbian novel *The Well of Loneliness* (1928) is instructive because her view suggests the novel "offers a meticulous account of the many outrages, failures, and disappointments that attend gender and sexual conformity in a homophobic world" (Love 2007, 107). Baldwin's and Vidal's reluctance is difficult to understand in light of their stature in queer literature, but it taps into the fact that sometimes being queer was burdensome in terms of one's personal understanding and broader social agency. Again, these feelings persist and inform the tentative relationship Quartet members have with identity and identity politics.

The sanguinity of the coming-out era functions almost as a form of forgetting and a nod to queer survival. The artificial break between cultural desire and a more liberated politics obscures how ongoing feelings of social ambivalence continue in the present. We must resist "a queer reading practice that assumes the movement from 'pathology to politics,' so that they come to represent, for better or for worse, what 'we' presume ourselves to have transcended: the closet, isolation" (Nealon 2001, 13). Historical ruptures are very seductive intellectually, but history does not work this way. Many of the same challenges queer artists faced prior to queer uprisings continue to inform their public identities. They also shaped the queer-identified artists and the users of queering tools who followed them, even indirectly. I raise this point because the Stonewall demarcation can easily shift attention away from the ongoing presence of homophobia, genderphobia, and other forms of anti-queer violence that constrain the expressive freedom and social equity of queer lives. If we understand historical ruptures as openings rather than closings, we are more poised to engage with the nuances of queer life that preceded political moments and the struggles that remain. I hope that readers feel poised to explore the eclectic ways Johnnie Ray, Little Richard, Johnny Mathis, and Liberace employed the "queering" tools to express themselves and continually engage their audiences, which is the focus of the remaining chapters.

CHAPTER TWO

A Freak Deferred

Johnnie Ray Navigates Innovation and Convention

They come to see what the freak is like. They want to know
what this cat has got. I know what this cat has got. I make
them feel. I disturb them. I exhaust them. I bring one or
another of their buried and controlled emotions to the surface.
That's enough for the present. There'll come a time when I'll
do something more for them. But I'm not ready for that just yet.
—Johnnie Ray, quoted in "Million-Dollar Teardrop," 1952

Freaks are called freaks and are treated as they are treated—
in the main, abominably—because they are human beings
who cause to echo, deep within us, our most profound terrors
and desires.
—James Baldwin, "Here Be Dragons," 1985

FEW DETAILS ABOUT Johnnie Ray conform to standard scripts of the
postwar era. Deaf, effeminate, bisexual, openly approving of black culture,
and loathed by many music critics, he was seemingly an anomaly. Arguably,
his commercial success and cultural notoriety points toward curiosity and an
openness regarding queer masculinity. Ray's recording career peaked from
1950 through 1960, a period of great musical and cultural transition, notably
the rise of rock 'n' roll. He attempted to downplay the oddities that gave him
his initial career, which also made him a forerunner to rock 'n' roll, by shifting
toward a mainstream blandness that failed to sustain his career. His career
represented a tug-of-war between representing an appealing freakiness and
striving to be as accessible as possible that has surfaced in the careers of other
queer artists. Instead of continuing to push himself into outré territory, he

tried to stick to the middle at a time when more radical musical styles and personas were gaining footing.

His initial success represents a break with conventional wisdom about the kinds of masculinity that circulated commercially in the postwar era. For example, though Baldwin is correct that the social mainstream of the twentieth century usually treats freaks poorly, the ability of certain "freaks" to gain fame and illuminate truths about the mainstream itself is important to consider. The interplay of the tools Ray used to navigate his popularity, most notably drawing attention to his "enfreaked" status and self-domesticating, speaks to uncharted territory other musicians, such as Liberace and Little Richard, also faced in their careers. The core questions that emerge from such careers is the following: When audiences embrace your queering of expectations, how much can you trust their interests, how far can you go in a queer direction, and is it essential to tone down these elements for greater mainstream accessibility? Liberace thrived, Little Richard retreated and returned (multiple times) as a public figure and performer, Johnny Mathis has persisted as a recording artist well into the 2010s, while Johnnie Ray faded. The book's chapters tell their individual stories, which includes highlighting overlaps and differences from other musicians. I am especially interested in using Ray's story to discuss historical openings and closings. Perhaps he could have achieved the stature of an Elvis Presley as a white translator of black music styles if he had stuck with his initial sound and image. He and his handlers second-guessed his initial success. Instead of viewing his queerness, which surfaced in various forms, as an asset that drew audiences, they seem to have underestimated the capacity of his audience to embrace the unconventional. Essentially, his audiences were not *queerphobic*; Ray and his management were. Part of telling his story is analyzing the forces that may have led them to abandon what was a promising path.

What Makes Johnnie Ray a "Freak"? Musical Traces

Johnnie Ray launched his career with "Cry," which was a radical pop song because it incorporated musical elements of black music that made it a pop and R&B hit. The song, written by Churchill Kohlman, was released October 1951, several years prior to civil rights landmarks such as the death of Emmett Till, *Brown v. Board of Education*, and the March on Selma that drew attention to the toll of racism and the promise of integration. The B-side of "Cry" is the highly sentimental "The Little White Cloud that Cried" and was atypical for white male pop in its themes of isolation and loneliness. Compared with most mainstream white male singers of the early 1950s, Ray was an anomaly, or, colloquially speaking, he was somewhat of a "freak."

Ray defied masculine vocal styles and "white" vocal styles of the late 1940s and early 1950s. He was so highly influenced by R&B singing, especially black female singers like LaVern Baker, that he was mistaken for a *black female* singer when his voice was mistaken for that of a black female singer. Danny Kessler, head of Okeh Records Artists & Repertoire (A&R), told Ray's biographer Jonny Whiteside, "I played the record for the sales force at Columbia and almost in unison they said, 'We don't think she's gonna make it.' They all thought I was pitching a girl who sounded like Dinah Washington! Finally I convinced them that she was a boy, and then I had to break the news that she was a white boy. I know they all felt that I had lost my head completely" (Whiteside 1994, 63). Ray's R&B inflections and sentimental tone were apparently such a contrast to the typical sound of white male vocals at the time that he stood apart instantly on sound alone. He favored highly emotional songs like his 1951 hit "Cry," and his vocal intensity was matched by a physical spasticity.

In the early 1950s Ray's sentimental singing and dynamic concert style led to a barrage of nicknames ("Nabob of Sob," "Prince of Wails"), variety show sketches, and song parodies (Stan Freberg's "Try"), which he accepted with humor. As he told *Billboard* in 1952, "I get the biggest kick out of take-offs on me—particularly Stan Freberg's record and the stuff that Jack E. Leonard and Sammy Davis Jr. do" (Martin 1952c, 19). Ray had to stand apart in some way if other artists felt compelled to coin these names. If he were a typical crooner, he would not have garnered this kind of attention.

Rock historian Charlie Gillett discusses Ray in his *The Sound of the City* as a transitional figure one step beyond Frank Sinatra and Frankie Laine, who capitalized on Sinatra's pioneering audience aesthetic. According to Gillett, "Sinatra's style involved audiences in his singing—and in him—as no previous singer had done, and stimulated devotion comparable to that previously aroused only by film stars like Rudolph Valentino. . . . Audiences expected singers to project themselves (or what was publicly known of their selves), and each listener wanted to feel as if the singer were singing to her (or him, if the listener was male) (Gillett 1996, 6). There was a succession of Italian American male singers who found success post-Sinatra, but Laine was a particularly successful follower. Gillett distinguishes Ray by noting that "in 1951, involvement rose to a new peak when another singer . . . inspired furores at airports, hotels, and backstage theatre doors—Johnnie Ray. In contrast to his predecessors, Ray lacked smoothness, precision of phrasing, or vocal control; instead, he introduced passionate involvement into his performance, allowing sighs, sobs, and gasps to become part of the sound relayed by the amplifiers" (6).

Gillett intends to contrast rock 'n' roll and pre-rock pop of the early 1950s, and in doing so he defines Ray as an almost purely contextual figure, "Even Johnnie Ray was hardly as remarkable as the enthusiasm of his supporters, or the distaste of his decriers, would suggest. Only in comparison with the generally emotionless music of the times, to which Ray, like Laine, were exceptions, could the silly and sentimental 'Cloud' have attracted anybody's interest" (Gillett 1996, 6–7). His harsh summary is perhaps too broad in its reading of pre-rock music, but it addresses the distinctive emotionalism Ray brought to 1950s pop and his unique appeal to audiences.

Some of the main elements of his musical appeal were his unique phrasings and the mechanics of his performing style. Rock historian Reebee Garofalo's *Rockin' Out* suggests that "early in the 1950s, the emotionally unhinged Johnny [sic] Ray could have provided Columbia with a way into rock 'n' roll. His uninhibited stage performances, during which he routinely ripped off his shirt, were at least in part the result of tutelage by LaVern Baker and her manager" (Garofalo 2005, 126). Here he refers to the influence of Baker, a black R&B singer who recorded many successful hit singles for Atlantic Records during the 1950s, on Ray. It is important to note, however, that various black musical figures directly influenced Ray's performing style. Whereas most white crooners were trained in big-band singing before transitioning to solo careers, Ray had more diverse mentors. In their 2003 *American Popular Music*, Larry Starr and Christopher Waterman note, "Ray created an idiosyncratic style based partly in African American modes of performance, and in so doing paved the way for the rock 'n' roll stars of the later 1950s," and this included being "the first white pop performer to remove his microphone from its stand and go down into the audience, seeking direct contact. His stage act was dynamic: Ray writhed, wept, and fell to his knees" (181). Other singers commonly associated with this kind of vocal intensity and physical emotion were black male performers like Jackie Wilson, James Brown, and Otis Redding.

Ray's chief childhood vocal influences were gospel, hillbilly, jazz, and black popular music. Blues and jazz-influenced popular singers Kay Starr and Billie Holiday strongly influenced Ray (Whiteside 1994, 29, 32; Guild 1957, 49). Profiles in both *Billboard* and the *Saturday Evening Post* noted Ray's roots as a performer on the Midwest club circuit including Detroit's "black-and-tan" (or racially mixed) Flame Bar. Ray developed his chops for blues-oriented singing under the tutelage of blues singer Maude Thomas and years of singing at the Flame, where he developed a rapport with numerous black musicians and endeared himself to multiracial audiences (Martin 1952c, 16, 19; White-side 1994, 49, 51, 54). The *Post* noted, "It was here, in all probability, that Ray developed his phrasing and vocal style which are reminiscent of so many top-flight Negro blues singers" (Sylvester 1952, 112). After he scored his initial hits Ray proclaimed his attitude toward segregation in the self-penned 1953 *Ebony* story, "Negroes Taught Me to Sing." Ray boldly expressed his outrage at Jim Crow laws and related to blacks when he noted, "Coming up the way I did—the hard way—and having been almost laughed out of existence ever since I was a skinny, unwanted kid, I know how it feels to be rejected," and "they have an innate sympathy with the underdog and a delight in seeing a handicapper come from behind" (Ray 1953, 48, 56). Though some of Ray's statements were simplistic, what stood out was the oddity of a white mainstream pop singer overtly identifying with and praising black culture at the time, and his open disapproval of racial segregation.[1]

Few popular white musicians of his time took this kind of political stance openly. Though many white musicians would participate in the civil rights movement in the 1960s (Tony Bennett, for example), Ray's article and statement were unusual (Raymond 2015b, 71, 197). As author of a book about the closet, I would argue that his ability to incorporate black musical elements and his comfort and acceptance among black musicians and audiences are notable for what such realities *uncloseted*. Notably, he demonstrated the constructed nature of racial differences and modeled possibilities in the entertainment world that could translate into daily life. I have yet to locate any record of fallout from his statement, especially since few whites probably read *Ebony* in the early 1950s. Nonetheless, it illustrates another way he stood out and remained viable commercially.

Music critic Will Friedwald argues that in vocal terms, Ray "was indeed the first-ever crossover R&B star—the first white entertainer to work in the contorted, hyphenated manner (in other words, "Cah-ry-hi" instead of "cry") that characterized rhythm and blues and then doo-wop and early rock. That style of singing was already highly exaggerated and mannered, yet Ray was even more so. . . . As the first white R&B headliner, he signified the first time many middle Americans had heard even a vague imitation of 'race' music" (Friedwald 2010, 684). The nature of his performing style and vocal approach has culminated in diverse opinions about Ray's relationship to rock 'n' roll. Gillett defines Ray as a slight contrast to pre-rock crooners but not as a rock 'n' roll performer; Garofalo posits him as a would-be rock 'n' roller; Starr and Waterman more overtly define him as "a crucial link between the crooners of the postwar era and the rock 'n' roll stars of the later 1950s" (181). Whiteside and Friedwald suggest a slight variation on this connection by defining him as a bridge between Al Jolson and Elvis Presley (Whiteside 1994, 117; Friedwald 2010, 683). Whiteside states,

> From the cornerstone of blackface (the earliest commercial 50–50 blend of African rhythm and European melody) popular music grew in entirely new and different ways. The general acknowledgement of such personal freedom brought with it a sense of individual power. That response led to a craving for the long denied taboo of primal independence. Jolson brought it to the Twentieth Century; Johnnie tore off the theatrical mask and offered it to people; Elvis gave it a threateningly tangible accessibility. (Whiteside 1994, 117)

Ray's differences from the mainstream made him a phenomenon in a decade fascinated by novelty. For example, the anthology *Widening the Horizon* (1999), by Philip Hayward, documents the commercial rise and social impact of postwar "exotica," defined as "music which features aspects of melodic and rhythmic structure, instrumentation and/or musical colour which mark a composition as different from established (western) musical genres (while still retaining substantial, recognizable affinities to these)" (7). Les Baxter, Martin Denny, Arthur Lyman, Korla Pandit, and Yma Sumac are among the musicians whose "exotic" sounds reached the commercial mainstream, peaking commercially from the early 1950s through the mid-1960s (9). Though Ray's music certainly fits within Western musical traditions, it was just different enough to stand out in a decade when America was actively reinventing itself. *Billboard* published a four-part series on Ray's rapid rise from obscurity to success. The second installment documented the numerous disk jockeys and club bookers who claimed to have discovered Ray. Key to this story is the line, "While Ray was working in the Ohio territory, several musicians and disk jockeys saw in him the big-time touch" (Martin 1952a, 19). The pervasive sense that he was "different" made Ray a unique commercial figure, and marketing him effectively was important. The appeal of "Cry" to pop and R&B listeners solidified him as the rare white performer with white and black appeal. In this sense, his ambiguous aural identity was beneficial.

Deafness, Performance, and Masculinity

Alongside Ray's initially unusual sound was his image: he was the first popular singer to perform as openly deaf (he wore a hearing aid in his left ear). Related to this was his unusual sense of pitch that caused him to writhe onstage in a manner that many critics found disturbing. The critics may

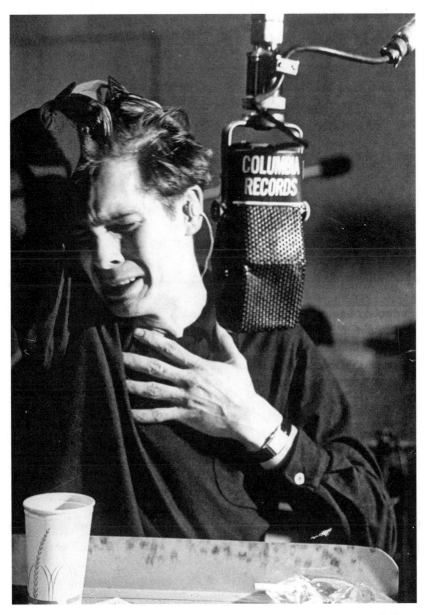

FIGURE 2.1. Johnnie Ray emotes in the recording studio wearing his hearing aid (photo by Leonard McCombe/Getty Images).

have despised his sentimentality, but teenagers made him a popular idol, and his vulnerable image offered an alternative to the emotional stoicism of most crooners.

As George McKay notes, Ray "performed with a highly visible electrical device protruding from a hole in his head (hearing aid in his ear) with a cable running from it to [a battery pack strapped to] his body" which made him America's only deaf pop singer of that time, a distinction which endures. Ray lost 50 percent of his hearing from a childhood blanket toss when he landed hard on his left side, "leading to concussions and hearing loss" (Whiteside 20). The impact of his disability was "its power or shock value—and the way it could construct a different form of masculinity" (McKay 2013, 125, 127, 128). McKay argues that Ray's "disability *feminizes* masculinity" (137; emphasis in the original), and though McKay does not fully develop this idea, the implication that Ray was less able to do something yet still triumphed and had a career made him an empathetic figure.

Most firsthand accounts of Ray's performing style suggest a lack of control and a heightened emotionality with feminine connotations. Robert Sylvester describes a 1952 performance in detail: "As a night-club and theater entertainer, he is startling and disturbing, to put it mildly. He takes the floor and thanks God or the orchestra leader for his good luck. Then he sits at a piano with a detachable microphone and starts to sing. Behind him, the band plays a set orchestration while Ray plays his piano chopsticks style and hollers out his lyrics" (Sylvester 1952, 30). Vocally, "In his singing he breaks rhythm constantly. He grimaces as though in pain. He punches the piano with a frustrated fist. He can shed real tears. He throws out his arms in desperate supplication and he reaches out open hands for some lost personal illusion" (112).

Music critic Howard Taubman described Ray's 1952 Copa performance with more pointed editorializing:

> He sings like a man in an agony of suffering. One number, at best two, may have a cheerful slant, and in such pieces Johnnie Ray's phrasing has a neat, rhythmic beat. The other songs are lachrymose in content, and when he gets through with them they are drenched in tears. Using the microphone to the full, he tears a passion to tatters and then stamps on the shreds. His voice, thanks to ear shattering amplification, shakes and quavers thunderously. Occasionally his misery sinks to a whisper, which makes for effective contrast, but soon its wracking pain is roared out in blasts of sound.
>
> Johnnie Ray accompanies his singing with a visual performance that is equally anguished. His face glistens with dew. Some observers say it is tears; some insist it is perspiration. It could be a little of both. His hair falls over his face. He clutches at the microphone and occasionally behaves as if he

were about to tear it apart. His arms shoot out in wild gesticulations and his outstretched fingers are clenched and unclenched. (Taubman 1952)

Sylvester's and Taubman's observations refer to the spastic tone of Ray's wrenching vocal style and full-bodied involvement, notably his pleading, outstretched arms. Interestingly, their reviews do not consider how his hearing impairment influenced the physicality of his performing style. I concur with Cheryl Herr that on some level "Johnnie Ray's music, at least the ample percentage of his act that was downbeat, is often viewed as a direct function of his hearing loss. That is, Ray's delivery is seen to be caused by his deafness" (Herr 2009, 327). McKay notes that his hearing aid was essential: "He needed to be able to hear more clearly what he was singing and playing, and where he was in relation to the band or orchestra's musical accompaniment," and he apparently turned the volume up loudly a times, which affected his pitch (McKay 2013, 128–29). His sense of balance is also key, since he struggled with balance after his accident, and "the functions of the inner ear are concerned with both the sense of hearing and of balance" (Whiteside 1994, 37; McKay 2013, 131). Both writers also attempt to diagnose Ray's appeal to teenagers. Interestingly, Taubman's review noted, "Those in the know contend that the teen-age set is the bulk of his public. But there were not many teen-agers in the Copacabana the other night" (Taubman 1952). Instead of delving into the presence of adults, some of whom "were there out of curiosity," Taubman assessed Ray's appeal to the young and suggested that he "speaks for young people beset by fear and doubts in a difficult time. His pain may be their pain. His wailing and writhing may reflect their secret impulses. His performance is the anatomy of self-pity." This conclusion was a logical outgrowth of the proclamation near the beginning of the column: "In the long run it will be clear that he has not added anything to the sum total of American art. But he and his audience reflect a significant aspect of the country's cultural pattern, and they both deserve study and analysis. Possibly the task should be undertaken by a social scientist rather than a student of music, but undertaken it should be, and without condescension." I invoke the Baldwinian concept of the "freak" here to point out the tension between the ideal American manhood Taubman normalizes, in this case normative notions of male physical and emotional expression, with the more complex and cross-gender appeal of Ray's embodiment.

McKay's argument that Ray's "disability *feminizes* masculinity" warrants further analysis. In the context of musical production and performance the implications are highly gendered. Ray was less musically able than other musicians, more dependent on his band, and thus more reliant on empathy and acceptance. Especially compared with the independence and strength expected of a postwar man. Extending this notion could lead one to ask: If Ray needed such high-level support in his professional life, how could he successfully fulfill the expected social role of serving as a husband and father?

Ray was not only different visually and physically but aurally as well, and the combination made him the face of male vulnerability among crooners of the 1950s. As Allison McCracken has noted in *Real Men Don't Sing*, from the 1920s onward crooning was stigmatized as part of a wave of low culture. With the advent of amplification and the surfeit of crooners in the 1920s and 1930s, crooners were perceived to show "an unseemly degree of ardent emotion and vulnerability for white men, and they used microphones and amplifiers to artificially enhance their soft, trembling, often sensually breathy sounds" (McCracken 2015, 3) and aligned symbolically with the gay "pansy" type that emerged in 1930s popular culture. This stereotype did not change much until Bing Crosby's baritone style and "common man" identity emerged (6). Ray was hardly a "breathy" singer, but in a formal sense his strident emotive sound adhered to these stigmas, even two decades later. More to the point, the notion of emotional excess and artificiality haunted many critical responses to his performing style.

"Freak" Sexuality: Stated, Implied, and Ambivalent

Underlying the odd specter of both Ray's visible disability and his bombastic style was his bisexuality and his efforts to manage his desire. Ray's pursuit of his desires thrust him into a liminal space between a penchant for soliciting public sex from men and publicly declaring his desire for a wife and children. Attempting to balance social conventions with clandestine access to queer sex is a notable aspect of postwar queer male experience that reflects uncertainty about meeting personal sexual needs and appearing socially acceptable. Though Ray was married to Marilyn Morrison briefly and had a long-standing (yet clandestine) affair with columnist Dorothy Kilgallen, many industry professionals perceived him as homosexual, and the tabloids exploited this perception. Curiously, Ray's biographer Whiteside notes that Ray's bisexuality was an "open secret" in the music industry and did not significantly deter Ray's ability to secure a recording contract or bookings in first-rate clubs and performing venues. For example, he quotes H. D. Hover, manager of the nightclub Ciro's, who said about Johnnie, "Someone told me that Johnnie was homosexual, but I didn't place any weight in that." He continued by noting it was not shocking, "because most of your top attractions are homosexual. It was so prevalent that it didn't matter. It's like having black hair—so what?" (qtd. in Whiteside 1994, 102). Industry knowledge, however, did not necessarily deter the rumor mill, as queerness was a commodity. Nor should we confuse the industry with the public; it is not clear that Ray's "open secret" was public knowledge. Tellingly, Hover said "homosexual," not "bisexual," which speaks to how anxieties about sexuality meant homosexuality overwhelmed the possibility of a person having hetero *and* homo desire.

Ray was liminal in an era that idealized certainty and stability. The press's confusion over how such a strange performer became a cross-racial, cross-generational sensation highlights Ray's liminality. As Joseph Vogel has noted, "In embodying a liminal space 'in the middle,' in ambiguity, the androgyne becomes problematic for those invested in protecting established borders of identity" (Vogel 2015, 467). The multiple anxieties over his persona encompass multiple questions about the performer and the kinds of people who are drawn to him or who could be in the future. It is not clear if Ray knew Columbia executives initially thought he was a black woman, but he did know about the rumors surrounding his past. Sylvester notes, "During the early months of his recording success when he was still unknown and unseen, it was 'reliably reported' that Ray was an Indian, a polio victim, a female impersonator, a copyrighted myth and a fugitive from a Kinsey report who wore a silver plate in his skull and had only six months to live. Most startling of all was the widely circulated report that he was a deaf mute who could somehow sing songs" (Sylvester 1952, 112). The fact that public rumors referenced female impersonation with such certainty as well as *Sexual Behavior in the Human Male* (Kinsey, Pomeroy and Martin 1948) (known colloquially as the *Kinsey Report*) subtly signifies a more intricate relationship between what is valued (normalcy) and what is *known* (deviance) than is typical in postwar rhetoric. One would have to have encountered an impersonator in some context to speculate on whether someone else was one. Similar observations could be made about other forms of so-called social deviants.

Actually, the rumor that was most startling *to Ray* was his supposed past as a female impersonator at a burlesque house. Ray tells Sylvester he regrets the way the mainstream press reported on his former gig as a pianist and vocalist at a burlesque show: "That's what caused the worst of these crazy rumors. . . . The one about my being a reformed female impersonator. Why, in that burly show I never even put on a woman's hat. I just banged away at those stale pianos" (Sylvester 1952, 112). The publisher of Sylvester's article is important; the *Saturday Evening Post*, famous for Norman Rockwell's iconic images, was a very mainstream commercial magazine in the early 1950s, and millions of readers were reading a major star deny being a female impersonator.

Ray's wildness was tempered by vulnerability, and his bisexuality was maintained within the industry, but the combination of these associations with more explicit rumors regarding his gender had great potential to undo his career or stall his momentum. He risked transitioning from a weird-but-intriguing figure, which perhaps gave him cachet with teenagers, to a pervert trying to force himself onto the public, including its vulnerable youth.

Ray was not immune to these questions and concerns. He relayed to Sylvester that he knew curiosity was part of his freakish appeal. In relation to the epigraph from Ray, the "they" he refers to is the crucial part of this statement. A performer like Ray had to understand the nature of his audience and their musical interests. He also had to protect them from having their taste undermined by external suggestions that he was an inappropriate and corrupt influence.

The initial lack of public transparency about Ray's sexuality did not mean his audience lacked some sense that he might be queer sexually; secrecy simply enabled him to *feel* queer without being officially "queer." The nascent homophile movement was not poised to provide men with tools to develop a personal identity around sexuality and move through the world confidently. Nor was bisexual desire the movement's focus. "Looking backward" at Ray, using Heather Love's critical lens, reiterates how we must reconcile our contemporary desire for collective pride with historical realities that fostered shame and isolation (Love 2007). The closet was a private space for queer men to struggle with articulations of desire on a personal level, which preceded public affiliations. They might have known *what* they desired sexually, but this did not necessarily translate into knowing *who* they were, how this could translate into an identity or *where* they could explore these questions more fully.

Ray's persona was queer, especially his blending of male and female, as well as black and white. Audiences had enough information about him to draw all kinds of conclusions. His queerness was part of the draw. He could not closet his deafness and declined to closet his integrationist perspective. In thinking about Ray, I continually return to the question: How did a deaf, effeminate, white integrationist succeed in the early 1950s? It turns out these were assets rather than liabilities in the early 1950s. For a time he was exactly what Americans, especially teenagers, wanted.

This unspoken contract was a distinct feature of the early 1950s. Since the late 1940s through the early 1950s, audiences were primed to define themselves against effeminate men, who were believed to be homosexual by definition, and simultaneously surrounded by resources that increasingly publicized homosexuality and by association made it a feasible identity. Much of the anxiety regarding queer figures was both the inappropriate effeminacy and, therefore, homosexuality of the performers and the potential nature of their audiences. Christopher Nealon argues, in reference to 1950s physique magazines that, "the mysteries of publication—not knowing who produced these fleeting but widely available print materials or who consumed them or with what desires and objectives—fed a heterosexual paranoia about a 'gay' audience with solidity and purpose that, ironically, was not even close to existing yet" (Nealon 2001, 116). There is a parallel here since Ray was feared for igniting passions in young women toward a man who lacked proper virility. He was also perceived as providing a poor role model for young men—whose consumption of Ray is rarely discussed during the 1950s—and even potentially attracting other "freaks," to use Ray's language. For example, the tabloid *Uncensored* suggested in a 1955 piece by Bert Mason that "one of Ray's big secrets is that he's got something for the boys too" (Mason 1955, 48). The issue here is not just Ray the individual performer but a larger fear that *perverse* versions of masculinity were rapidly infiltrating mainstream popular culture, an anxiety also present in Liberace's career during the 1950s. These fears undoubtedly shaped the ability of queer male performers to feel capable of expressing aspects of their sexuality that would have associated them with queer political and social communities.

Johnnie Ray and the "Sex Police"

In addition to Ray's black-influenced gender-vague music, deafness-inspired performance, and public rumors regarding his masculinity, he had a criminal record. The underbelly of his initial access, however, besides negative reviews, were creeping suspicions that his image was too polished and that he was overexposed. Ray's high profile in scandal sheets was a significant source of irritation, which contradicted the image Ray's handlers conveyed. What is less clear is that tabloids undermined Ray's commercial appeal *directly*. Though his audience loved him, tabloids may have diminished his confidence about his image.

The careful promotional materials that defined Ray's image suggested an almost desperate feeling among his managers that he needed overt displays of conformity to survive, a notion Ray's perpetual tabloid presence reinforced. *Hollywood Life, Confidential, Low Down* and *Hush-Hush* published a series of stories from the mid-1950s through the 1960s that "accused" Ray of being a social misfit and gender deviant. In the midst of the rock 'n' roll "sexual revolution" some writers asserted that Ray's press coverage and career opportunities dwindled because the rumors of his queerness grew too strong (Whiteside 1994, 148–49, 162, 196–200, 273, 292; Ehrenstein 1998, 161). I focus on *Confidential*'s coverage of Ray because of its mission to target rumored homosexuals. Though it is easy to dismiss tabloids, we must note that the genre exploited social taboos of the time because there was an audience for such material. Just as audiences warmed up to musical "exotica" and embraced anomalous figures like Ray, they sought out things outside of the norm. As Henry E. Scott's *Shocking Story* notes, "Recurring themes in *Confidential* such as homosexuality and miscegenation were good for sales because they pandered to popular fears and preconceptions. *Confidential* publisher Robert Harrison's focus on gays was extreme in the eyes of at least one of his editors, who remarked that his boss was 'queer for queers.' . . . There were stories about homosexuality in most of the magazine's issues" (Scott 2010, 80). Furthermore, *Confidential* was the most popular scandal sheet, and though they are "low culture" literature only sporadically archived, its articles are more obtainable from libraries and special collections than most tabloids. Two representative examples of *Confidential* stories on Ray that I was able to obtain combine several typical tabloid techniques. Notably, their stories build from previous public information, which made them appear credible and protected them from libel.

For the record, Ray *did* accumulate a history of near-arrests and actual arrests throughout the 1950s, usually the result of his struggles with alcohol. Before Ray was a national act he had accumulated an arrest record. In the early 1950s he and LaVern Baker were arrested in Detroit at what Baker described as "an after-hours spot," likely an African American club being subjected to police harassment (Whiteside 1994, 55). It is unclear if this was officially documented, but Baker recounted it to Whiteside in 1992. On June 5, 1951, after a performance at the Flame Club, he went to the Stone Theater burlesque house. The Detroit Vice Squad had been targeting the Stone because of its reputation as a homosexual gathering spot. Around 1:45 A.M. he went to the men's restroom, struck up a conversation with an officer, and was arrested for "Soliciting and Accosting" after reportedly offering oral sex to the arresting officer. This incident was a key example of Ray's bisexual desire and his navigation of what was available to him: public sex. Ray plead guilty and could either spend thirty days in the Detroit House of Correction or pay a fine. He paid the fine and left town (65–66). Ray's arrest could have instantly jeopardized his career but remained hidden from the mainstream public for years, and he did not treat the encounter as more than a lapse in judgment. Whereas Liberace was willing to sue tabloids for suggesting he was homosexual, an act whose very litigiousness suggested proof of innocence, Ray placed himself in situations where his behavior was overtly interpretable sexually as queer.

Several of his police run-ins were alcohol-fueled mishaps that garnered minimal publicity. In 1952, after a performance at Blinstrub's Theater in Boston, he was drunk and parked his car on the sidewalk, which led the cops to bring him into the station. Whiteside states that he was "reprimanded and released immediately" (Whiteside 1994, 132), though it is unclear if he was formally arrested. Shortly after this, he and comic Gary Morton got drunk after a performance in July 1952. They then purchased skates and skated through the lobby and restaurant of the hotel where they were staying in Minneapolis. They were charged with disorderly conduct and quickly bailed out. Later that year he and his manager were in Boston about to depart when Ray, who was drunk once again, urinated into a plant and passed out in Logan Airport. Ray was arrested for drunkenness and released the following morning (135).

But by the end of 1952 this behavior became more worrisome. On December 12, 1952, the subscription-only tabloid *Hollywood Life: Newsweekly of the West* published the cover story "Johnnie 'Cry' Ray Arrested on Homosexual Charge" (Whiteside 1994, 148–49). Because of *Hollywood Life*'s limited circulation, the story probably had limited direct impact on Ray's career. His newfound visibility nevertheless made him more vulnerable to public scrutiny, which is similar to Liberace's increased presence in tabloids after his first years of fame. Whether any of these incidents were reported publicly or covered up to avoid embarrassment is unclear.

Confidential's story by Jay Williams, published in its April 1953 issue, was the next major piece to insinuate that Ray was queer. The headline "Is It True What They Say about Johnnie Ray?" is significant because the "It" alludes to some form of prior knowledge about Ray. By doing so the tabloid represents the notion that something present but unarticulated pervades Ray's career, and the publisher's mission is to unearth this buried "truth" (J. Williams 1953, 37–39, 63–64). Tabloids viewed themselves as a form of "alternative" media that saw through the publicity machines of most public figures. Scott notes, "The very existence of so obstreperous a publication was another in a growing number of signs, albeit initially a small and easily overlooked one, that the studios were losing their tight grip on the film industry, its stars, its theaters, its public, and even its sense of magic" (Scott 2010, 6).

The story focuses on Ray as a gender-deviant possessor of a virulently contagious sexuality and supports this by presenting him as a sexual late bloomer incapable of satisfying his wife, as a pre-fame female impersonator who suffered from gender confusion and cashed in on his abnormality, a claim it supported by quoting "eminent psychiatrist" Dr. Louis Berg, who characterized Ray's feminine hysteria in his performances as the outgrowth of being surrounded by and affirmed by women (Williams 1953, 64). In Wini Breines's *Young, White, and Miserable*, she recalls the 1950s as a decade in which experts were trusted to explain human motivations and behavior, so Berg's presence was an attempt to add credibility to the article (Breines 1992, 25). Finally, the story cast Ray as a powerful celebrity whose press agents and publicists distorted his drag past and arrest records for morals charges and public lewdness, referred to as alcoholic rages and feminine fits of anger, but that actually involved solicitation and disorderly conduct charges (Williams 1953, 38).

Even though Ray had been arrested in Detroit in 1951 (Whiteside 1994, 65–66), *Confidential*'s story only mentioned his arrest in Boston for public drunkenness (135). Whiteside reports that Ray's press agent, Art Franklin, who had requested more pay from Ray's manager Bernie Lang, was actually an informant for *Confidential*'s story. He told Ray's management the story was going to be a "legitimate profile" of Ray rather than a smear (162). In reference to Ray's criminal past, the article said that despite newspaper reports suggesting an arrest record, "there are no records on police blotters to support these stories," and though *Confidential* spoke with policemen, they got "plenty of off-the-record comment," but "in all cases, the complaint had been smoothed over" (Williams 1953, 37–39, 63–64). Clearly, Ray's "secrets" became increasingly vulnerable to scrutiny.

The story's primary thread was the notion that Ray's popularity could be harmful especially to his young audience. Couched in the language of contagion and panic, the article quotes Dr. Berg, who says, "Once presented to an audience, the phenomenon very often generates a mass effect much like the frenzied religious revivals which have astonished the globe's more phlegmatic citizens since the days of the cave man" (Berg, qtd. in Williams 1953, 39). The article supports this assertion with a quotation from a Philadelphia concert attendee who recounted the hysteria during a Ray concert. Visual elements of the story support the article's notion of Ray as a solicitous type. On one page, there is a photo of Ray in front of a police station; he's flanked by policemen but still signing autographs for teenagers. Beneath the photo runs the caption, "Admiring teen-agers greet Ray after release from Boston police station. Despite frequent brushes with law, Ray's name is mysteriously absent from official arrest records." This pointed juxtaposition of text and image frames Ray as a distorted figure and a hidden threat to his vulnerable young constituency, a notion the photo amplifies by presenting him as the idol for American children (Williams 1953, 37–39; 63–64). The article was a shrewdly manipulative piece that posed as both a sympathetic portrait of a troubled musician and an exposé of corrupt industry practices.

Yet *Confidential* still had not yet reported on Ray's 1951 arrests for soliciting and accosting. Instead, his 1951 arrest reached the larger public when the tabloid the *Lowdown* published "*Lowdown* Demands Michigan Governor Pardon Johnnie Ray!" in its August 1955 issue, which recounted the arrest, reproduced his mugshots, and cited details from the arresting officer's testimony (Whiteside 1994, 195). There in plain view was the text of Ray's rap sheet, printed above a right-profile shot of Ray and a forward-facing shot with a Detroit Police sign hanging from his neck. At stake in the tabloid's story is not whether Ray solicited a man but the perception that the public would want him pardoned. His audience was imagined as a forgiving one that could separate his effeminacy from the rumors surrounding his sexuality and private life; thus, they participated in what Margaret Thompson Drewal termed a "conspiracy of blindness" (Drewal 1994, 150).

Lowdown's story opened the door for other tabloids to exploit the 1951 arrest for future stories relating to Ray's homosexuality. *Confidential*'s November 1955 story by Francis Dudley, "Knock, Knock! Who's There? . . . Why Did Johnnie Ray Try to Break Down Paul Douglas' Door?" defined Ray as a man-hunting predator who vainly attempted to seduce a well-known *real man*, though this was merely a hook to "out" Ray and expose his contrived image. According to the article, Ray, "that strange Yankee creature who'd made millions out of being maudlin in front of a mike," stood "stark naked and plainly three sheets to the wind" at Paul Douglas's door; "lunging inside the room he made a determined grab for Douglas" (46). In response, the "husky and he-mannish" Paul Douglas, who "was strictly for girls," violently resisted Ray. To amplify the text, a doctored photo of Ray with his arms stretched out in front of him on one page faced Douglas standing in a doorway with a cigar in hand blankly staring out on another page prefaced the article. The article also noted the possibility that Ray's fans might be shocked—"Their idol . . . the tenor with a million tears . . . making a pass at a man? Never!"— and stretched a thread from the April 1953 story that Ray had a criminal past (Williams 1953). Leaping from this aside, Dudley claimed the Douglas incident fell into line with Ray's June 5, 1951, Detroit arrest and noted how "the sob singer's managers and agents made every effort to cover up Ray's blunder." Dudley concluded by reiterating the dishonesty shrouding Ray's career when he noted that "his advisers have never been able to hide from insiders the facts about Johnnie" and how "every now and then—as Paul

Douglas discovered to his surprise—the girl in Johnnie Ray just has to come out" (Dudley 1955, 23, 46). Though briefer than the Jay Williams's 1953 story, this article more overtly accused Ray of being a sexual deviant without calling him gay, homosexual, or queer, and used factual evidence with a location and a date to sound credible. By reiterating the spin control his managers had, the article highlighted the distorted nature of Ray's image. The tension between soliciting sex, being a divorcée, and now being framed as a predator speaks to what may have been an urgent need to assure his audience that he was "normal" (23, 46).

The two stories represent a small but demonstrative selection of articles addressing Ray as a sexual deviant. Because of *Confidential*'s massive circulation, its stories probably reached more readers than any other scandal sheet. Scandal sheets' calculated perception that an audience would be interested in sexual deviance indicated their hunger for something extraordinary and unusual in a time of conformity. Audiences may not have approved, but they were fascinated by difference because it was so lacking in popular culture. The articles' shrewd emphasis on revealing previously hidden information enabled them to carry out their mission to provide an alternative to studio- and press-generated notions of celebrities as free from vice.

Audiences Embrace "Freaks"

Audiences' interest in "freaks" like Ray and his 1950s counterpart R&B and jazz singer Jimmy Scott speaks to a longing for alternative renderings of gendered possibilities. Rosemarie Thomson ruminates on how audiences have processed "freaks": "The extraordinary body symbolized a potential for individual freedom denied by cultural pressures toward standardization. . . . Sympathy and affiliation surely flowed along with smugness and differentiation, as some onlookers probably used the shows to explore the limits of human variation" (Thomson 1997, 68). Though she is speaking to "freak shows," the notion of "difference" as a site for audiences to develop empathy and envision other social possibilities beyond established norms relates to my ongoing discussion of enfreakment herewith. Music is perhaps a safer, subtler method for expressing this yearning. Ray's appeal to young women is especially relevant here.

As noted in the introduction, musicians become objects laden with a range of meanings for audience members through their "consumption" of musical performances (Frith 1996, 205, 211). Ray's maudlin vocal style and dramatic gesticulations enabled audiences to empathize with him and render him as an icon of the vulnerable male. These elements attained a poignancy that particularly endeared him to women. By 1956, despite the tabloids, he had a well-established reputation for appealing primarily to young females. Regarding this, Ray said, "Women see reflected in me all of the emotion and tenderness that, unfortunately, the American male doesn't have time for today" (Whiteside 1994, 179). In *Queer Noises*, John Gill interprets Ray's appeal to young women as "a form of catharsis, and bonding, in which the individual fan's feelings towards a star can take a variety of forms, from a desire for companionship to a sadistic urge to control" (84–85). Clearly, in the context of the 1950s Ray represented a kind of male fantasy for many of his audience members. By physically letting his audience in during his performances Ray personalizes his presentation and enriches "our fantasy of what the offer might be, that it might be just for us" (Frith 1996, 215). These diverse responses to Ray's performing style reflect Philip Auslander's observation that "an audience actively *constructs* the performer's identity in ways that speak to what it wants and needs that performer to be" (Auslander 2006, 233; emphasis in the original). Ray's performance was especially useful for certain segments of his audience to "perform" their identity through his recordings and performances (Gracyk 2001, 202). Notably, he performs the audiences' anxieties about enforced conformity and normalcy.

Ray's vulnerable appeal to audiences is not an isolated phenomenon. A similar interest in transgressive sounds also influenced the early career of "Little" Jimmy Scott in the 1950s. Because of Kallmann syndrome Scott did not reach puberty and therefore sang in a feminine vocal register (Ritz 2002, 15–16). His sound led some audience members at his live shows to openly declare, "He sounds like a freak, he looks like a freak, he *is* a freak," according to R&B singer Ruth Brown (70). Ultimately, he enchanted audiences in the 1950s, beginning with his first hit "Everybody's Somebody's Fool" (64). Music critic David Ritz's *Faith in Time* astutely describes the tenor of the moment, noting that Scott's "straight-from-the-heart style was only a few degrees off the mainstream mark. A year after 'Fool,' for example, Johnnie Ray hit the top of the charts with 'Cry.' Deeply influenced by Jimmy (as well as Kay Starr and Dinah Washington), Ray would be the biggest singer in the country" (67–68). Scott is not typically perceived as a teen act, but many of the performers who were influenced by him, such as Marvin Gaye and Nancy Wilson, were actually teens when they were exposed to his music.[2]

One of the most peculiar aspects of critical responses to Ray is the suspicion of him as a teen act, especially considering his apparent appeal to adults. A 1952 *Life* article, "Johnnie Ray Sings and Sobs His Way to a Quick Fortune," featured a teaser headline that noted how "a tearful new singer leads his young followers to the brink of frenzy." Above the headline are photos of young women waving autograph books in their hands reaching for an unidentified man to sign them. Below is a similar picture without the man. The opening paragraph complements the photos and establishes his audience by defining Ray as "the young man on the previous page who is being buffeted by a female tidal wave." On the adjacent page Ray, photographed during a performance, appears incredibly tender and fragile with his head angled to the left, his eyes closed and mouth partially open as if crying, and his left hand clutching his upper chest. These words and photos deftly portray how Ray embodied and defined the male idol of the early 1950s. He possesses heteronormative appeal to women and simultaneously defies codes of masculinity by appearing vulnerable (*Life* 1952, 99–101). Ray's image suggests that young women had a separate version of masculinity from the broader culture, one with room for tenderness and vulnerability; this was apparently worrisome.

This vulnerability appealed particularly to young women, though it also attracted adults. Sylvester and Taubman both reviewed Ray's 1952 Copa appearance. Sylvester's review is highly descriptive, as it is part of a profile, whereas Taubman is more overtly critical (Sylvester 1952, 30, 112, 114; Taubman 1952). Both infuse their discussions with attempts to address the teen psyche. Sylvester notes, "Ray jammed the place and divided the audiences into two loud stubborn camps." He notes how the "nylon-soxers" Talullah Bankhead and Marlene Dietrich are openly affectionate toward Ray's style. But, he says, "Other observers were less enthusiastic" (112). Notably, "Robert Ruark, a columnist usually concerned with the light side of weighty matters, wrote what was basically a challenge to Ray to come outside and fight like a man. Dorothy Kilgallen and Dick Kollmar, the husband-and-wife radio team, almost came to crockery throwing during early-morning discussions of Ray's talents" (112). Kilgallen was embarrassed to admit that she admired him in her "Voice of Broadway" column. Though she was married, she and the bisexual Ray eventually entered into a secret romantic relationship until her mysterious death in 1965 (Whiteside 1994, 101, 114, 334).[3] Again, his ability to be intimate with women potentially complicated his willingness to frame himself, personally and publicly, in queer sexual terms since certain aspects of his desires were "normative" (Taubman 1952).

Sylvester also described a scene of teenagers mobbing Ray at a Philadelphia concert and uses this occasion to address the youth's fixation on Ray by quoting a psychiatrist who claimed, "Kids are simply lost today. A young boy can't plan his life because the Army is about to grab him. Girls can't marry who and when they want for the same reason. And there's always that potential war and potential violent death hanging over us. Plus the fact that we're all upset financially. Kids feel that they have no place to go, nothing they can plan. They're sad and frightened and lonely. And here's a boy who's also sad and frightened and lonely. He's singing what they feel" (114).

In a 1954 story on popular male singers, "Crooners, Groaners, Shouters and Bleeders," Taubman refined his thesis on teenagers and Ray. He explained the appeal of emotive crooners to young listeners by noting that these adolescent listeners are "filled with inchoate yearnings. If their fantasies are romantic, their favorite singer sets their senses aquiver with tones that seem intimate and tender. If they feel abused and misunderstood by their busy elders, here is a voice that is comprehending and as comforting as some nameless unguent. If they feel inwardly outraged and would like to scream at the indignities of the world, they find a voice that rages and agonizes for and with them" (Taubman 1954b, 27, 54). Perhaps teens sought an alternative to the conformist nature of the era, which may have required separation from their parents. He also observed an increased emotionality among post-Sinatra male vocalists and cites Ray, noting, "This breed reached its height or depth (depending on one's point of view) in Johnnie Ray. When this young man did his lacerating threnody, 'Cry,' he tore a passion and himself to tatters. As you listened, you felt sure he would not get over it: your fear was that you would not either. He agonized in alternations of crooning and shouting until you wondered whether he would survive the song. Johnnie Ray twisted and turned and his face was contorted as his body was cracked by the tortures of his song" (54–55). His conclusion reiterated the psychiatrist's view of the vulnerability adolescents feel during times when war seems imminent: "It may be that these changes in style reflect the world we have lived in and the emotional attitudes of the youngsters in each period. . . . There was fighting abroad again when a Johnnie Ray came along. Now that the shedding of blood has ceased and many of the boys are back home Eddie Fisher seems to have the popular style" (55). While it is pretentious and strange for journalists to devote these (quasi) social scientific energies to Ray, he triggered such a sense of bewilderment, as did his audience, that teenagers became convenient targets for naming and defining something palpable yet elusive about Ray's rhetoric.

The truest test of the public's ongoing interest in Ray was an infamous solicitation case that reached the mainstream press. This case also amplified Ray's liminal position between existing in the mainstream and turning toward the more sordid edges of society to express himself sexually, perhaps by necessity. The outcome was surprising acceptance from his audience. On November 21, 1959. After watching a performance at the Flame Bar in Detroit, Ray and friends had a few drinks and signed autographs for a man named "Gene." Afterward, Ray went outside to what he thought was a private area to urinate. Before he finished, "Gene" reappeared, Ray invited him for a nightcap and then suddenly two men joined "Gene," who was a cop, and arrested him for accosting and soliciting. The next morning major papers, including the *New York Post* and *Los Angeles Mirror News*, published stories on the "morals charges" that Ray faced (Whiteside 1994, 265–66). This could have easily confirmed finally that Ray was not just an entertaining "freak" but also a pervert and thus a social threat.

On December 1, 1959, Ray went to trial; after deliberating for fifty minutes, the jury found him not guilty. His celebrity status and the insinuation of entrapment seemed to have partially contributed to the jury's reading of the case. Ray was understandably nervous about his public image leading up to the trial and after, especially since he had booked a performance for December 10 at Harrah's. *Variety*'s reviewer commented, "If publicity re: the Detroit incident will have any adverse effect on the marquee values of Johnnie Ray's name, it's not obvious at the South Shore Room." His fans embraced the jury's verdict and "gave him an ovation that should have assured him he was well received" (qtd. in Whiteside 1994, 270).

Ray confided to Boze Hadleigh, as he writes in his book *Sing Out!*, that Ray's perception was that scandal sheets had significantly contributed to the decline of his career. In a 1986 interview, he relayed that during the height of his career, "it was really such a perverted, paranoid time. They attacked me for everything, but almost always without saying why. Anyone who wasn't square was a menace to society" (Hadleigh 1997, 91). Despite some harsh reviews and incessant tabloid harassment, it is unclear that either was actually enough to *end* his career. Even during the harshest of attacks, he remained commercially viable as a concert performer, though his sales declined in the late 1950s. My brief look at the historical commercial record reveals that tabloids actually had a negligible effect on his sales. The fact that Ray did not behave or sound like a "square" actually *launched* interest in his career.

Ending on a Bland Note

Rather than mobilizing his initial appeal, Ray *self-domesticated*. Ray did not enter the music industry trying to provoke audiences and critics, but he became aware of how he was perceived. The proverbial middle of the road is always a seemingly safe place for retreat, and Ray ventured toward it when needed, musically and culturally. He oversold the image of himself as a conventional white male crooner, which led him to publicize his marriage and desire to have a family aggressively, record blander pop material, and try desperately to counter tabloid coverage of his alcoholic antics and homosexual solicitations. Ironically, his audience was as indifferent to his bland pop music as they were to the insinuations in the press that he was homosexually oriented. His audience did not abandon him because he was "queer," he did. Bachelorhood was highly suspicious as a sign of immaturity and pathology during the early 1950s (Coontz 2000, 32–33), and Barbara Ehrenreich's perspective that homosexuality "was a diffuse possibility that haunted every man, a label that could be hurled against the man who was 'irresponsible' as well as the one who was overly 'effeminate'" pertains to Ray's public image (Ehrenreich 1983, 129). The most overt gesture toward the image of sexual normalcy was Ray's rushed, arranged marriage to Marilyn Morrison in 1952.

Before Ray met Morrison there were several attempts to pair him with female companions. Dancer Tempest Storm told Whiteside that in 1952 she saw Rock Hudson enter into Hollywood's Mocambo nightclub with a group of other men, including Ray. Though she was taken by what she describes as "a fantastic lookin' guy," her friends warned her against pursuing him: "Forget it. Hands off—he doesn't like women" (Whiteside 1994, 98). Her dismissal is somewhat inaccurate, since he was bisexual; but homosexual/gay was clearly a blanket term for queer men. Shortly after this encounter Storm's manager encouraged her to pursue Ray, based on a contact he had, because, he said, "It would be great publicity if you and Johnnie Ray got together." Based on his advice, she met with Ray, who charmed her, but she ultimately declined the opportunity. Her reservations about his sexual ambiguity put her off: "I could have fallen in love with him very easily, but because of those rumors, I just did not want to get into that" (98). Ray was actually bisexual; he had multiple relationships with various Los Angeles entertainment industry figures, including disc jockey and singer Eddie Smardan (42) and a threesome with the couple Jan Grayton and Bob Mitchell, who were professional mentors, around 1949 (36). Whether Storm or her friends knew the specifics of these relationships is perhaps less important than the blanketing of male bisexuality or any hint of queerness as equaling male homosexuality. The standards of the time led people to equate effeminacy with homosexuality.

Ray met Morrison in 1952 at an industry event held at a Hollywood lounge called The Interlude. The event aimed to introduce Ray to various press and radio personnel. Also in attendance were Charlie Morrison (owner of Mocambo's), Marilyn, and Herman Hover (owner of Ciro's). Both men wanted Ray to book shows at their venues. Ray performed in response to a request, and afterward he and Marilyn left together (Whiteside 1994, 98–99). This infuriated Hover, who questioned whether Marilyn was there with the explicit purpose of wooing Johnnie, an impression reinforced by the fact that she was his constant companion (100, 123). On April 30, 1952, Louella Parsons's popular radio program announced Ray and Morrison's engagement, which set off a barrage of stories on the promising young celebrity couple. Hover's fears were ultimately moot, since Ray's manager booked him to perform at Ciro's in homage to the kind treatment Ray received when he first arrived in Hollywood. This reportedly angered Charlie who was claimed to have initially opposed the marriage (124).

Marilyn appeared at Ray's concert performances at New York's Copacabana and Chicago's Oriental Theatre (Whiteside 1994, 124–26), and the press was abuzz about their impending marriage. The *Chicago Herald American* asked Ray about the wedding in an interview; Parsons's radio show reported the wedding date of May 25. Marilyn actively promoted the wedding, holding a press conference on May 15 at the Beverly Wilshire Hotel in which she described Johnnie's proposal and claimed that her father approved of their marriage (127). A high degree of hyperbole accompanied the announcement, including Ray's infamous statement, "I'll say we're getting married—she's the first woman who ever made me feel like a man!" and a dramatic public reunion in a New York airport. The couple married on May 25, as scheduled, and Ray told a reporter he "couldn't get over how nice that 'Mr. & Mrs.' sounds" (128). I reference this because there is something desperate about the whirlwind courtship. Keep in mind that this came less than a year after his 1951 arrest.

The 1955 fan magazine *The Complete Life of Johnnie Ray*, written by Clifford Roberts, reproduces press photos of Ray and Morrison's courtship and marriage in a section labeled "Part Three: The Wedding" (Roberts 1955). The three pictures dominating the two-page spread that begins the section convey a genial intimacy between the couple but have the generic, staged quality of publicity stills. The photos tend to depict the couple in series of default poses that do not seem particularly personal or spontaneous. Collectively, these photos establish Ray and Morrison as a legitimate couple with chemistry, signified through their smiles and physical closeness, and other stock visual indicators of intimacy. For example, one photo in the spread shows the smiling couple leaving the wedding surrounded by Ray's young fans and police escorting them, which indicates the conscious choice to render the wedding as a significant public celebrity event. On the following spread, the left page features Ray holding Morrison, which the caption describes as "Johnnie carries Marilyn across threshold to reception," a standard wedding-album shot (Roberts 1955, 26–29).

Symbolically, Ray is depicted as a "normal" heterosexual young man entering into the first step of the nuclear family "tradition" expected of adults in the 1950s. The wedding and reception photos featuring the couple with their families also solidify Ray's lineage within the institution of marriage and as contributors to the generational legacy signified by their parental ties. Perhaps the most important element of the photographs is the opportunism implicit to celebrity publicity. The effort to publicize as many aspects of their relationship as possible broadcasts to the public Ray's normalcy and his status as a family-friendly act. Ray exacerbates the transparency of these overly self-conscious gestures through his nervous behavior. *Confidential* eventually latched onto his statement regarding Morrison as "the first woman who ever made me feel like a man!" because it perfectly encapsulated his effort to perform heteronormativity (Williams 1953, 38).

The questionable influence of the tabloids did not curtail the efforts of Ray's management to sanitize his image, though arguably this process *preceded* the tabloids. Since people within the industry knew or perceived him to be "queer," various domesticating efforts were made throughout his career. The most obvious gesture was his short-lived marriage to Morrison, which ended in divorce ("on the grounds of incompatibility of character") in 1954 after a brief separation (Whiteside 1994, 135, 171). But prior to his marriage he told *Downbeat* magazine, in December 1951, "All I want anyway is to have a wife and kids and a nice home where I can sit down and sing to myself" (92). This quote does not mean he was disingenuous, it merely illustrates his sexual complexity. He did *not*, however, share with the press his relationship with male model Stan Halpert, which lasted from 1953 to 1955 (145). In February 1953 he also announced the founding of the Johnnie Ray Foundation for Hard of Hearing Children on the *Ed Sullivan Show* (Herr 2009, 324). Whiteside interprets his announcement as a bid for public respectability. As was not the case with his marriage, though, Ray remained committed to funding the Foundation and similar organizations throughout his career (Whiteside 1994, 154). The musical gesture was a shift in his recordings from emotive contemporary material like "Cry" and "Whiskey & Gin" toward more emotionally neutral songs like his duets with Doris Day (for example, "Let's Walk That-a-Way"), religiously themed collaborations with Frankie Laine, and traditional popular standards (Ray 2003, in the *Hysteria! The Singles Collection*).

These singles reflect an intentional strategy to essentially whitewash Ray's sound and broaden his appeal. R&B-inflected music may have established the public's interest in Ray but Columbia feared his becoming overly associated with black popular music. Mitch Miller told Whiteside, "'The white audience, at the time, just couldn't accept it from a black artist—like Big Maybelle, Little Richard—but I didn't want Johnnie to be noted for just his black-inspired singing,' Miller said. 'I knew he was an original, and obviously the sales of the records provide it. But you'll notice, in the rotation of releases, that on the next record I came out with a standard 'Walkin' My Baby Back Home.' And of course it was Johnnie himself who decided to record the song" (Whiteside 1994, 102–3). The single went gold in 1955 and confirmed the audience's openness to hearing other styles from Ray. Achieving success on the singles charts was important for establishing Ray's presence on commercial radio. Radio, however, was rapidly changing, and the long-playing record (LP) was about to emerge as the ultimate artistic expression in pop music aimed at adult listeners.

Ray's peak as a tabloid subject occurred during his last period of consistent commercial success, roughly 1955 to 1957.[4] By 1958 Robert Harrison at *Confidential*, who had spent more than $500,000 defending the tabloid against libel charges, avoided a second trial by agreeing that neither it nor its sister publication, *Whisper*, would publish stories on movies stars' private lives (Scott 2010, 187). Thus began the decline of its sales and its eventual demise, which was a boon to its competitors.

In the late 1950s Ray was musically out of touch with rock 'n' roll and R&B, and by the late 1950s he was also unsuccessful at recording albums that appealed to adult pop tastes. The rock 'n' roll commercial revolution began in 1955, the year Chuck Berry and Fats Domino debuted two of rock 'n' roll's quintessential songs "Maybellene" and "Ain't That a Shame" (Whitburn 2007, 79, 249). Little Richard hit the pop charts in January 1956 with "Tutti Frutti" (504). Then, in January 1956, Elvis began his run of twenty-six charted singles between 1956 and 1957 with "Heartbreak Hotel" (669). Buddy Holly and the Crickets followed in August 1957 with "That'll Be the Day" (389).

Where was Ray when this was occurring, and how did he perceive the increasingly prominent style? He was very prolific during the 1955–56 period; he recorded the unsuccessful "Johnnie's Coming Home," which peaked at #100 (Whitburn 2007, 221), "Just Walking in the Rain" (#2), "You Don't Owe Me a Thing" (#10) backed with "Look Homeward Angel" (#36), and three duds, "In the Candlelight," "Weaker than Wise," and the unreleased "If I Had You." He and Laine also recorded the duets "Up Above My Head" and "Good Evening Friends," released as a double-sided single (Whiteside 1994, 221–23).

Despite this steady output of songs, Ray was somewhat oblivious to chart placements because he was touring abroad as rock 'n' roll was gaining its commercial footing. His tour included South America, the Philippines, and South Africa (Whiteside 1994, 204). Miller was more aware of the changing tide and had Ray record a few attempts to appeal to teens with "Ooh, Ah, Oh, (This is Love)" and the country ballad "Why Does your Daddy Have to Go" (205), but neither was released commercially. In a telling moment in 1956, reporters asked him his opinion of Elvis Presley, and he replied "What is an Elvis Presley?" (205–6). Such ignorance about the industry did not serve him well for the remainder of the decade as he scrambled to catch up, bouncing between genres and trends in hope of appealing to someone, and never successfully landed.

Ray recorded five LPs: *Johnnie Ray* (1952), a pop album; *The Big Beat* (1957), which focused on pre-rock blues and R&B; *'Til Morning* (1958), focused on popular pre-rock standards; *Johnnie Ray in Las Vegas* (1958), a live concert of hits and standards; and *On the Trail* (1959), featuring country and folk songs, including originals. *Johnnie Ray*, released on the heels of "Cry" and "Little White Cloud," peaked at #2 in March 1952 on *Billboard*'s Albums chart, and remained on the chart for twenty-two weeks (Whitburn 2007, 121). But instead of fully devoting himself to an album-driven career, Ray concentrated on touring and recording singles.

Commercially, *The Big Beat* set peaked at #19 and became Ray's only album to chart during the early 1955 to 1959 rock era, so it was successful. It is not clear what demographic purchased the album, so perhaps it did grab the attention of adults and teenagers. What is clearer is that 1957 was the peak of his rock-era commercial momentum. He had five more Top 100 singles from 1957 through 1959; two reached the Top 40 in 1957 ("Look Homeward Angel" and "Yes Tonight, Josephine"), so Ray and his musical collaborators had reason to believe they could continue down an eclectic path. The remaining three albums were anachronistic stylistically and irrelevant commercially.

Ray's lack of commercial awareness continued at other labels. He signed a short-term contract with Decca Records; when the singles failed, the label dropped him. The two singles he recorded for Cadence were also sentimental ballads and commercial flops. Liberty Records signed Ray in 1961, and he recorded two albums (not yet reissued) and a duet with female pop singer Timi Yuro (Whiteside 1994, 272, 277, 294). These failed to restore him as a mainstream recording act; he spent the rest of his career touring. Though his U.S. career had diminished commercially, he remained a popular performer in Europe and Australia. Ray died in 1990 from liver failure, likely tied to years of his struggle with alcoholism.

Johnnie Ray's mainstream acceptance in the early 1950s is more salient than his demise because his success reflected an opening for queers, in terms of affect, music, ability, and racial norms, tempered by the ways the rhetoric of the Lavender Scare era led him to second-guess his own success. Briefly, a "freak" was the most popular singer in America, and this opened the door for rock 'n' roll stylistically and symbolically—but, even more important, to a rhetorical space in the popular imaginary for other queer freaks to enter into the industry, risks and all.

Ray's recordings are only one part of his persona, but their contents ground some of the speculation about why he ceased being a major recording artist in the U.S. market. This sounds benign, even obvious, but it challenges the conventional wisdom. For example, Whiteside's liner notes to the compilation *High Drama* argue, "By 1959, his offstage antics . . . combined with the lurid attacks of the scandal mags . . . had nearly wiped out Johnnie Ray's mainstream career" (Ray 1997). His personal struggles with who he was and what he wanted personally, and publicly, seem more salient as factors in his decline. His musical confusion is equally salient. It is difficult to quantify how closely Ray's audience read tabloids and whether they would have been as willing to abandon him if his music appealed to them commercially.

Beyond music, Ray made no impact as a film star (*There's No Business* was a commercial and critical failure) and never quite translated his persona to television. Extensive efforts were made on 1950s variety shows "to stage—and soften—Johnnie's appearances," but "alone, under a spotlight, he was too inflammatory" (Whiteside 1994, 183–84, 208). Given these circumstances, we could understand why he was unable to endure as a recording artist, a profession which required careful control of image and, increasingly, media versatility. In a sense, his sexual and gender queerness were only branches of a larger queer relation he had to the era. For a brief moment before rock 'n' roll emerged fully, Johnnie Ray's "freak" persona merged aspects male and female, black and white, pop and R&B, and young and adult tastes in a queer manner outside of the industry's norms that felt like the future of popular music. His persona forecast many of the transitions that occurred, but he could never quite handle the potential revolutions his career foretold. Ray attempted to downplay the very things that made him interesting. He went for the middle of the road instead of propelling himself forward musically and culturally in the lane he had already carved out. Broad social pressures to conform to social norms, especially around masculinity, undoubtedly haunted his career, and he was understandably cautious. The struggle to locate himself personally and socially in terms of his desires is a recurring theme within his struggles. In his career, the tension between embodying the freak and seeking broad accessibility clashed. Historically speaking, it is profoundly ironic that a performer who won over the mainstream by being a "freak" underestimated his appeal by assuming the mainstream was incapable of maintaining its complex affair with his complexity.[5]

CHAPTER THREE

Spectacular Vacillations

Little Richard Charms and Disarms America

We sometimes underestimate how many styles of black masculinity there are. . . . We sometimes forget how much of the feminine and the homoerotic can be found here. The dandy, the gent and the tough emerge with the church choir leader and the queen: think of Little Richard.
—Margo Jefferson, *On Michael Jackson*.

They called you "sissy" back then. Or "freak." Or "faggot." That's the common name for it.
—Little Richard, quoted in Charles White, *Life and Times*

As much as he has tried to renounce the spirit of abandon he had advocated with his first important recordings, exchanging it for the spirit of religion, Mr. Penniman, two years short of 60, always seems to return to the carnivalesque secular style that made him famous.
—Peter Watrous, "Back to Basics"

I SHARE THESE EPIGRAPHS because they represent a fundamental tension in the career of Little Richard (Richard Penniman). When he was a child, his family and various community members in Macon, Georgia, stigmatized his effeminacy and flamboyance. But regional and, eventually, national audiences embraced his queer masculinity and made him a star. He rejected this fame for a religious lifestyle that he abandoned for secular music, a cycle he repeated over the course of several decades. Little Richard is a consummate manipulator of queering tools. No matter where he is, he never quite escapes his ability to queer a space. The elasticity of his falsetto whoops, the playful bitchiness of his abrupt signature phrase "Shut up!" and his ongoing use of facial makeup that borders on drag linger in his career, even as he has disavowed queerness as something belonging to his past.

Little Richard's self-conscious enfreakment in his music and visual presentation were central to his commercial persona that attracted his national audience. Alongside *self-enfreaking*, we will see how the tools he uses intersect and feed off each other initially, in service of navigating racial and gendered territory. Eventually, he employs new tools to *domesticate* himself and broaden his appeal, but ultimately these tools fail to thwart the impact of his initial queering strategies. Despite his resistance, his presentation of gender is too transgressive to tame or quell his queer deviations from normative masculinity fully.

Chapter 3 traces his elaborate use of tools to establish and continually refocus his image. Embedded in his use of tools is an ongoing process of becoming. During his initial burst of fame, teenaged audiences celebrated him, but it has never been clear where the persona and person overlapped; there are layers of ambivalence that continually inflect his vacillations between religiosity and secularism. Little Richard *played the race card*, which had multiple impacts on his career. He *self-enfreaked* and *self-neutered* situationally in service of navigating intra- and intercultural expectations.

Little Richard Plays the Race Card on Both Sides

Little Richard was acutely aware of the racial context of the 1950s and had an abject relationship to the "race man" construct that informed the careers and perceptions of black male icons like Belafonte and Poitier. He was aware of his social location as a black man and his need to conform to certain tropes of blackness to fit. He seemed simultaneously aware that he would never quite fit with black normative masculinity, especially the respectability trope. Therefore, he played with race to his advantage; two sterling examples are his hair and his music.

From the 1940s through the 1960s black male entertainers commonly wore the conk hairstyle (Craig 1997, 405, 407), "a style of wearing straightened hair that was often combed into a swirl of waves atop the forehead" and "was achieved by 'processing' the hair with a lye-based cream" (404). There was ambivalence among blacks about the style, including whether it was an imitation of "white" straightened hair or if it was proper for males.

For example, a woman interviewed by Maxine Craig noted, "To me it looked feminine" and she comments on how "some African Americans never accepted it as a legitimate expression of masculinity and saw it as a feminizing style." "Straight, flowing hair," she maintained, was a look that "marked a man as a dandy" in many black circles (Craig 1997, 409). Regardless, many blacks associated it with black cool, sophistication, and street life (405, 406, 408). By the mid-1960s, especially with the rise of the natural hair movement, the style fell increasingly out of favor among entertainers (410–11).

Despite this ambivalence toward the conk, at its height respectable "race men" such as Nat "King" Cole wore the style (Craig 1997, 407). Little Richard developed his sense of style from two black queer men—his predecessors Esquerita and Billy Wright, who also had processed hair.[1] Recalling Little Richard's pre-fame years, David McGee's entry in the *Rolling Stone Album Guide* notes, "On the style front, Penniman, who often performed in drag, or in pancake makeup, found his models in Billy Wright, a Savoy recording artist who favored makeup, mascara, and a multi-level pompadour; and in a strange character named Esquerita, he of the mile-high pompadour and unconventional piano technique" (McGee 1992, 429). The references to pompadours are important here. Where Cole's "process" was compressed and sculpted, Little Richard and his influencers wore their hair high in a flamboyant pompadour style. Wearing a "processed" hairdo located them within the black male aesthetic of the time, but it also set them apart. They did not merely wear it; they pushed it to new literal and figurative heights. Located simultaneously within and outside of black male celebrity norms, Little Richard complicated the image of the race man. Below his "beauty shop, not barbershop hair" was his makeup, notably his "face powder, eyebrow pencil and lipstick" rendered in exaggerated shades (Jefferson 2006, 103).

As I noted in the book's introduction, drag was mainstream entertainment in black communities during the postwar era. Little Richard fused conventional male clothing, a suit, with a feminized version of male hair and with makeup that blurred the gender boundaries. This made him different enough to be interesting but still palatable. He consciously "enfreaked" himself because it was marketable in the mid-1950s. Johnnie Ray was somewhat of a blueprint of a marketable freak, but Little Richard pushed it further and even more consciously.

Musically his recordings were located in the urban R&B style black musicians had been pioneering since the mid-1940s. George Lipsitz's *Time Passages* (1990) describes Little Richard's signature 1956 hit "Good Golly, Miss Molly": "It employs a three-line, twelve-bar blues structure with an AAB rhyme scheme, uses call and response between instruments and voice, displays falsetto and similar 'impure' tones, relies on blues chord progressions and blue notes, utilizes a rolling bass line in 8/8 time, and expresses a playful wit and joyous hedonism in its lyrics" (109–10). He follows this description illuminating its lyrical, harmonic, and rhythmic parallels with African American musical forms, ranging from work songs to the blues.

Beyond employing these generic black music elements, Little Richard's performance brought a palpable exuberance, playful sexuality, campy affect, and colloquial gospel aspect via falsetto, flourishes, phrasing, and rhythm that was different from jump blues or "soul." He was recognizably part of the black music continuum, but he was on the louder, more flamboyant end. Susan McClary includes him in her discussion of "soprano masculinities," noting, "In a more innocent time Little Richard could sport high vocals and spectacular grooming without creating sexual panic; most rock 'n' roll fans remained oblivious to the connotations of Richard Penniman's stage persona when he performed songs like the frenetic 'Tutti Frutti'" (McClary 2013, 37). Despite this impact, he is strangely absent from many important books on black music, including books on the blues. As Marybeth Hamilton points out, the history of drag and gender transgression in black nightclub life is often absent from blues and R&B histories, though this has changed gradually (Hamilton 1998, 160–76).

Drag's visual and performing aesthetics shape Little Richard's story significantly. From age fourteen onward, Penniman left Macon, Georgia, and performed throughout the South as a singer, pianist, and female impersonator on the circuit before becoming the national figure known as "Little Richard." As Preston Lauterbach notes in *The Chitlin' Circuit and the Road to Rock 'n' Roll* (2011), during the 1940s, "Southern cities and towns that had been inconsequential were growing into lively hubs, with nightclub work, recording opportunities, and strong connections to national talent agencies," and Macon, where Penniman's family lived, was a key spot on the circuit (147). In 1947 Penniman performed at a national talent search held at the Macon City Auditorium. He had grown up in a community with an active gospel music scene whose nuance he absorbed heartily. Gospel star Sister Rosetta Tharpe was also a great influence on his sound. In October 1947 he also opened for Tharpe. By 1949 he left to become a performer, including stints as a singer with snake-oil showman Doc Hudson and a tenure with the B. Brown Orchestra, where he was christened "Little Richard." Shortly after this, he performed as Princess Lavonne with the Sugarfoot Sam from Alabam minstrel show (White 1984, 21–24; Lauterbach 2011, 215–16).

Drag was a fundamental part of the eclectic variety-show format of the "chitlin' circuit."[2] Hamilton notes that during the 1940s and 1950s, "Pompadoured, effeminate, and raunchily funny" black male performers were commonly featured in "the black showbiz circuit: the world of minstrel shows, cabarets, tent shows, and black vaudeville that took performers from the north to the south in the early twentieth century" (Hamilton 1998, 168). These circuits included female "classic blues" singers and "blues-singing drag artists who made their homosexuality the core of their act" (168). Frankie "Half-Pint" Jaxon, Gladys Bentley, "Gloria Swanson," and George Hannah are examples of circuit performers. Lauterbach links Little Richard's drag persona to "a popular tradition of black transvestite entertainers. From Billie McAllister packing chic Chicago cabarets, to Patsy Valdalia strutting her hairy legs through New Orleans's rough joints, there are as many impersonators as blues singers in black clubs" (Lauterbach 2011, 216).

As part of his *self-enfreaking*, Little Richard "spectacularizes" via his hair and music in a way that garnered attention, if not always appreciation, from black audiences. Regionally his combination of effeminacy, drag, and R&B helped him thrive in black spaces. Sometimes, however, black audiences shunned certain songs. James Miller's *Flowers in the Dustbin* (1999) recounts how certain Little Richard's songs did not play well with black audiences. For example, "Tutti Frutti" was not a big hit when he performed it for black audiences, but it was received well in segregated white clubs. Miller implies the song's sexual content may have been too suggestive for black audiences wanting to hear traditional blues rather than rock 'n' roll, and it may have leaned too far from respectability politics (110–11).

Little Richard was also aware of the hypersalience of blackness for whites and his inability to trump race. He *played the race card* in the 1950s and beyond by using visual spectacle to neuter himself sexually. He used his Baldwinian freakishness—his blending of male and female elements—to be more acceptable to a white audience. In this respect, he mirrors jump blues performer Louis Jordan's antics that were so comic he barely projected a sexuality. As Lisa Diane McGill notes in *Constructing Black Selves* (2005), Jordan was "featured in colorful ensembles with a wide smile and welcoming body gestures in various mass media [and] encoded black masculinity with comic levity and an unthreatening public image" (37). Unlike Jordan, Little Richard was effeminate and sexually queer.

Race was a minimal commercial barrier for the pursuit of the commercial mainstream by the white musicians featured in this study. Race, however, explicitly shaped Little Richard's self-presentation as a sexual commodity and must be understood in the historical context of black men in the U.S. public sphere and commercial pressures for black musicians to be crossover artists. For example, in the 1991 film *Good Rockin' Tonight* Little Richard commented on the strategy behind his feminized appearance during the mid-1950s. "By wearing this make-up I could work and play white clubs and the white people didn't mind the white girls screaming over me. I wasn't a threat when they saw the eyelashes and the make-up. They was willing to accept me too, 'cause they figured I wouldn't be no harm" (Ward 1998, 53). In a 1995 interview he confirmed his influence, stating, "I worked like a dog for what I got, 'cause they wasn't used to no person at the time bein' flamboyant like I was. Before Elton John and David Bowie, I was dressin' like that" (Gill 1995, 4). His racial identity was a key part of the innovation Bowie and John would not have to navigate. Comparatively, a certain kind of racialized wholesomeness has cushioned performers like Liberace, and whiteness has afforded many of the musicians, particularly those who have incorporated black music traditions like R&B into their music (like Ray) historical cultural cachet and access to markets beyond pop.

Little Richard was keenly aware that mainstream audiences might reject his blackness and his sexuality. "We were breaking through the racial barrier," he said. "The white kids had to hide my records cos [*sic*] they daren't let their parents know they had them in the house. We decided that my image should be crazy and way-out so that the adults would think I was harmless. I'd appear in one show dressed as the Queen of England and in the next as the pope" (White 1984, 85–86). Instead of projecting a clearly defined sexual persona, he projected a sexually ambiguous one more notable for its eccentricity and unpredictability than its romantic or carnal appeal. This does not discount the existence of an erotic current between him and his audience, but there is a fascinating irony to queerness, which was associated with sexual deviance, being employed to deflect attention *away* from sexuality. In terms of queer ambivalence it is hard to get a grasp of Little Richard's sexuality since he was manipulating his sexual appeal in so many directions.

His ascent is significant because of the precision of his calculation. James Miller observed that "Richard intuitively grasped the issues at play" during the era and that "by exaggerating his own freakishness, he could get across: he could evade the question of gender and hurdle the racial divide," which astutely captures the brilliant reconfiguration of the artist's outstanding features (Miller 1999, 112). His commercial success also contributes to my argument that audiences of the period craved alternative representations of masculinity.

For example, Wini Breines argues that rock 'n' roll played a unique role in the developing emotional subjectivities of young white women during the 1950s. Notably, the genre prompted repressed sexual yearnings and opened them to alternate representations of masculinity. According to Breines, "the enormous popularity of rock and roll, while not merely a sign of rebellion—since it was also a sign of being a teenager—suggests that teenage girls were drawn to otherness. Interest in outsiders and others, values and people excluded or occluded in postwar America, is the thread that connects the Beats and rock and roll, and links both to black culture in the lives of young white women" (Breines 1992, 129). Fandom also "offered girls a way 'not only to sublimate romantic and sexual yearnings but to carve out subversive versions of heterosexuality'" (157). In the context of ambiguous figures like Little Richard she notes the attraction of alternative racialized masculinity, observing how "vaguely androgynous men—playful, sexual, tender even, and often dark—provided young women with alternate visions of masculinity and femininity, of identity, and as Barbara Ehrenreich suggests, of heterosexuality. Music that spoke to young people of the body, of sex, and of people and experiences they did not know provided them with a glimpse of difference. Teenage girls used the music to imagine themselves outsiders just as they imagined themselves Beat adventurers" (159). Brian Ward, whose history of R&B is sympathetic to Little Richard, specifically cites him as a pioneer who "presented a potent challenge to cherished sartorial and heterosexual norms" (Ward 1998, 52–53). Lipsitz also recognizes the complex scope of Little Richard's cross-racial appeal: "Facing a choice between the sterile and homogenous suburban cultures of their parents or the dynamic street cultures alive among groups excluded from the middle-class consensus, a large body of youths found themselves captivated and persuaded by the voices of difference" (Lipsitz 1990, 123). Little Richard played the race card from multiple angles by establishing a recognizable sense of belonging within black performing norms and tweaking this enough to appeal to white audiences through playing with gender.

Even if the predominantly white teenage audiences of rock 'n' roll expected its performers to be more subversive than pre-rock pop singers, Richard needed to project an image that was not *too* threatening. This expectation led him to shift attention away from his sexual orientation by performing multiple acts of gender play that were on the edge of queerness but collapsible into a more general spectacle. It would be naïve to presume that his strategy *fully* quelled white audiences from imagining him as a sexual *other* by virtue of his race, or that it inhibited audiences' ability to detect something queer about him. But performing these tacit racial and sexual equivocations must have felt necessary for him to reach broad audiences.

Despite the common historical trumpeting of rock 'n' roll's ascendency as a symbol of a racially progressive era, significant gaps existed prior to and during the genre's birth. Compared to Little Richard, the white queer performers I explore possess a mobility that reflects what Diana Taylor has

defined in *The Archive and The Repertoire* (2003) as "representational options" that accommodate white racial identity (119). The way "blackness" as
a category has pushed Little Richard and Johnny Mathis to equivocate has
important implications for the study's white artists. Racialization is difficult
to comprehend in the context of whiteness, which is frequently invisible,
unremarkable, and thus naturalized. This has particular consequences in the
postwar-era music industry, wherein a racialized double standard segregated
commercial markets even in the racially expansive rock 'n' roll era.

Stated plainly, crossing over to the white pop market has historically been
the primary commercial trajectory for black popular musicians seeking mainstream audiences. Black musicians have typically had to succeed in black
commercial music markets—including promotional spaces and performing
venues with primarily black constituencies—before being granted access to
promotional and performance spaces with a wider commercial demographic.
In an insightful analysis of the backlash directed toward Michael Jackson's
post-*Thriller* success, critic Dave Marsh's *Trapped* (1985) noted how the term
crossover "implied that there was a boundary that needs to be reached. It also
hinted that maybe there was no easy way back once you'd made the move
to the other side" (203). Heightened levels of scrutiny that can limit what
musicians choose to reveal and conceal about themselves are often the price
black performers of the 1950s, and beyond, have paid for commercial access.

Though Taylor employs "representational options" specifically to describe
the sexually ambiguous Latino male astrologer Walter Mercado's racial ambiguity as a "white Latino" and his bourgeois pretensions, it also speaks to
the contortions men-of-color have frequently performed for mainstream
access. It also amplifies the minimal racial burden for white public figures.
Taylor notes how "Walter the white, oh-so-affluent Latino flamboyantly calls
attention to his body and background, only to emphasize that what he has to
offer is not about sexuality or ethnicity, but about the spirit, the soul" (Taylor
2003, 128). He employs his mastery of mainstream codes and his physical
readability as "white" to deflect from his ethnic and sexual difference. The
wholesomeness of whiteness is thus implicit to his performance and safety.
There is a parallel here with Little Richard; he performs a rendition of black
masculinity—nonthreatening and/or *other*—that is commercially palatable,
and he gains commercial access at the possible expense of a fuller and more
expansive expression. This mirrors the constraints of black male figures like
Belafonte, Cole, Jordan, and Poitier who constrain their masculinity to appear acceptable.

The representational options of these men of color confined them to defining themselves against the racial and sexual mainstream through various

forms of closeting, whereas the study's white subjects have a wider range of options. Being a "race man" meant closeting sexuality itself, regardless of a race man's sexual orientation, which was ironically "queer" in a heteronormative culture. Regardless of Little Richard's sexual orientation, the fact that he was a *black sexual* being meant that he was probably self-conscious on some level about publicly presenting his body. This is clearly true of other black male performers of the era, including Cole, as well as Little Richard's rock 'n' roll contemporaries like Chuck Berry and Fats Domino. Each of these figures conformed to certain masculine norms and could cloak potentially threatening sexuality. Domino could do so via his corpulent body, which was usually confined to playing his piano. The combination of age (Berry was thirty years old in 1956) and an often comic image (for example, the duck walk) neutered Berry symbolically. White male musicians played the race card differently, and queer white male musicians had a different path of sexual deflection. Critical consideration of these racial differences enriches our ability to understand the incomplete and somewhat distorted historical accounts of Little Richard's status as a sexual, racial, and musical pioneer. His public profile emerged only from him suppressing other aspects of his identity. As I noted in the book's introduction, this is a racial equivocation that Wallace and Blassingame have pointed out, is integral to the public identities of black male public figures. This element of contortion and equivocation informs my frustration with the way rock 'n' roll histories historicize Little Richard. They celebrate the disruptions of whiteness Breines, Ehrenreich, and Lipsitz describe, but they overlook the tools he used to become commercially palatable. He is an easy figure to celebrate and appropriate for rebellion but harder to understand as a person navigating the complex racial and sexual climate of his time.

The Many Phases of Little Richard: Retreats, Comebacks, and Integration

This section outlines Little Richard's manipulation of tools in various phases. From 1957 to 1963 he domesticated himself, studying religion, marrying, and attempting to launch a gospel music career. In 1964 he returned to secular music, which extended into a late-1960s comeback as a rock 'n' roll nostalgia act well into the mid-1970s. In the 1970s through the mid-1980s he grew more fervently religious, a phase captured by the singer's rhetoric in Charles White's 1984 biography. By the mid-to-late 1980s, he began tempering some of this fervor and leaned toward a more integrated sense of himself. Embedded in many of these vacillations between the spiritual and the secular is his complex relationship to queerness as a form of intimate desire and public identity.

The regional homegrown star had been developing a following in the early 1950s and was aspiring to a national profile. He had toured successfully with the band he had formed, The Tempo Toppers, in 1952 (Lauterbach 2011, 227). Unfortunately, their live energy failed to translate in the recording studio (229). In 1953 Little Richard left the band and formed a new group, The Upsetters (229). In 1955 he met Lloyd Price, who, having recorded several R&B hits on Specialty Records, recommended he audition for Specialty (Lauterbach 2011, 248; Whitburn 2010, 529). Similar to his Tempo Toppers experience, his raucous concert style was not translating well in the studio, but after a spontaneous performance of an early version of "Tutti Frutti" at a local club, producer Bumps Blackwell helped him capture this energy in the studio, and the song became a Top Ten *Billboard* R&B hit. The song crossed over, his bookings increased, and he needed a band and support. Ultimately, his success was a sign of change: "With radio behind black music . . . and the pop record market desegregated, there was a new way to make it big, open for the first time to chitlin' circuit artists. This caused a simple, seismic shift—following Little Richard's breakthrough, chitlin' circuit performers could think seriously about making a living, perhaps a fortune, in the recording studio" (Lauterbach 2011, 267).

From 1956 to 1959 Little Richard charted sixteen Top 100 hits before taking a self-imposed hiatus (Whitburn 2007, 504). He also appeared in two 1956 rock 'n' roll films, *Don't Knock the Rock* and *The Girl Can't Help It*. He retreated from rock 'n' roll during the 1957–58 period to study theology at Oakwood College, a Seventh-Day Adventist college in Huntsville, Alabama. Specialty Records continued to release singles he had already recorded through 1959.

The choices he made after his initial fame complicated the carefree spirit of the man on the radio. I now turn my critical attention to his *self-domestication* (late 1950s through the early 1960s), his "comeback" as both a contemporary recording artist and nostalgia act wherein he reiterated and expanded on his "enfreaked" image (mid-1960s through the mid-1970s), his second period of *domestication* (late 1970s through the mid-1980s), and his current, more integrated status wherein he balances his freakiness with his faith.

Retreat and Domestication (1957–1963)

Some of the key signposts of Little Richard's initial self-domestication included abandoning his secular musical career to study Theology at Oakwood in 1957, marrying Ernestine Campbell in 1959, and recording gospel albums in 1961 and 1963. My critical concern is the extreme nature of his vacillations, as they tend to negate the qualities that gave him his initial appeal. They may also reflect a challenge similar to Johnnie Ray's of navigating same-sex and opposite desire and feeling limited affiliations with straight or gay culture. Celebrities often turn to religion, and religious music, for a variety of personal reasons, as seen in the careers of Little Richard as well as Candi Staton, Al Green, and Bob Dylan. This is a highly subjective matter exceeding the scope of my interests. Similarly, his queer public gender behavior is compatible with his apparent bisexuality. His faith and his marriage are not my immediate concerns then. What interests me are the performances involved in his gospel albums, aurally, visually, and symbolically. Though he has frequently framed his flamboyance as a strategy, which is certainly believable, much of his flamboyance feels far more natural than he is willing to concede. His ability to amplify and "enfreak" himself to differing degrees is relevant, since style is part of his celebrity identity. If he is able to amplify his queerness, he is then equally capable of ramping up his performance of normalcy.

He returned to the studio in 1959 to record an album called *The King of Gospel Singers: Little Richard* for Mercury Records. On the cover, he wears his hair short, his face has no discernible makeup, and he wears a suit.

He poses at an angle with his hands clinched as he looks upward posed in front of a stained glass window. This is the most gender normative image of him featured on an album cover. The songs are all hymns, such as "Peace in the Valley" and "Joy Joy Joy (In My Heart)." Selections from the album have been reissued periodically under various titles such as Polygram's 1989 reissue *It's Real*.

In 1963 he recorded *Sings Gospel*, and it also focuses on hymns like "Precious Lord, Take My Hand," "Everytime I Feel the Spirit," and "Milky White Way," among others. In 1995 ten of its selections were reissued as *Little Richard Sings the Gospel*. Listening to it digitally (via the digital streaming service Spotify), I was confused. He sings in a robust, almost operatic baritone, with occasional choral backing, that is almost unrecognizable. He sounds more like gospel singer turned R&B stylist Roy Hamilton than Richard Penniman. As pleasant as everything is, it is hard not to agree with Joel Selvin and Kevin Burke's observation that, "although his powerful rock 'n' roll singing might lead one to reasonably suspect a great gospel singer lies beneath, Richard records deliberately tame, unexciting ballads sung without any flair or color" (Selvin and Burke 1999, 677). The *All Music Guide* has a similar response, noting, "He was nevertheless in good voice, and he delivers fine performances throughout *Sings the Gospel*, even if the production and overall feel of the album are a little bland" (Erlewine 2017).

FIGURE 3.1. The cover of Little Richard's first gospel album, released during his first retreat from secularism (Mercury Records).

Though turning toward domestic life and religion is conservative, Little Richard took a major risk during his retreat. Symbolically, he challenged who he was and how he wanted to present himself publicly. His time studying at Oakwood, his marriage, and his initial gospel recordings suggest a radical turn from his initial image. Though there are probably multiple motivations, one of the observable impacts was a self-conscious redefinition of his masculinity. His newly sober image, defined by his streamlined appearance, marriage, and religiosity all feel like gestures toward appearing "respectable." Alas, he made no commercial impact as a gospel singer and witnessed the ascent of performers he influenced, most notably James Brown and The Beatles. The combination of his stalled "second" recording career and envy may have influenced his return to secular music in 1964.

Comeback-Reiterated and Expanded Self-enfreakment (1964 to the late 1970s)

From the late 1960s through the mid-1970s, Little Richard thrived on the comeback trail he had been on since his 1964 return to secular music. Arguably caught between being a contemporary artist and a nostalgia act, he capitalized on the nostalgia boom in 1970s pop music by playing his classic hits wearing a newly flamboyant visual style and performing in a self-consciously campy, crowd-pleasing mode. A 1968 concert review, "Little Richard Draws Crowd in Central Park," cited him as "among the first to have developed the fully visual side of pop, using all the flamboyant movements since standardized by soul and pop singers (New York Times 1968). The review cited his "dynamism, showmanship and charisma" as superior to peer musicians at the same Central Park concert. His flamboyant energy ("He camps it up and camps it down") and command of his audience distinguished him. "Involved they were, whether squealing for encores, singing along in nonsense scat lyrics or scuffling for the star's shoes and shirt thrown from the stage." A year later reviewer Mike Jahn of the *New York Times* noted Richard was "as inflammatory as ever" and described his newly cultivated visual style: "Richard wore bright red velvet pants and vest and a ruffled shirt, and had his long hair teased into a greasy plume standing six inches over his head" (Jahn 1969, 29).

Poised to begin a new decade in 1970, he released the acclaimed album *The Rill Thing* on Reprise Records, led by the moderately popular single "Freedom Blues," which peaked at #47 on the pop singles chart and #28 on the R&B chart (Whitburn 2007, 504; Whitburn 2010, 401). Both coincided with his reappearance on the talk-show circuit as queer as ever. As critic Don Heckman noted, "If you've been watching late television at all lately, you know that Richard is back and at it again. Dressed in the primary colors of an Alice in Wonderland vision, his face smoothed to perfection with pancake makeup and eyeliner, his long, shining black hair swirled into a bouffant hair-do, he comes on stage like some extraordinary, modern-day shaman of the absurd" (Heckman 1972, 89).

Little Richard was more than a recording artist—he was an increasingly notable visual and verbal *presence*. The viewer's ability to get a fuller picture of his visual style and personality, beyond even his most thrilling recordings, was the benefit of a visual medium like television. I explore his identity phases through three talk show appearances recorded in 1970, 1982, and 2000. What the video clips show over the thirty-year span is not a progression or regression but a navigation of the complex terrain of queerness. In his career, we witness his initial "freak" phase, followed by a period of self-imposed domestication, a return to a more elaborate freakiness, and a return to a more domesticated image, one informed by a certain ambivalence. Since the late 1980s he seems to have integrated elements of queerness with his faith identity more seamlessly. It is unclear how he has reconciled religion with his queer masculinity, but he is not openly hostile toward it. The video clips illustrate key aspects of these phases.

With regard to his post 1960s through the early 1970s comeback, I examine his February 17, 1970, appearance on an episode of the highly popular *Dick Cavett Show*. Little Richard appears onstage in a lime-green halter-top showing his upper clavicle, with fringe on the sleeves, and skintight pants. He is wearing a wig and pancake makeup. Though he is clearly a cisgender male, his outfit places him somewhere between "explicit 'female impersonation,' which is often designed to confront, scandalize, titillate or shock" and what Garber terms as *unmarked transvestism* (ABC 1970; Garber 1992, 354, 359). After the initial shock of his appearance he sits down and sings and plays his 1957 hit "Lucille" at the piano, then transitions into a cover of "Lawdy Miss Clawdy," which he recorded in 1956.

The camera periodically cuts to his band members, who are all black men dressed in suits, but he is clearly the focus. After playing a few bars of "Lawdy," he gets up from the piano with a handheld microphone and dances while he sings (ABC 1970, 0.27–5:56). After his musical performance, he sits down next to former NFL-player-turned-actor Jim Brown, who epitomizes the rugged black masculinity of the time, and chats with Cavett. Brown and Cavett both seem charmed and amused by Little Richard's effervescence. He repeats his famous line, "I am the bronze Liberace" punctuated by the audience's laughter, and he responds with a stinging "Shut up!" Cavett asks a series of questions about hair, makeup, and hobbies, all of which fails to deter the clever performer. After this banter, Little Richard asks if he could do something he has always wanted to do. Cavett obliges, and Little Richard leaves the stage and runs a circle around the studio to a drum roll and the audience screaming "Whoooo!" (ABC 1970, 11:41–11:56).

The spectacle of Little Richard's behavior was a package with his spectacular sartorial choices. In November 1970 he was one of the featured performers in a series of Rock & Roll Revival Shows performed by such icons as Chuck Berry and The Shirelles. Little Richard, dressed in "a mirrored, fringe midi-vest" ably "brought the crowd to its feet" as he performed his classic hits in his ineffable style and was "the high point of the evening" (Jahn 1970, 84). Critics showered him consistently with similar acclaim for his 1970s concert performances. When reviewing a 1972 Madison Square Revival gig, Heckman referred to him as the "star of the show" who understood that "pop/rock music works best when it balances theater with song." He described the act as "outrageously campy, filled with preacher-like admonitions and interactions with the audience, screaming, dancing, and, at the close, a modified strip in which he hops on top of the piano and throws boots and assorted articles of clothing to a voraciously eager audience" (Heckman 1972, 75). During a March 1973 performance at the Garden, when Little Richard asked his audience if they were ready for him to leave, the reviewer noted how they "urged him to stay." Inspired by his presence in "silver lamé trousers" and performing masterfully, the reviewer noted, "Students of the current rock vogue for gaudy glitter and flash can observe the roots of this approach in Richard's eccentric style" (Dove 1973, 59).

Three things stand out regarding his late-1960s through the mid-1970s persona: He was still vital as a performer despite his relegation to the nostalgia circuit; he continued pushing gendered boundaries in his hair, makeup, and fashion choices; and audiences *loved* him. Words like "campy" and "eccentric" underline the queer nature of his performance, and critics' references to these veiled terms clarified how much audiences enjoyed this aspect, alongside his musicianship. The more outrageous he was, the more they wanted him. The audiences these reviewers continually reference are especially crucial. They appreciated his music, humor, style, and overall aura. His queer masculinity transcended trends, identity, or politics; it appeared to be his core persona, whether on record, on television, or in concert. Despite his winning appearance in D. A. Pennabaker's documentary *Keep On Rockin'* (filmed in 1969) and ongoing praise for his performing prowess (Canby 1973, 49; Dove 1975, 45) this acclaim was not sufficient for Little Richard. By the late 1970s, his comeback had withered and his 1980s persona offered a striking turn toward an almost aggressive *self-domestication* and normativity, rooted in his overt Christianity.

Domestication Part 2: Inflected by Ambivalence (late 1970s through the mid-1980s)

In a May 4, 1982, appearance on the *Late Show with David Letterman* Little Richard made a very different impression than he had more than a decade earlier on *The Dick Cavett Show*. He drew an explicit boundary between flamboyance and religion and attempted to distinguish his old self from his newly domesticated self. His success executing this mission is debatable. Visually, a neatly coifed Afro replaced the wig, and a beige business suit replaced the colorful halter top and skintight pants. Letterman mentioned his newly religious image, and Little Richard noted that he grew up in a religious community in Macon, Georgia: "I've always loved God" (NBC 1982; ABC 1970). As they discussed his early career, the singer illuminated some of the dark corners of his past image. Referring to his record label, he noted,

> LITTLE RICHARD: When I would wear makeup, they would let me sing for the white girls. When I put on eyelashes and all that, they would let me sing. But when I went on as a straight dude, they wouldn't let me sing.
> DAVID LETTERMAN: Now, why is that?
> LITTLE RICHARD: They thought I wanted the girls. So, if I came out straight guy, they wouldn't let me sing. But, when I came out with the makeup and all the eyelashes and all the hair they said Richard is a good boy. I thought I was a good man. But, I was a goody boy. [*Audience laughs.*] (NBC 1982, 0:34–13:50)

Though Little Richard has discussed his intentional flamboyance as a conscious strategy before, this is one of the only times he has claimed the record company imposed this on him. As the interview continued, Letterman asked about the tension between his newfound religiosity and his flamboyant past. The singer noted the childhood roots of his personality and his father's disapproval:

> LITTLE RICHARD: I was gay, and he says, "I want seven boys and you're messing it up."

This quip amused the audience. He continued:

> I was really flamboyant, so my people didn't like it; so my daddy said, "You either follow this rule or get out." So I got out because I wanted to wear all my stones and all of my beads. (NBC 1982, 0:34–13:50)

He said that this happened around age sixteen or seventeen but quickly rescued what could be a traumatizing memory of his father throwing him out as a teenager by citing his beliefs:

> LITTLE RICHARD: But God gave me the victory. I'm not gay now but you know I was gay all my life. I believe I was one of the first people to come out. But God let me know that he made Adam to be with Eve not Steve. [*Audience laughs.*] So I gave my heart to Christ.
> DAVID LETTERMAN: But let me ask . . . you keep saying one provocative thing after another. You used to be gay but now you're not.

LITTLE RICHARD: I'm a man for the first time in my life. I know how you
   feel now.
[*Audience laughs. Letterman pauses. Audience claps.*]
DAVID LETTERMAN: Ugh, this is, this is getting more and more fascinating
   with each new term. (NBC 1982, 0:34–13:50)

Little Richard drew a binary between being gay and being Christian and
framed gayness as malleable. Though many people may have found much of
this to be offensive, he, the clever showman, was able to couch it in humor.
Further, in the context of the early 1980s it is crucial to remember that Ronald
Reagan's presidential victory was attributed to his call "for a return to simpler
times and ideals: traditional values, unambiguous strength, order, and power,"
(Vogel 2015, 465). It is highly likely that many people in the audience agreed
with Little Richard's rejection of queerness and embrace of Christianity and
manhood. The rise of the Christian Right, which was central to Reagan's victory, represented a cultural tide against 1960s liberalism toward a more rigid
codification of social ideals. Culturally, this shift was mirrored by a return to
postwar-era gender norms, notably the cinematic success of white hypermasculine figures like, as Joseph Vogel notes, "Clint Eastwood, Burt Reynolds,
Harrison Ford, Sylvester Stallone," and, later in the decade, "Bruce Willis and
Arnold Schwarzenegger. For the most part they played cowboys and boxers,
cops and renegades, military men, and cyborg assassins. They toted guns and
battled enemies. They exuded superhero-like strength" (Vogel 2015, 473).

Letterman showed a 1975 clip of Little Richard wearing a wig and a cape
and singing "I Saw Her Standing There" in front of a filmed backdrop. The
follow-up dialogue finds Little Richard disparaging himself.

DAVID LETTERMAN: When you see yourself in action in the old days is it,
   you want to get back into it at one level?
LITTLE RICHARD: I'm just so glad God brought me out of that. I never knew
   I looked like that. I'm just so glad that God was able to clean me out and
   wash me up. Thank you, Lord. (NBC 1982, 0:34–13:50)

Little Richard concluded the interview portion sharing how he had become
an evangelist who travels all over the world. He relayed that he turned to
God after years of losing various people in his life, including his brother, to
drug-related violence, and he noted how fortunate he is to be alive given his
own history of drug abuse.

He ended the show performing a four-minute version of "One Day at a
Time," a Christian hymn written by Marijohn Wilkin and Kris Kristofferson

and popularized in 1980 by gospel and country singer Cristy Lane. Other than singing the hymn with a pedal steel as part of the band, there was nothing remarkable about the performance. He sang it unusually "straight," devoid of the gospel inflections and asides he usually incorporated, until the last ten seconds or so, when he ended on the same falsetto note that defined his signature rock 'n' roll tunes (NBC 1982, 13:50–17:50).

Little Richard's performance on *Letterman* was a kind of *coming in*. He remade himself visually in a sober-looking suit that could function equally well in an office or a church; renounced his old ways by attributing them to outside influences; and mocked the image he created a decade earlier to great acclaim. Yet, despite these choices, the injection of a kind of campy, knowing humor throughout the interview, and his ending falsetto note hinted at the paradoxes of his new image. His effusive vocalizations of his renewed Christianity feels in tension with the person we see performing in the clip. As much as he insisted he was unaware of what he looked like in the past, he crafted it too meticulously and consistently for him to claim ignorance. Letterman's audience played along, but Letterman seemed characteristically skeptical throughout, and even the audience appeared a little unsure of how to react, though they applauded politely. Perhaps they could also see a gap between the exuberant man in the clip and the uptight man sitting in front of them trying not to claim his not-too-distant *past*. I interpret this less as inauthentic or dishonest than as a reflection of maneuvering to stay relevant. As homophobic as he appears to be in this clip, religious and cultural forces frequently create self-doubt and confusion in queer people. Because they receive the same homophobic rhetoric as straight people, traces of internal homophobia and self-loathing can also inform their public rhetoric.

The tension between the newly religious, masculine Christian rendition of Little Richard and the queer "freak" version also appears in Little Richard's account in Charles White's 1984 biography, *The Life and Times of Little Richard*. The core narrative depicts the artist's tortured childhood in Georgia, his musical training, career ascent, professional retreat, and underwhelming mid-1960s commercial comeback. This predictable trajectory concludes with a grandiloquent pseudo-apocalyptic sermon in which Little Richard disavows his queerness and, by association, homosexuality. Two of his most pertinent statements include the following:

> I want to tell you something, I enjoyed being a homosexual. I didn't give up something that I hated. I enjoyed being gay. I enjoyed being unnatural. It was fun to me. . . . But I want to tell you tonight, that's from Hell.
> [. . .]

That's the reason a lot of people go to homosexuality, because of loneliness. They're so lonely, they want people to love 'em. Homosexuals are the nicest people that you can ever meet. They're kind, they're artistic, they are lonely people. You can't hate 'em to Jesus, you got to love 'em to Jesus. (208, 215)

These statements, which duplicate some of his dialogue with Letterman, feature some of the most common tropes of anti-gay reasoning, including homosexuality as being unnatural, caused by improper parenting, against God's will and punishable by death, and an orientation that can be changed. Given his cavalier tone, it is surprising that he would end with a statement that actually features traces of empathy and compassion, even if they are broad pleas for tolerance and redemption. But the fact that these words are from a book from 1984 and leap from vitriol to pseudo-tolerance speaks to what appears to be a negotiation within Little Richard's own mind. The brief disruption he offers provides a glimpse into his ambivalence about queerness at the time. His words fall somewhere between heteronormative sentiments, bathed in religious rhetoric, and a concession that gay people are people who possess merit. Beyond the extremity of the condescending stereotypes lies a fascinating affective and rhetorical negotiation. Julia Kristeva's *Powers of Horror* (1982) defines the abject as "something rejected from which one does not part." Rather than being a lack or opposition, it is "the in-between, the ambiguous, the composite" (4). As Shane Phelan states, "Neither acceptable nor removable, the abject persists within a culture or a psyche that seems to expel it" (31). This liminal quality strongly defines Penniman's persona as Little Richard in more recent decades. His post-1984 recording and performing career provides several examples of this liminal positioning between identifying as gender and sexually normative but signifying through gender transgressive elements associated with queer-inflected performance. His abject sentiments play out in complex ways for the remainder of the decade in ways that ultimately shape his contemporary persona. The ghost of Harlem Renaissance performer Gladys Bentley haunts my understanding of Little Richard's transitions from hot to cold. I turn to Bentley because I see fascinating parallels between her career and Little Richard's vacillations.

* * *

Interlude: Gladys Bentley and Little Richard

Gladys Bentley was a large, African American woman whose dapper white tuxedo and raunchy blues performances defied a slew of gender, racial, and show-business conventions. Though even at her career peak, from 1929 to 1937, she was controversial, an essential icon of Harlem's freewheeling 1930s social scene. Immortalized as a character (or character inspiration) in novels like Carl Van Vechten's *Parties* (1930), Clement Woods's *Deep River* (1931), and Blair Nile's *Strange Brother* (1931) and highlighted as an icon of Harlem on artist E. Simms Campbell's 1932 drawing *A Night Club Map of Harlem*, Bentley's boldly queer persona was something audiences embraced (Vogel 2009, 148).

It must have been shocking to her loyal followers to learn in the August 1952 issue of *Ebony* magazine that Gladys Bentley, who had performed regularly in front of a chorus of male "pansies" and married a white woman in a civil ceremony in New Jersey wrote an article called "I Am a Woman Again" (Faderman 1991, 72; Bentley 1952, 92–98). Despite her apparent outer *joie de vivre* as a performer, she revealed, "In my secret heart, I was weeping and wounded because I was traveling the wrong road to real love and true happiness" (Bentley 1952, 93). The happiness she refers to include receiving an alleged medical intervention ("female hormone injections") that "corrected" her deformed sex organs and "extreme social maladjustment," marrying her first husband Don, and discovering God. She concluded the article hoping her forthcoming biography could help others "find someone in the opposite sex who can teach us love as love really ought to exist" and could prevent "some un-knowing youths . . . from succumbing to the shame and instead turning to the path of righteousness" (98).

Conflating gender deviance with homosexuality, medicalizing gender and sexual deviance, articulating crudely gendered stereotypes, and framing gender deviance and homosexuality as social problems were common tropes in African American magazines, notably *Jet* and *Ebony*. I drew these themes from analyzing the content of three articles printed in *Jet* from 1952 to 1954 and from Bentley's piece as well (Bentley 1952, 92–98; and see Jet 1953; 1954a; 1954b). Further, my analysis parallels earlier observations from Gregory Conerly (2001) and Stephen Knadler (2002) about depictions of gender and sexual deviance in African American magazines. I mention these because Bentley's stands apart from the usual sensational news stories about queerness because she was a celebrity providing a juicy autobiographical account of her conversion from queerness to a *normal* life. Interestingly, she never states that she ever loved women exclusively or that she stopped loving women. She simply states that she married a man. What is Bentley's story?

In 1928 Bentley, who was a singer, pianist, and songwriter, began performing in Harlem. Before performing as a proto-drag king in her signature tuxedo, she recorded eight singles for Okeh Records in 1928–29 in the "classic blues" style pioneered by Bessie Smith. The sides were not big sellers, but she cultivated "her cross-dressed, mannish persona" through rent parties and private appearances in the late 1920s (Wilson 2010, 173). Her bawdy parodies of popular songs were the highlight of her act, and she crossed over to the Harlem cabarets and speakeasies like Mad House and Harry Hansberry's Clam House. As her star rose, various writers and artists took notice; in 1930 she sang blues and jazz songs on a weekly radio program; by 1933 her act gained prominence in mainstream nightclubs and legitimate theaters. Her revues, which featured her risqué song spoofs, were especially popular, though they upset many critics. In 1934 she headlined successfully at the newly renovated Ubangi Club and from 1934 to 1937 her revues made her a celebrity in New York and sustained her career.

Around 1935 she altered her act, including changing her name from "Harlem's King" to "Broadway's Queen of Song and Jazz," focusing more on her persona than her music, which included no longer playing piano in her shows. By 1937's *Brevities in Bronze*, her last show, she was performing with female rather than male background singers (Wilson 2010, 179–82). During the period of her celebrity, Harlem was in decline financially and lost much of its tourist appeal. In 1937 Bentley moved to Los Angeles to live with her mother (Mitchell 2001, 221). From the late 1930s through the mid-1940s she made some sporadic club appearances in Los Angeles and New York but reportedly sanitized her act, wearing dresses and tempering some of her infamous vulgarity (Mitchell 2001, 221; Wilson 2010, 185). Little was heard from Bentley publicly until *Ebony* published her 1952 confessional. Many critics have argued that the conservatism of the era was central to her choice to change her act and publish the article (Wilson 2010, 188; Mitchell 2001, 222). James Wilson draws explicit parallels between the postwar-era role of women and her domesticated image in the article, an image that contrasted starkly with the image of lesbians as single, tragic women (Wilson 2010, 189).

In the 1950s Bentley married newspaper columnist J. T. Gibson, divorced, and then married Charles Roberts. She also became a devout member of The Temple of Love in Christ Inc. (Mitchell 2001, 222). In her only performance on film, she appeared on Groucho Marx's game show *You Bet Your Life* in 1958. She wore a "plain-colored, short-sleeve blouse, a matching skirt falling below her ankles, pearl necklaces (two), pearl bracelets, large daisy-like earrings, and flowers in her scooped-up and scooped back hair" (183). In essence, she projected a matronly image quite different from the cross-gender tuxedo-wearing performer of her youth. This is not entirely surprising, since in the 1952 article she wears a dress exclusively in the numerous pictures included in the *Ebony* article (Bentley 1952, 92–98). All are gender normative, including images of her posing with male figures, Billy Eckstine, Louis Armstrong, and Crip Heard, one of her in front of her jewelry box deciding on her wardrobe, and one of her typing on a typewriter at a desk (93, 95, 97). After introducing herself on the show, she sits at the piano and plays a dynamic rendition of "Them There Eyes." Despite her rather bland appearance, her musicality excites the audience and the host. James Wilson also remarks on the remnants of her previous persona, describing a "revealing moment in which the audience gets a glimpse of Bentley's legendary toughness and swagger. She defiantly shakes her head and tells Groucho, 'I don't want no part of that wheel'" (Wilson 2010), referring to a spinning wheel where contestants can risk losing the money they have won on the program. Her infamous article and her appearance conveyed a domesticated version of Bentley, but the film captures another dimension. Bentley died in 1960 of Asian flu and remains a subject of critical interest for scholars in multiple fields.

I reference Bentley because many of the same tropes that surfaced in her life paralleled Little Richard's later rhetoric. Like Bentley, he was an innovator whose musical and visual blurring of boundaries challenged conventions and elicited excitement from audiences. His innovations continue to influence performers, but at various times in his career he retreated from the very things that distinguished him in favor of a normative gender identity framed in religious terms. Bentley retreated in the postwar McCarthy era, and many have speculated that she had to change her image to survive. Little Richard's initial gospel recordings occurred as rock 'n' roll was transitioning to rock, which became even bigger commercially. Americans were shocked by The Beatles's long hairstyles in 1964, and Barry Goldwater was considered a radically conservative presidential candidate, but the political tenor differed greatly from a decade earlier. Little Richard's second retreat occurred in the early 1980s when conservative organizations like the Moral Majority helped elect Reagan twice and evangelism gained stem as a cultural and political force. Like Bentley, he employed multiple media, print and television, to convey normative renditions of himself. Also similar to Bentley is the visible evidence that his former self always lurked below the surface even when he attempted to *domesticate* his persona. Whereas Bentley remains a mystery in many respects, somewhat related to a lack of an audiovisual archive, audiences are very familiar with Little Richard's well-documented changes of personae, especially his wavering between being a freak and being normal. Since the mid-1980s he may have reached a more integrated equilibrium.

* * *

Toward Integration: Little Richard Balances Faith and Freakiness

Tracing the period between Little Richard's conservative Christian rhetoric and his shift toward a more balanced integration of freak and faith requires continued attention to his recordings and his media appearances. From the mid-1980s through the early 2000s, audiences witnessed Little Richard modulate his religious beliefs more cohesively with his signature visual spectacle and freak persona. Rather than framing himself so overtly as a Christian artist he blended elements of the past and present in a more accessible and endearing fashion. I examine a music video, several key recordings, and a talk show appearance to illustrate what seems like an enduring phase of his persona.

The singer's biggest commercial single since 1970 was the 1986 "Great Gosh A'mighty! (It's a Matter of Time)" written for the comedic film *Down and Out in Beverly Hills*, starring Bette Midler, Richard Dreyfuss, and Nick Nolte, which also featured the singer in a minor role. The song was a mild pop hit, peaking at #42 (Whitburn 2007, 504). The official music video is a hodgepodge that jumps from excerpts of the film to scenes of teen actor Evan Richards (an actor from the film) inputting various commands into a computer to shots of the 1986 version of Little Richard singing and playing alone at a white grand piano to archival footage of Little Richard performing in the mid-1950s. His appearance is less obviously flamboyant than his 1950s look. Instead of tails, a pompadour (or wig), and conspicuous makeup, he wears a black jacket, a black bowtie and a light gray shirt, (relatively) understated makeup, and a tapered hairstyle.

The video quickly shortens the initial distance between the new version of him and his past through the use of archival black-and-white footage that pays homage to his role as a rock 'n' roll pioneer.

There are multiple scenes of the 3:37 length video that salute Little Richard's 1950s rock 'n' roll persona. Each is framed by a miniature television screen that is part of a series of screens stacked on top of each other and presumably connected to actor Evan Richards's computer (Richards is featured in the film): First, viewers see black-and-white footage of teenagers dancing

FIGURE 3.2. New, streamlined Little Richard circa 1986 ("Great Gosh A'mighty" video; screenshots by author).

together to a rock 'n' roll rhythm and a collage of headlines, including "Singer Mobbed!" with a photo of Little Richard seated in a convertible with fans rushing toward him.

In the second scene, the singer, dressed in a white suit with tails, stands at the piano pounding the keys, and there is a close-up shot of him singing to the camera (MCA Soundtracks 1986, 1:31–1:37).

The third clip is a wider shot from the same shoot, but this time viewers see him playing in front of a band of musicians, who are on a slightly raised stage a few feet behind him. In the scene he turns and plays the keys with his backside and then turns around and plays with his right leg on the piano and gyrates forward (2:03–2:08).

After a brief scene of a black couple dancing (2:09–2:11) it returns to him playing the piano with his right front leg on the piano continuing to gyrate (2:11–2:13).

The fifth shot of the "old" Little Richard is a close-up of his face on the TV screen (2:46).

I interpret the video's juxtaposition as a way of contrasting the new and old Little Richard and thus tracing his *transition into the present*. Another interpretation of this evolution might emphasize the differences between the

FIGURE 3.3. Footage of Classic Little Richard playing and performing in front of his band ("Great Gosh A'mighty" video; screenshots by author).

FIGURE 3.4. Classic Little Richard playing piano with his back turned ("Great Gosh A'mighty" video; screenshots by author).

FIGURE 3.5. Classic Little Richard playing piano with his leg up ("Great Gosh A'mighty" video; screenshots by author).

performer of the two eras rather than continuity. Evan Richards complicates both interpretations at the video's end by mimicking the teenagers of the 1950s. Dressed in a satin tuxedo, at the end of the video (3:12) he appears on a mini-TV screen lip-syncing the song and dancing.

Thus, Little Richard's music animates teen listeners in his old and new guises. Because the video seems rather hastily constructed, what interests me primarily about the video is its inclusion of the archival footage. Little Richard's biographical disavowal of his past homosexual image two years earlier would seem to make the video's emphasis on his past somewhat contradictory. But close attention to the abject tone of his words indicates that he is unable or unwilling to abandon his past career and persona. There are probably multiple reasons that would motivate a director to include the 1950s footage, such as reminding older viewers of the singer's legacy and introducing it to younger viewers. But what is compelling here is how Little Richard's past becomes intertwined with his new persona; perhaps the mellower visual rendition of him in the 1980s signifies his soberer image, but the 1950s version of him always lurks, which indicates an ambiguous attitude toward queerness.

FIGURE 3.6. A modern teenager of the mid-1980s is moved to dance to Little Richard's music ("Great Gosh A'mighty" video; screenshots by author).

FIGURE 3.7. A modern teenager transforms into a Classic Little Richard rock 'n' roll clone ("Great Gosh A'mighty" video; screenshots by author).

This quality is exacerbated in other contexts. For example, during his live performance of "Great Gosh A'mighty!" on *The Late Show Starring Joan Rivers*, he wears eye shadow and foundation and punctuates his vocals with falsetto flourishes (FOX 1986, 1:10, 1:22, 2:34, 2:40, and 2:52 in the 3:49 clip). In other words, he continues to *enfreak* through his feminized visuality and spectacular performing style, which are virtually identical to his 1950s persona. He sits rather than stands at the piano, and he does not gyrate, but elements of his look and his energy are highly reminiscent of the 1950s. Incidentally, "Great Gosh A'mighty" appeared on his 1986 album *Lifetime Friend* that blended broad Christian ideals into seemingly secular songs. I have not heard the album (it is out of print), but based on a thorough review by John Rockwell of the *New York Times*, it seems like an early example of Little Richard's transition away from religious extremism toward a more inclusive vision of the human experience (Rockwell 1987, H29).

Other high-profile examples of his more integrated persona include a 1994 duet with country singer Tanya Tucker on "Somethin' Else" and a 1996 recording of "I Feel Pretty." The Tucker duet, recorded for the cross-genre set of duets *Rhythm, Country and Blues*, has a heterosexual lyric in which a man and woman express lustful admiration for each other (Little Richard and Tucker 1994). Little Richard sings the lyric faithfully, but his performance is almost exaggeratedly lustful and he laces it with his trademark falsettos. In the video clip, which shows the duo recording the song, he wears shades, eye shadow, and thin lip liner and has shoulder length hair (MCA Records 1994). Similarly, the character Maria usually sings "I Feel Pretty" in the musical *Westside Story*, but he sings it on the 1996 *The Songs of Westside Story* without changing the lyric, except for altering the female pronoun to a male one. Little Richard has a long history of proclaiming his beauty (he did so on *Dick Cavett* for example; ABC 1970) so this is simply understood as a natural extension of his persona. The song has a rock rhythm rather than the original's waltz tempo, but otherwise he does very little that radically masculinizes the song. In addition to the expected falsettos, he throws in his humorous catchphrase "Shut up!" at the end of the song—perhaps directed to the female background section listed in the liner notes as Female Vocalist & Lady Provocateurs. He may have rejected his association with queerness in his biography a decade earlier, but these notable recordings, performances, and appearances tie him to the queer tools and associations that made him famous. Peter Watrous observed these vacillations in the opening epigraph from 1992.

If the Little Richard of the late 1960s through the mid-1970s was the newly invigorated king of the rock 'n' roll nostalgia boom, and the Little Richard of the 1980s strained to be taken seriously as a Christian, the Little Richard of the 2000s seems more believably human. In a February 18, 2000, appearance on *Donny and Marie Show* (FOX 2000), he was invited to promote the NBC TV telefilm of his life *Little Richard* (2000), for which he served as executive producer.

Little Richard sports a slick, shoulder-length, processed hairstyle, defies age with his customary pancake makeup and sculpted eyebrows, and sparkles visually in an embroidered jacket and gold ankle boots. Along with heralding him as a pioneer and making small talk, all punctuated by Richard's well-known campiness, the hosts show several clips and interview him. After watching the dramatization of his father throwing him out, Little Richard cries and tearfully explains how he always struggled for his father's approval. Marie cries as he wipes tears away, Donny praises him for all of his accomplishments, and the audience leaps to its feet, applauding his courage (FOX 2000, 7:20–11:15). Rather than disparaging his flamboyant past, he endears himself to his audience and generates understanding.

Incidentally, the telefilm was one of the more recent efforts to relay Little Richard's story. There is no clear record of his exact level of involvement, as producing is typically a hands-off kind of position. But the text itself, as directed by Robert Townsend, attempts to be comprehensive and definitive about certain aspects of his life (Kerby and Tiplitz 2000).

In *Little Richard: The Birth of Rock 'n' Roll*, biographer David Kirby views the film as "the one attempt to serve up the whole story" and as "a failure" (Kirby 2009, 181). The film's depiction of sexuality is central to his complaint: "The big thing about this Richard Penniman, though, is that he's straight" (182). He notes the film's depiction of several autobiographical details including its portrayal of the "casual cross-dressing" and grabbing of "male band members swimsuit area" that occurred among Little Richard and his band members. He objects, however, because "his main relationship, which takes up most of the movie, is with a certain Lucille, a goodtime gal who eventually wants Richard to marry her. The closest the film comes to saying he's gay is when he echoes God's answer to Moses in Exodus by telling her 'I am what I am' and that while 'part' of him wants to marry, there are 'other parts'" (182). While there is definitely a sense of distortion in the film, I challenge Kirby's tendency here to subsume Little Richard's sexuality to being gay. First, he does not acknowledge the singer's bisexuality. Second, his focus on sexuality overlooks the broader queerness the singer embodies and conveys through the tools I have described.

Little Richard previously revealed that the song "Lucille" was actually modeled after Queen Sonya, a female impersonator from Macon, Georgia (White 1984, 75). The song's lyrics are ambiguous in this regard. As Hamilton notes, "They give no indication that Lucille is anything other than genuinely female and the song a rather anodyne anthem of teenage romance" (Hamilton 1998, 173). In this light Kirby's objection, "The only problem is that the real Lucille was a female impersonator in Macon" (182), seems to miss the film's intended audience. A hardcore Little Richard fan may already know this information. I doubt that Little Richard or the teleplay's writers Bill Kerby and Daniel Tiplitz were stricken with amnesia, especially since Penniman had revealed this information in his biography. The film's narrative license seems intentional since the film targets a general audience rather than a specialized audience familiar with his story. In a sense, the film performs a reinvention. Regarding the song, Kirby notes, "True, Richard sanitizes homosexuality in his song," but he is disappointed that the film seems to skirt Richard's homosexuality: "By whitewashing the singer's sexuality in the film, director Robert Townsend makes him smaller than life" (Kirby 2009, 182). When we consider the biography, the ongoing cycle of post-1984 recordings, and videos that flirt with queer signifiers, the film's depiction is not surprising, and it extends the singer's attempts to distance himself from the past and retell his story. Yet Little Richard remains impossible to contain.

Kirby's response is overly concerned with an objective sense of fundamental truths about Little Richard rather than considering the instability inherent to the performer's construction of his persona. Essentially, he obscures Little Richard's ambivalence about his identity and chooses to render his primary identity as a gay man. The historical "truth" about Little Richard extends beyond sexual orientation. He capitalized on his freakish appeal to regional audiences and translated this into national success through carefully enfreaking multiple aspects of his persona. He was recognizably black yet simultaneously presented a new version of blackness spectacularized and neutered for a broad, white, teenaged audience. While it has never been exactly clear why Little Richard suddenly shifted from secular to religious life, there was clearly a shift that has often felt like an attempt to reinvent himself as a "normal" man who is also a dynamic musical performer.

Musically and culturally, he influenced generations of future rock musicians, but it is not clear that he ever pushed his audience as fully as he could have if he'd persisted with his initial image and music. Rather than telling the full story, the telefilm presents a version of the singer for mass audiences. But we cannot be too sure the general audience is too blind to read the codes embedded in the film or takes the film at face value, especially if they have seen and/ or heard Little Richard. Even if we argue that he wants audiences to perceive him as *straight*—a heteronormative God-fearing Christian—he cannot quite let go of traces of queerness, which means his audience cannot either.

Too Queer to Be Contained? Little Richard in Music Histories

Despite his rhetorical efforts to domesticate himself and draw some distance between his secular and Christian persona, Little Richard is almost
too transgressive for traditional linear music histories. White rock 'n' roll
historians flatten out and overly romanticize him, emphasizing the radical
break without addressing his struggles. Being a black "freak" was difficult,
and they typically evade substantial discussion of his post-fame conflicts.

The nature and appeal of rebellion is integral to the racially divided responses to Little Richard. For white listeners Little Richard's music, image,
and persona represented a subversive challenge to middle-class normalcy and
conformity. This is the most common interpretation of his impact in rock 'n'
roll and popular music histories. For example, in *The Sound of the City* Charlie
Gillett argues, "With Little Richard, the rock 'n' roll audience got the aggressive extrovert to enact their wilder fantasies, and his stage performance set
precedents for anyone who followed him. . . . Compared to [Fats] Domino,
Little Richard, musically and stylistically speaking, was coarse, uncultured,
and uncontrolled, in every way harder for the music establishment to take"
(Gillett 1996, 26). David Szatmary's discussion in *Rockin' in Time* emphasizes a
wildness motif noting: "Little Richard and Chuck Berry, significantly younger
and wilder than most R&B performers, became heroes to white teens who
had discovered rhythm and blues," describing Little Richard as "a wild-eyed,
pompadoured madman who crashed the piano keys and screamed nonsensi-
cal lyrics at breakneck speed" and noting his "wild stage show" (Szatmary
2004, 16–17). In *Rock & Roll*, Robert Palmer refers to him as, "an outsider's
outsider—black and bisexual and proud of it, the self-designated King and
Queen of Rock and Roll. Had he belonged to an earlier generation of performers, he would have had to keep his sexual predilections well hidden under a
veneer of highly stylized masculinity, and doubtless subordinate his natural
exuberance to a smoother crooning style. But Little Richard was a rocker,
and this is one way you can tell: Rockers don't sublimate their idiosyncrasies,
they exaggerate them, revel in them" (Palmer 1995, 140–41). Reebee Garofalo
describes Little Richard as the "archetypal rock 'n' roll screamer" and notes
how "Tutti Frutti" "instantly established Little Richard as the most outrageous
rock 'n' roller of them all" (Garofalo 2005, 80, 88).

These excerpts emphasize the aggressive sexuality and boisterous, outrageous image that defined Little Richard's early career, as well as the fantasies
he fulfilled for teenage audiences. Symbolically the performer represents

"rock and roll at its most subversive" for white listeners, according to Bruce Tucker. As Hamilton has noted, "In an era of grey-flannel suits and backyard barbecues, of sexual conformity and suburbanization, white teenagers' passion for rock and roll could be interpreted as an unarticulated social rebellion, an implicit endorsement of sexual flamboyance that forecast the sexual revolutions to come" (Hamilton 1998, 173).

This point of view favors a sociological interpretation of Little Richard and other black rock 'n' roll performers as providing a cultural antidote to white middle-class social conformity and emotional repression and symbolically providing them with a form of resistance. Missing from these stories are important details such as the way the singer had to sue to receive proper royalties for his compositions and the severe commercial decline he experienced during the mid-1960s (Watrous 1992). Perhaps the most important detail these stories exclude is how his symbolic role for white audiences, partially the result of exaggerations that skillfully catered to white racial and sexual fantasies about blackness, was politically and socially irresponsible to many blacks. Despite his initial fame, Little Richard was not *respectable* by 1950s black cultural standards.

His strategy is a telling calculation of how to push boundaries far enough to stand out but also to avoid igniting certain pre-established racial and sexual tensions. The national spotlight that singles like "Tutti Frutti," "Long Tall Sally," and "Rip It Up" afforded him had to be balanced against the mounting fears of a transition toward desegregation in education, public facilities, and cultural consumption. The music marketed toward mid-1950s teens, particularly white teens, inspired an array of objections, ranging from the sobriquet "leerics" to describe the sexual content of R&B and rock 'n' roll to organized efforts to eliminate certain "vulgar" recordings from record shops and radio airplay lists (Gillett 1996, 17–22; Martin and Segrave 1993, 15–26). Traditional pop crooners and song publishers of traditional pre-rock pop songs (particularly those represented by the American Society of Composers, Authors, and Publishers [ASCAP]) were also mutually opposed to rock for fear that it was dominating airplay and sales (Garofalo 2005, 140–43; Szatmary 2004, 23–24). Fears that black musicians and R&B-derived music was going to contaminate white youth and incite miscegenation was a particular concern, best exemplified by the organization and mobilization of White Citizens Councils in Northern Alabama, Birmingham, New Orleans, and other Southern regions (Martin and Segrave 1993, 41–43). In 1956 Asa "Ace" Carter of the Birmingham branch defined rock 'n' roll as "the basic, heavy-beat music of the Negroes" and one component of a "plot to mongrelize America" (Szatmary 2004, 22). As Garofalo noted succinctly, "Rock 'n' roll represented everything white, middle-class parents feared: it was urban, it was sexual, and most of it was black" (Garofalo 2005, 125).

Histories of black music frequently ignore Little Richard or criticize him for buffoonery. These dismissals seem to exclude him tacitly for not adhering to the standard "race man" script of respectability. Little Richard's appeal to white teenagers and his challenges to postwar masculine norms in particular alienated many black audiences during the mid-1950s and has affected his historicization (Miller 1999, 110–11; Ward 1998, 52–53). For many historians of black music his act reinforced regressive stereotypes. Little Richard figures into Samuel A. Floyd Jr.'s discussion in *The Power of Black Music* (1995) of 1950s-era R&B recording artists who helped the genre reach "the pinnacle of its popularity outside the core culture" (177). He devotes several pages to discussing Richard and Chuck Berry, including their musical influences, and surveys critical opinions of their role in rock 'n' roll. He concludes by noting, "[Little Richard] therefore took on an ambiguous sexuality and developed a ridiculous stage manner and persona that made him appear to be exotically harmless to parents of white teenagers. In other words, he became Esu, male/female, a symbol of androgyny. In this, Little Richard donned a new—and truer, I might add—minstrel mask" (180). Floyd's assessment is missing the power of Little Richard's strategies, especially how he un-closets cross-racial desire through gender. Just as Ray's immersion in black musical communities challenged white segregationist norms, Little Richard upset racist fears that exposure to black music would corrupt white youth.

Anxiety about sexual ambiguity and androgyny also figures into these critiques. As Hamilton notes, negative or dismissive responses to sexual and gender transgression suggest they lack historical awareness of the pre-1950s role of the "freak" figure within black masculine traditions of performance (Hamilton 1998, 174). I believe the scope of her argument reaches even further if we consider Mathis, whom I discuss in chapter 4. His success with white and black audiences suggests that black audiences embraced black queer public figures *if* their sexuality was *implied* rather than *stated* by their gender behavior, and if their demeanor adhered to principles of "respectability." Mathis had a very subdued persona, and his success as a romantic crooner positioned him as an heir to the black male crossover pop music tradition that made Eckstine and Cole musical and cultural icons. In many ways he could be considered a "New Negro" in the vein of Mark Anthony Neal's definition in *What the Music Said*: "The New Negro figure of the late '50s and '60s, personified in figures like Sammy Davis Jr., and boxer Floyd Patterson, simply did not aim to be accepted as part of the bourgeois liberal establishment but firmly believed that on the basis of their talent, hard work, and work ethics, they were already a part of such an establishment, as witnessed by their presence in mainstream culture" (Neal 1999, 43). Mathis's career suggested an alternative way of understanding the different possibilities of what constitutes "subversion" alongside the obvious disruptions Little Richard performed. In essence, though he and Little Richard made a commercial impact around the same period (circa 1956), he represented a different variation of the black "open secret" that was a better political fit for black politics of the time than rock 'n' roll performers.

Like the black gay writers who claim the famously anti-identitarian James Baldwin as a literary father, black queer writers want to claim Little Richard as a queer forefather (Brim 2014, 27–43). This ancestral effort is admirable, but these writers struggle to integrate his own ambivalence about his queerness, especially his effeminacy, which he himself codes as homosexuality. Little Richard's sexuality and genderplay, and the drag tradition he rose from, have limited his presence in black music surveys. They are central, however, to his inclusion in queer critics' recollections of his historical role. Similar to rock 'n' roll histories, these histories have also favored a *happy ending* that fixates on a particular moment rather than addressing the toll of his equivocations. The tone of queer discourse on Little Richard focuses on him as a pioneer for queering rock 'n' roll and for serving as a kind of heritage/legacy figure for queers.

In *A Boy Called Mary* critic Kris Kirk expressed disappointment in the White biography's failure to "deliver the serious critical evaluation that musical buffs may have been expecting" in favor of the "lurid" details of Richard's homosexual past, "much of it in the words of the Pompadour himself" (Kirk 1999, 36; White 1984). Kirk briefly describes the singer's career as "a lifelong symbiotic struggle between homosexuality and religion" and recalls various details gleaned from the biography. Amid this recital he reminds readers that despite the singer's claim that black audiences were uninterested in his music, other musical performers were interested, including Pat Boone, Elvis, The Beatles, and Prince, "another frail black kid convulsed by sex and God, who at least admits his debt" (Kirk 1999, 37). He builds on the discussion of Little Richard's legacy by noting that the rock 'n' roller "was the world's first outrageous pop squealer" (38) and ends by ultimately endorsing the book to readers who want to "learn what it means to be a Living Legend" (39). In expressing what is ultimately an appraisal of Little Richard's historic importance, Kirk skirts the distance between Little Richard and black audiences. The performer's influence and legend status provide a happy historical ending that feels incomplete because it overlooks his struggles to clarify his identity.

Boze Hadleigh's book *Sing Out!* defines Little Richard as a pioneer for opening up the sexual climate of the repressive 1950s: "On either side of the sexual fence, 'queer' was a '50s obsession. It was the first decade in which the closet door opened a crack to shed some light on the worlds of song and film" (Hadleigh 1997, 64). He discusses Little Richard in this context as a kind of pioneer who changed the mainstream: "That was in the 1950s, when rock was new, people were sexually naive, and America didn't know what to make of or quite how to label frightening newcomers like Elvis Presley—with his banned-in-Boston hips—and Little Richard—with his eyeliner, wild-man antics and womanish demeanor" (67). This brief reference accurately addresses Little Richard's contrast with the era's general expectations, and in the context of Hadleigh's book it also asserts him as a highly visible queer hero. Once again, the performer's complex identity and the messy racial political issues he encountered are overlooked for a more transcendent and finite narrative.

Isaac Julien and Kobena Mercer, who are black and gay British scholars, employ Little Richard in an essay that reviews the possibilities for engaging with established attempts to critique "traditional concepts of [black] masculinity" (Julien and Mercer 1991, 172). They end it by suggesting, "As a way forward to debates on race, sexuality, and culture, we need to reclaim these resources to make visible the positive ways black men have been involved in a political struggle around the very meaning of masculinity" (173). Their analysis employs Little Richard as an example of one of these potential symbolic resources:

> Once we reclaim the camp and crazy "carnivalesque" excesses of Little Richard—the original Queen of Rock 'n' Roll—we can appreciate the way black men in popular music have parodied the stereotypes of black masculinity to "theatricalize" and send up the whole charade of gender roles. Little Richard's "outrageousness," the model for many who have deployed the subversive rhetoric of irony like George Clinton and Parliament-Funkadelic, Cameo, and perhaps even Prince, affirms the plurality of black male identities and draws critical attention to the cultural constructedness of sexual identity. These figures remind us that our pleasures are political and that our politics can be pleasurable. (173)

Because they address race, sexuality, and his musical and cultural legacy, this is one of the more nuanced discussions of Little Richard. In many ways their discussion complements my alternate masculinity argument by suggesting that he has offered possibilities to other black male performers rather than framing him exclusively as an icon for white audiences and/or queer audiences. Yet this argument also feels a bit too complete in light of Little Richard's ambivalence about his queerness, public image, and career.

What I hope my argument illustrates is how the wide range of tools Little Richard used to define his persona—*self-enfreaking, self-neutering, playing the race card, spectacularizing*, and *self-domesticating*—requires attention to his synthesis of these elements to navigate social expectations regarding race, gender, music, and persona. Kicked out of his home for being a "freak," he used this to his advantage as a teenager, which culminated in regional and then national fame. Different audiences embraced different parts of Little Richard, but he felt compelled to retreat. His initial attempt at *domestication* failed to sustain him and he returned to the mainstream spotlight bolder than ever. As this ebbed, he retreated more deeply into a kind of *domestication* that paralleled the culture's turn toward conservatism and binaries.

Gradually, we witness him navigate his secular persona with his faith. The result is a figure who performs the queer feat of fusing many elements typically defined as opposites. He can excite audiences nostalgic for classic rock 'n' roll fervor, garner the respect of people of faith for his sincere expression of belief, and still embody and express unabashed spectacular queerness in his verbal wit, musical expression, and hair, makeup, and clothing choices. In his career we witness ongoing navigations between struggle and acceptance, ambivalence and enthusiasm, freakiness and normativity that represent the needs and desires of his audience as much as it does his personal story. If the society defines and maintains norms, and openly embraces figures who flout these conventions, therein lies a collective potential for drawing more attention to the artificial constraints imposed by normalcy and embracing the true complexity of our nature, our inner "freaks."

CHAPTER FOUR

Fine and Dandy

Mapping Johnny Mathis's Negotiations of Race, Sexuality, and Affect

IN 2017, AT AGE eighty-one, Johnny Mathis spoke openly about his sexuality to reporter Nancy Giles on *CBS Sunday Morning*.

VOICEOVER: In 1982 Mathis told *Us Weekly* something personal he has rarely discussed since. He said, "Homosexuality is a way of life that I've grown accustomed to."

NANCY GILES: You got death threats once that happened as well, when you spoke about your private life.

JOHNNY MATHIS: And that was a revelation for me. I come from San Francisco. It's uh . . . it's not unusual to be gay in San Francisco.

NG: No. Uh-uh.

JM: I've had some girlfriends.

NG: Uh-huh.

JM: Some boyfriends, just like most people. But, I never got married, for instance. I knew that I was gay. I didn't want to do anything about that.

NG: Right.

JM: My dad had a wonderful, wonderful way about accepting things as they are. As opposed to the way . . . we think in which they would be. He said, "Son a lot of people are not going to like you out there you know." [*Laughs.*]

NG: Well, that's an amazing thing that he was so loving and accepting.

JM: He was my pal. I could tell him anything. And I did. (CBS Sunday Morning 2017b, 4:43–5:38)

To my knowledge, this was the first time he has discussed his sexual orientation on television. In addition to posting the edited television segment on YouTube, CBS also features a "Web Extra" with the subtitle "Johnny Mathis on Coming Out." (CBS Sunday Morning 2017a, "Web Extra," 3:25). Based on the "coming out" framing, viewers could easily interpret his verbal declaration on television (and the internet) as his *official* coming out. Though queer people frequently "come out" multiple times in a variety of settings throughout their lives, celebrity disclosures garner unusual attention. Since his 1982 off-the-record declaration to *Us Weekly* that he was gay (Petrucelli 1982, 58–60), he later retracted his statement, which Giles references in the interview; consequently, viewers might assume he was ashamed or closeted back then and only now has he come to terms with his *true* identity (CBS Sunday Morning 2017a). These kinds of presumptions are understandable, since audiences commonly interpret coming out as a journey from secrecy to publicness, and by association shame to pride, but ultimately this is an incorrect assumption.

I argue against this type of interpretation because it imposes generic expectations of how public figures manage their gender expression and sexuality. Chiefly, Mathis's queerness, notably the ways his public persona subtly challenges male gender norms, has been discernible *throughout* his career. While queerness often refers to both sexuality and gender, his performance of gender has been his most accessible challenge to normative masculinity and is arguably his most influential legacy socially and artistically. As a vocalist and public figure, he has employed several tools, especially *self-neutering*, *playing the race card*, and *self-domestication*, to construct a persona that has given him tremendous access to a wide range of audiences. As discussed in chapter 3, whereas Little Richard toyed with the "race man" that was constructed by employing black conventions, with a spectacular queer twist, Mathis adhered faithfully to the race man idea by projecting a quiet dignity devoid of scandal, notoriety, or anything divisive.

Chapter 4 depicts Mathis as a masterful navigator who queered expectations and mostly thrived. I map out the queer nature of his vocal style, his navigation of white and black musical expectations, the ways he negotiated heteronormative sexual expectations, and his cultivation of a contemporary black queer dandy identity. In the 1970s, when he experienced a resurgence, he was more overt about his personal ties to gay liberation, yet he modulated them in a manner that neither denied his sexuality nor made it the most salient part of himself. He continues to maintain a gentle grip on his image as a smooth, unimposing crooner who can be who and what you need him to be.

A Novel Sound for the 1950s: Johnny Mathis's "Queer" Voice

In the original liner notes of 1963's classic jazz album *John Coltrane and Johnny Hartman* writer A. B. Spellman lauds Hartman's membership among "a strong lot of big-voiced crooners" (Coltrane and Hartman 1963), which also includes black baritones like Earl Coleman, Billy Eckstine, and Arthur Prysock. He celebrates Hartman for combating what he views as a steady decline in jazz singing since the demise of bebop bands "especially among male singers." Central to his almost elegiac tone is a concern that "replacing the masculinity of the crooner with the effeteness of the lark is only another kind of premature destruction of artists by factors which have nothing to do with their art, which destruction we are the passive witnesses of in these times" (Coltrane and Hartman 1963). These pointed notes highlight the pervasive nature of gender norms in multiple facets of society, including popular music. I interpret the remarks as a slight to the rise of female singers and effeminate voices or, more simply, to the feminization of popular music. The notes also imply that the rise of such voices is more about commercialism than art. Beneath these words are layers of assumptions about art, gender, and expression that instantly make me think of Mathis.

By the 1963 release of the Coltrane and Hartman album, Mathis had become one the most consistently popular rock-era crooners. He had placed twenty-seven Top 40 pop hits on the *Billboard* Hot 100 singles charts and twenty albums on its albums chart. He ranked second only to Sinatra as an albums seller during the 1956–1959 period and #11 among singles artists of the 1955–1959 era. Central to his broad appeal was a signature vocal sound; as James R. Morris in his *American Popular Song* (1984) pointed out, "He, more than any other contemporary singer, recalls the virtues of the high sentimental tenors" of an earlier era. He also praised Mathis's "reflective and yet concentrated" style, his "very sensitive" approach to melody and rhythm, and "beauty of tone" (98). In a 1981 review of a compilation album, critic Peter Reilly noted "the sweetness of his sound, the high voltage charge given certain key words within a lyric" (Reilly 1981, 72). Sentimental, sensitive, beautiful, and sweet represent a few of the adjectives commonly applied to Mathis's signature tenor sound.

Though Morris and Reilly employ these terms as forms of praise in the two instances above, the words also have feminine connotations that speak to the "effeteness" Spellman's liner notes mention. Music critic Will Friedwald argues that "Mathis's technique and tone production are indeed impeccable" but believes he "often sounds merely piercing" and "annoyingly mannered" (Friedwald 2010, 689). Taste is a highly subjective matter, but certain terms, like "piercing," can have gendered connotations. This becomes particularly clear if one believes Friedwald's anecdote that Frank Sinatra (one of Mathis's idols) "cast aspersions upon the younger singer's lifestyle by referring to him as 'the African Queen'" (689). Friedwald supplies no specific date or place for such comments, but the implications are clear. "Queen" is slang for "gay man," and queenliness is associated with effeminacy. The specific root of Sinatra's sobriquet may be based more in inference than actual knowledge about Mathis's' "lifestyle" (to use Friedwald's unfortunate term), but his voice is part of his affect.

From a vocal perspective, the link between effeteness and Mathis grows clearer when we recall that one of his most famous recorded moments is his falsetto passage during the bridge on his 1959 hit version of "Misty," a ten-second passage, sung between 2:39–2:48 in the 3:34 single (see Mathis 1993). In *The Queen's Throat* (1993), Wayne Koestenbaum notes the historic connotation of male falsetto voices as "profoundly perverse: a freakish sideshow: the place where voice goes wrong" (164). He links it to gender by recalling its gender ambiguity,

> The falsetto is part of the history of effeminacy—a compelling saga yet to be written. Long before anyone knew what a homosexual was, entire cultures knew to mock men who sang unconventionally high. Plutarch disparaged "effeminate musical tattling, mere sound without substance"; John of Salisbury discouraged; "womanish affectations in the mincing of notes and sentences"; St. Raynard insisted that "it becomes men to sing with a masculine voice, and not in a feminine manner, with tinkling, or as popularly said, with false voices to imitate theatrical wantonness." (165)

Susan McClary's discussion of "soprano masculinities" notes similar perceptions that men singing in higher registers signifies "damaged manhood," the kind associated with seventeenth-century male castrati (McClary 2013, 34). Linguists Ron Smyth, Greg Jacobs, and Henry Rogers argue that North American listeners frequently correlate sexual orientation to vocal sounds and have developed conceptions of what constitutes a "gay voice." Though their research reveals how imprecise this approach is in practice, it is nonetheless a sound that "can be stigmatized both within and outside the gay community(ies)" which makes sense, as such a construct could only exist "within a homophobic culture" that feels compelled to demarcate bodies so rigidly (Smyth, Jacobs, and Rogers 2003, 347).

McCracken's discussion of "white masculine vocal performance" notes how the rise of crooners led many people to commonly connect "a male pop singer's high pitch (or use of falsetto), emotional vulnerability, and demonstrative female audiences with his effeminacy, arrested development, likely homosexuality, and, consequently, his critical devaluation" (McCracken 2015, 313). Despite the history of stigma toward male falsettos in classical music and crooning discourse, the falsetto holds a different value in African American popular music. As Peraino notes, "The male falsetto voice in African-American gospel and soul had a long history . . . and was not in itself a marker of effeminacy or artifice, but rather an ideal romantic or earnest voice, marked as emotionally sincere" (Peraino 2005, 189). McClary echoes this observation by noting how the African American church "frequently features male gospel singers who produce high falsetto moans and melisma. Although they scale the heights of their ranges, their high-pitched vocals rarely have anything to do with gender bending" (McClary 2013, 35).

For example, Tony Cummings has described the influence of Rebert (or R. H.) Harris of the gospel quartet The Soul Stirrers, which also launched Sam Cooke's career. Notably, Harris "had a high tenor and, by utilizing falsetto, introduced the soaring false soprano which was to become fundamental to gospel" (Cummings 1975, 11). Several writers have reiterated his unique influence, as well as the way male falsetto singing became a church convention, "probably because it has always been so adventurous, if not theatrical" according to gospel scholar Anthony Heilbut (Guralnick 2005, 4, 26, 60; Ravens 2014, 203; Heilbut 2012, 255).

Beyond gospel, falsetto pervades the blues, doo-wop, Motown, soul, and disco genres. Specific examples of black male singers whom writers commonly reference in this context include Phillip Bailey (Earth, Wind, and Fire), D'Angelo, Marvin Gaye, Michael Jackson, Al Green, Eddie Kendricks (the Temptations), Frankie Lymon, Curtis Mayfield, Aaron Neville, Prince, Smokey Robinson, Sylvester, and Jackie Wilson (Ravens 2014, 203; Royster 2013, 118; McClary 2013, 35; François 1995, 446–48). This rich history may contain the reason Mathis did not face a significant stigma during the 1950s, and beyond, for his vocal style; his style fit into the mainstream of black popular music.

Despite the masculinist gender economy of the postwar era, and implications that Mathis's voice sounded "queer" to some ears, he embraced male and female elements in his vocal approach. Within the liner notes of the boxed set *The Music of Johnny Mathis*, Mathis cites male and female pop- and jazz-oriented stylists like Nat "King" Cole, Ella Fitzgerald, Judy Garland,

Frank Sinatra, and Sarah Vaughan as his interpretive models, so he openly acknowledges how male and female singers inform his style (Mathis 1993). Clearly, based on sales data, the public embraced his stylistic blurring of gender conventions. His voice occupied a relatively safe space between the conventional and unconventional—enough so that even when critics like Spellman drew attention to a sea change in vocal norms among men, Mathis remained unscathed.

His voice is inseparable from his complex public affect. In the context of the postwar male expectations Kimmel outlined, Mathis was too young to have served in the military. But, beyond that caveat, Mathis was not married, did not have children, and, based on his voice alone, did not project a virile image. So why did people not single him out for diverging from the era's masculine norms? As I have noted, the black popular press of the postwar period depicted queerness in explicitly gendered terms such that female impersonators dominated its lens of what constituted male gender deviancy. As Gregory Conerly notes, "One common construction of same-sex sexuality was the association of 'homosexuals' and 'lesbians' with gender nonconformity. That is, homosexual men had feminine characteristics, and lesbians masculine characteristics, in terms of clothing, walk, and mannerisms" (Conerly 2001, 386). In promotional materials like album covers, singles sleeves, and press profiles, Mathis always wears gender-normative clothing like tailored suits or "preppy" clothing like sweaters and slacks. Though his hair is "processed," which, according to Maxine Craig, could mark "a man as a dandy" within black postwar communities, this look, patterned after idols like Nat "King" Cole, was common among black male entertainers and did not attract any attention for Mathis (Craig 1997, 409).

Even if Mathis had pushed gender boundaries a bit more overtly, Conerly notes that "the field of entertainment" was a space where "male homosexuality was tolerable" (Conerly 2001, 385), evidenced by numerous stories about nightclub performers and masquerade balls published in *Ebony* through 1953 and *Jet* through the early 1960s (386–90). As I note in chapter 3 in the discussion of Little Richard, when he was a young regional performer, he regularly performed in drag, and this did not hamper his career. As biographer R. J. Smith recalls, "[Little] Richard was the ultimate product of a little known, extravagant, underground scene. Like a number of other acts, he got his start playing the role of the 'tent show queen': cross-dressing song-and-dance acts that played to black audiences. As a teenager Richard performed in drag, billed as 'Princess LaVonne,' a chair balanced on his chin, in Sugarfoot Sam from Alabam's minstrel show" (Smith 2012, 65).

The contrast between Mathis and black female impersonators related directly to the race man construct. As Stephen Knadler reminds us in *Fugitive Race*, "In its frequent running of stories about gender deviants, the black popular press sought to recoup black male adequacy, setting up clear boundaries between the effeminate male and the masculine and clearly heterosexual race man" (Knadler 2002, 160). By virtue of not being a radical gender nonconformist Mathis was spared the potential stigma of being seen as queer and could function within the confines of the race man construct. This relative safety net shaped his navigation of racial and sexual anxieties.

Managing Queerness and Racial Difference

In *The Black Bourgeoisie* (1965) sociologist E. Franklin Frazier argues that "Negro men" (in the parlance of the 1950s) "are not allowed to play the 'masculine role' as defined by American culture. They can not assert themselves or exercise power as white men do. When they protest against racial discrimination there is always the threat that they will be punished by the white world" (220). In *Manning the Race* (2004) Marlon Ross has described this dilemma as one of "the contradictions of masculine self-making" for black men (190). Critically and politically, I want to interrogate rather than valorize the notion of a "masculine role" and its associated racial hierarchies. But my immediate critical concern is acknowledging that gender roles functioned as social currency for postwar black America, and to survive, a variety of black male figures felt compelled to maneuver around the conventions Frazier describes.

In the context of Mathis, he is visible as a black man, which makes him vulnerable to racist conceptions, and is discernibly queer to some listeners, which also makes him vulnerable. Yet Mathis was able to launch his career seamlessly. The remainder of the chapter examines how he embodied these vulnerable positions without either detracting from his access to black and white audiences or inhibiting his earning power. Like Little Richard, Mathis's navigation of race and sexuality required the careful coordination of various tools to build and sustain his persona. He needed to locate himself within black America to establish social credibility and simultaneously win over white audiences, who were still reluctant to accept black pop stars.

Musically, Mathis's management figured out that Mathis could appeal to a broad audience by cultivating a "raceless" sound (Christgau 1998, 19). In this sense, he *played the race card* musically and in the process neutralized and domesticated any potential *threat* a more *ethnic* sound would have conveyed. Though he debuted in 1956, during the early days of rock 'n' roll, Mathis's talent for singing melodic, romantic pop music in his classically trained tenor did not feature significant traces of the urban or rural styles that informed rock 'n' roll. His management directed him to downplay any racial and ethnic traces intentionally in his music to broaden his appeal and avoid pigeonholing as a racial act. He also downplayed jazz technique in his music, though jazz musicians were fond of him.

Mathis is synonymous with the pop genre, but his 1956 debut album *Johnny Mathis: A New Sound in Popular Song* was arranged by jazz arranger Gil Evans (Mathis 1956). Todd Everett's liner notes to the boxed set *The Music of Johnny Mathis: A Personal Collection* state that the album's commercial failure led his manager, Helen Noga, and Columbia Records producer Mitch Miller to steer him in a more pop-oriented direction (Mathis 1993, 20–24). The shift in Mathis's sound from jazz-oriented to pop made him more accessible to a broader audience, as did the careful tailoring of him as a "colorless" crossover artist to white listeners. In the liner notes Mathis noted how Noga and Miller urged him to sing in a soft, romantic style, to avoid overt association with R&B: "I think most people were very surprised when they saw me . . . they thought I was white because I sounded white on records" (24). In an appraisal of Cole as "the greatest of the crooners," critic Robert Christgau's *Grown Up All Wrong* (1998) declares Mathis as Cole's logical "inheritor" or successor and labels him "the most raceless star in the history of American pop" (19). Christgau's observation and Mathis's impression are also supported by the following caption from *Ebony* magazine's 1957 story on Mathis: "Boy with the Golden Voice." "Because of his lean, Latin look, he is often mistaken for Mexican, Italian, or Spaniard. Young white girl, who had requested signed photograph, stammered, 'What are you? I know you're not colored.' Johnny looked at her and smiled, 'Yes I am,' he said" (Ebony 1957, 28).

In a sense, his musical style represented a middle-of-the-road aesthetic that appealed broadly to younger and older audiences, blacks and whites, album buyers and buyers of singles, and other demographics. Though his manager steered him musically at the outset of his career, I would argue that vocally he lacks the grit and sensuality associated with rock 'n' roll and the melodic improvisation synonymous with jazz. Once he emerged commercially, he'd already conformed to the ideals of postwar tranquility and did not have to contort his sound or image to appear nonthreatening; he was already edgeless.

Somehow, Mathis managed to convey a somewhat "raceless" sound and still appeal to black audiences, based on a combination of factors. He plays the race card deftly with the black audience as well. Ross argues that sexually queer people represent multiple cultural groups and bring their traditional cultural orientation with them when they enter into queer culture. As such, for many queers, queer cultural affiliation is often secondary (always succeeding acculturation in some other racial, ethnic, religious group) and invisible (Ross 2000, 502). There was a modicum of private and intraracial "tolerance" for sexual deviance in black communities, largely informed by the de facto aspect of racial segregation. Among many African American queer people there is "not a binary of secrecy versus revelation" but instead "a continuum of knowledge that persists at various levels according to the kin and friendship relations within the community. Although sometimes imprecisely referred to as an 'open secret,' such attitudes express instead a strong sense that it is impossible *not* to know something so obvious among those who know you well enough. In such a context, to announce one's attraction by "coming out" would not necessarily indicate progress in sexual identity, and it would not necessarily change one's identity from closeted to liberated as conceptualized in the dominant closet narrative" (Ross 2005, 180). Mathis's willingness to play to certain aspects of black respectability but to maintain a certain distance from queer identifications speaks to this dynamic. I discuss his appearances in *Ebony* magazine to illustrate his fidelity to the black community.

Ebony has been an arbiter of African American community standards since its founding in 1945 and has consistently engaged in rhetorical gestures that highlight Mathis's conformity to notions of black "progress" by emphasizing aspects of his life, which affirm a traditionally masculine image of heteronormativity. Mathis was the subject of *Ebony* cover stories in December 1957, March 1965, and March 1976. A close reading of these stories reveals several efforts to define Mathis within black heteronormative conventions. Mathis played along gamely, but he gradually asserted his queer identity in subtle ways that grew more prominent in the 1970s.

Ebony self-consciously highlighted Mathis's *authentic* blackness by portraying him as a black role model who exemplified the social, economic, and sexual ideals of respectability. Respectability, particularly sexual respectability, has endured as a trope of African American consciousness "racial uplift" ideology spanning the late nineteenth and early twentieth centuries, which emphasized "social purity, thrift, chastity, and the patriarchal family" (Gaines 1996, 1–17; Higginbotham 1993, 185–229). A consistent emphasis on the nuclear family lives of black celebrities in black magazines like *Ebony* and the emergence of masculinist Black Nationalist politics of the 1960s focused on reproducing the black family and maintaining separate gender roles as "cultural values," prominent elements of black cultural thought that emerged during Mathis's career (Thomas 1998, 116–35). The culmination of these examples is the expectation of heteronormativity as a social norm for black public figures. Rhonda Williams addresses this pressure on black gays and lesbians: "Whether viewed as the products of broken families or betrayers of family life together, black gays and lesbians are a potential anathema to straight African Americans whose resistance to racist narratives inspires them to 'clean up' images of black sexuality." A substantial national history of sexual exploitation and suspicion toward black bodies and the pressure for families to mold future citizens inform many nationalist notions of families as "*the* sanctioned site for the reproduction of authentic national racial ethnic culture." This policing has resulted in efforts to "sanitize and normalize popular perceptions of black sexuality" away from the "hypersexuality, promiscuity, and danger" signified by black queerness (Williams 1998, 144).

The politicized currents of black heteronormativity, as a political project played out in cultural forms, operated complexly in *Ebony*'s reportage. Its articles simultaneously reified Mathis's presumed heterosexuality *and* suggested he was nontraditional by presenting him as incomplete and underdeveloped because he was single. A reading of Mathis's comments to the magazine reveals a discernible sexual ambiguity to Mathis, who navigated the pressure to be sexually normative and signified sexual difference to attentive readers. In the mid-1960s Mathis subtly alluded to his distance from traditional heterosexual romance and later acknowledged his homosexuality with little consequence. Black cultural tolerance for Mathis's "open secret" in the 1950s through the 1970s opened a space for future queer-vague or sexually ambiguous African American singers such as Michael Jackson, Prince, and Luther Vandross whose perceived "queerness" has generated controversy but never deterred their ultimate cultural acceptance among black audiences. Mathis tested the waters and floated onward without losing his audience.[1]

Ebony aimed to authenticate Mathis to black audiences by positing him as a role model. The authenticating strategy emerged during a period of heightened political investment in assimilation and acceptance among blacks. As previously mentioned, two of the most prominent 1950s-era black male singers were Eckstine and Cole. Throughout the 1950s *Ebony* published numerous feature stories on Cole, Eckstine, and Mathis. The stories are of comparative interest for understanding Mathis because *Ebony* focused on Cole's and Eckstine's interior lives, including their spouses, children, friends, and home lives. Such stories defined them as financially successful and "traditional" family men making an obvious "contribution" to black culture—raising strong black families (Cole 1953; 1958a; 1958b; Robinson 1965b; and Eckstine 1952a; 1952b). Representing black participation in the nuclear family and defining families as anchors from social pressures like racism, as well as a source of moral training and strength, imbued family with iconic significance for the politics of respectability.

In contrast, *Ebony*'s coverage of Mathis almost suggested that he had no interests or acquaintances outside of his career and parents. Despite Mathis's virtually absent sexual self, *Ebony* subtly used gender to assert Mathis's connections to black life. Through careful choices *Ebony* assured readers that Mathis conformed to 1950s notions of white and black "manhood"—and focused on his financial independence, competitive athletic background, and close immediate family ties.

Ebony's framing of gender in the text and photos of their Mathis articles vacillated between presenting Mathis as a traditional heterosexual man and images that signified liminality. *Ebony*'s stories marked him as potentially queer, because he was young, style conscious, artistic, and, most important, unmarried—all potential signs of queerness in 1950s America. There were numerous subtle signifiers in the written text and photos that suggested his gender deviance. For example, the December 1957 Mathis story featured a photo of producer Mitch Miller chatting with several black-suited white male executive types and Mathis standing behind Miller drinking from a cup. The caption reads, "At recording session, Johnny sips coffee while bearded Mitch Miller and recording executives talk shop" (Ebony 1957, 28, 30, 32). The caption juxtaposed Mathis, who is black, young, and a singer, against the ostensibly serious male executives who were white, middle-aged business people. While the male executives talked shop, Mathis drank coffee, deferred, and was a nonparticipant. *Talking shop* typically describes a male conversational ritual about business or sports and usually excludes women. Mathis's physical separation positioned him as an outsider to the masculine communication that surrounded him. The same article ended with Mathis virtually proclaiming himself as the proverbial mama's boy when he said, "I wanted to spend Christmas at home with my family. I promised Mama I'd be home for Christmas" (28).

The magazine offset these potential queer signifiers by emphasizing masculine signifiers, such as Mathis's financial success and athletic past. Because Mathis emerged in both a virile era and during the early years of the civil rights movement, *Ebony* predictably emphasized his identity as a cultural role model. Unspoken assumptions that black performers were cultural role models formed a unique expectation that heightened pressure for Mathis to appear "normal" and distinguished him from his white peers of the era. *Ebony* also focused on his budding manhood, especially his financial and managerial independence from the controlling Noga and, as I discuss in the "Self-neutering Strategies" section below, simultaneously questioned his bachelor status.

A March 1965 story on Mathis's split from Helen Noga described him as "often shy, quiet and sometimes child-like," which infantilized and even feminized him (Robinson 100). The story also contrasted Mathis with the domineering Noga and noted, "Once early in his career when Mathis wore a wristwatch which Mrs. Noga did not feel was masculine enough in its design, she did not bite her tongue in telling him so; Mathis did not bite his in reply. 'You can say what you want to,' he retorted, 'but it's my watch'" (Robinson 1965a, 100). The wristwatch incident performed several functions: it showed Noga's concern over Mathis's image, especially in terms of gender; it showed Mathis's casual attitude about his choices; and it showed that Mathis could defend himself, as any "man" should.

Ebony's March 1976 follow-up article went further in its focus on Mathis's post-Noga career. The article recounted his managerial lawsuit against Noga and found him owning up to his subordinated history under Noga, "We came to a point in our relationship where I was bored and tired of living with someone else . . . I was a man now; when she found me I was a boy. I had also decided that I wanted a choice in matters that pertained to my career and personal life. I didn't have a choice when I was with Helen" (Robinson 1976, 48). This was a loaded series of statements because it almost implied a romantic relationship and/or mother-son relationship. Perhaps more important, it reiterated the article's thesis that he was now, finally, at forty years old, a "man." Neither Mathis nor the article's author ever explored what the specific personal and career issues he was referring to were, but there was a slight suggestion of a queer subtext that *some* force was preventing his full exploration of a self. Mathis's affective investment in asserting his "manhood" reinforces patriarchy uncritically, which reflects a social norm and reminds us that using "queering" tools does not prevent the Quartet from reproducing hegemonic ideas.

Mathis complemented *Ebony*'s careful deflections from his queer signifiers through his resistance to revealing personal information. Though it is arguable what constitutes "personal" information, social, sexual, and familial relationships generally constitute contemporary notions of the personal. Mathis has always been reluctant to claim the identity of a "performer," which allowed him to avoid taking personal risks. Though he was primarily a romantic balladeer, he resisted the identification and did not identify as a particularly romantic person. Mathis sold the *idea* of romance rather than the *experience*, perhaps because his personal desires likely existed on the periphery of the romantic ideals of the era. The longing and unrequited affections he sang of were palpable but existed on the cusp between the generically accessible and personal. There was not necessarily a clear space for organizing and articulating such desires. Thus, the *audience* could swoon to Mathis without necessarily engaging with the notion that *he* had a clear sexual identity.[2] Such ambiguity gave him a broad appeal and accessibility safe for audiences of multiple racial backgrounds and sexual orientations. He was a multicultural conduit of his audiences' fantasies who never overpowered the flow of their fantasies with his personal desires. That he frequently chose to sing romantic material with intentionally fantastical and surreal conceptions of love, such as the material he sang on 1964's *The Wonderful World of Make Believe* (rereleased in 2012), complemented his broadly accessible approach (Mathis 1964/2012).

Self-neutering Strategies

Mathis has defined his persona through deflecting attention away from his personal life, or *self-neutering*. Anyone who examines his press profile sees no traces of specific romantic partners, almost no allusions to marriage or children, and few discussions about his sexuality, beyond the fact that he sang romantic songs and was adored by his fans. This suggests many things, such as public disinterest or even unspoken assumptions about him. Note that none of these divergences from heteronormative expectations has hampered his career. In a parallel to his musical idol Cole, and the then-emerging actor Sidney Poitier, he was a palatable black male figure because he was nonthreatening sexually. As mentioned earlier, this denial of sexual desire was actually queer in the way it positions black men between the expectation of conforming heteronormativity but avoiding overt expression of sexual desire and passion. Several key examples illustrate the ways Mathis neutralized the suggestion of sex as a component of his sexuality, beyond nominal heterosexuality.

During the 1960s when sexual behavior made significant shifts, reflected in rock 'n' roll's cultural impact, Mathis became more explicit in his cynicism toward romance and more defensive of his bachelorhood. As with many stars of his era, Mathis's representatives occasionally hired young women to pose as escorts, lest Mathis appear as a conspicuous eternal bachelor in the postvirile era. For example, a March 1965 *Ebony* article noted model Beverly Gillohm's $40,000 lawsuit against Mathis for not being fully paid for such an appearance. Gillohm was hired to accompany Mathis at the Seattle World's Fair for photo ops; of the arrangement, Mathis said, "I did none of

the foolish things people in my profession would do by trying to court affection. I thought people would want me to go to the World's Fair and be
photographed with a pretty girl. I never asked anything of Beverly that wasn't
a mutual agreement between both of us. She was angry that this association
didn't last longer. I found out she wasn't the girl for me. But my intentions
were very honorable" (Robinson 1965a, 102). Mathis's comments regarding
their failure to continue afterward vaguely alluded to pressure from some
force outside of himself to appear with a woman for a photo op, illustrating
the sex/gender expectations of the time (102). His tone was quite perfunctory; there is nothing leering about his comment or remotely indicative of an
interest beyond the job, despite the fact that Gillohm ostensibly represented
a heterosexual beauty ideal as a model. By declaring that Gillohm was not
his type Mathis made a somewhat honest statement that allowed him to be
sincere without disclosing his sexual orientation.

The same article noted a Las Vegas altercation wherein a man who perceived Mathis to be arguing with his wife assaulted him. Rather than re-
taliating, Mathis left town, though he was supposed to perform. The Vegas
incident left Mathis sounding like either a peacekeeper or a coward. The
article quickly followed this moment of "weak" behavior with a discussion
of Mathis's romantic future with the "opposite" sex, noting, "Johnny maintains that he still envisions a future life with at least one of its members. He
is not, however, rushing the moment of matrimony" (Robinson 1965a, 102).
The sequencing seemed to reassure readers that despite Mathis's dismissive
attitude toward Gillohm and his "soft" nature, he was still a traditional man,
thus heterosexual. However, Mathis's discussion of his marriage plans was
functional and detached: "Of course I'm going to get married. But when it
happens, I'll probably just meet somebody and that will be it" (102). These
words did not resemble those of an impassioned heterosexual desirous of
marriage but also did not overtly mark him as queer. Such ambiguity was a
recurring aspect of his public comments during this era. The fact that Mathis
said, "Of course" indicated the taken-for-granted nature of marriage at the
time. It was also notable that Mathis said "somebody," not a woman or girl.
He continued on in a more cynical vein, "I don't think you can expect too
much out of marriage. Just wait and enjoy the surprise of marriage. My *salvation* as far as marriage is concerned is I've just been too busy" (102; emphasis
added). There is a discernible ambivalence here. Mathis seemed to be having a candid internal dialogue where he weighed the socially constructed
joys of marriage with his personal doubts about it. His reference to work as
"salvation" from marriage pressure was a blunt admission that suggested
his disinterestedness in the union was more of a personal preference than

an overt political statement. Again, his overall tone disdained conformity with a casual rather than declarative candor, which was fundamental to his negotiation of sexuality.

During the mid- to late 1970s in press interviews, Mathis disowned any semblance of himself as a romantic person and questioned the pursuit of love and romance. In a June 1974 interview he said, "I think love chose me. . . . I didn't choose it. It just happened. I don't know why I ended up being the love song singer" (Renee 1974, 30). The article also noted, "His love life was traumatic, moving from the ridiculous to the sublime—full of fantasy. 'I've finally gotten over all of my fantasies,' he says, 'like falling in love, being spurned, and of course getting revenge and not seeing your lover as miserable as you'" (31).

Mathis's references are noticeably broad and perfunctory but generated no controversy or questions. I attribute this partially to his relative conformity to certain gender norms and his ability to satisfy his audiences' musical needs. Additionally, Mathis has spent his whole career flying under the radar, carefully deflecting attention away from himself. His lack of personal scandals, which is tied to his lack of a personal life, is integral to his ability to project an ambiguous and highly interpretable image.

"Nothing to Speak of . . .": Skirting Controversy through Absence

A major theme I discussed in the introduction that is central to understanding Mathis is how the postwar era catalyzed a new era of black visibility. Public figures like Belafonte, Cole, Davis Jr., Eckstine, Poitier, and younger emerging figures, like Mathis, were at the forefront of defining the white mainstream's understandings of black Americans. One outcome of this new context was an unprecedented era of black artistic, commercial, and social achievements.

In popular music, the generation of vocalists who emerged between the early 1940s and the mid-1950s achieved several milestones. Cole, Eckstine, Hartman, Herb Jeffries, cabaret singer Billy Daniels, and Mathis were "part of a movement in which black male singers became known for singing love songs, something that had been denied them before because the entertainment industry did not want black men to become sex symbols" (Early 2003, 60). Among this group, Eckstine is historically considered the "first black singer of romantic ballads" as well as "the first of his race [who] was sexually attractive to white as well as black audiences" (Ginell 2013, xvi). Despite the industry's fears, audiences widely embraced the recordings of black male singers. Harry Belafonte's album *Calypso* became the first album by a solo performer to sell a million copies in 1956, and its thirty-one-week run at #1 was unprecedented (Smith 2014, 113; Belafonte 2011, 158). In 1958 Mathis's *Johnny's Greatest Hits* was the first "Greatest Hits" album ever released, and in addition to reaching #1 on the albums chart, it remained on the albums chart for an unprecedented 490 weeks (Mathis 1958; Whitburn 2006, 669). Mathis was the second-most-successful albums artist of the period 1956 to 1969; Cole ranked eighth. In the 1960s Mathis ranked tenth and Cole twenty-seventh (Whitburn 2006, 1402).

Belafonte and Davis also broke many racial barriers as live performers. From 1953 to 1955 Belafonte was the first black performer at multiple cabaret rooms and supper clubs, including the Cocoanut Grove lounge at the Hotel Ambassador (Los Angeles), the Empire Room at the Waldorf Astoria (New York), and the Palmer House (Chicago). In 1955 he stipulated in his contract that he, as a black man, have all access to facilities at Miami's Eden Roc Hotel (Smith 2014, 121). Sammy Davis Jr. was the first black performer signed by the Copacabana, and he insisted on integrated audiences in Las Vegas (Raymond 2015b, 17).

Black male performers made significant inroads on Broadway, film, and television during the 1950s as well. In March 1954, Belafonte became the first black actor to win "Distinguished Featured Musical Actor" at the Tony Awards for his performance in *Almanac* (Smith 2014, 99–101). In the 1956 Broadway production of *Mr. Wonderful* Davis had enough influence to insist that the cast and crew were at least 50 percent black (Raymond 2015b, 17). By 1964 he was earning $10,000 a week for *Golden Boy*, the highest salary of any performer on Broadway (Early 2003, 47). Belafonte and costar Dorothy Dandridge were the leads in 1954's *Carmen Jones*, which many critics consider "the first all-black film to be a commercial success" (Smith 2014, 104). Dandridge also became the first black woman nominated for the Oscar's Actress in a Leading Role category based on her performance. Poitier "became Hollywood's first black actor to achieve stardom solely for his dramatic talents. He did not sing, dance, or joke" (Goudsouzian 2004, 155). He was the first black man nominated for an Oscar in the Actor in a Leading Role category for his performance in the 1958 *The Defiant Ones*, and, for his performance in the 1963 *Lilies of the Field*, he became the first to win the award (156, 217). Cole became the first black network television star with the debut of *The Nat King Cole Show* on NBC (Epstein 1999, 269–70). Though the show ended after one season, which I will address shortly, it set an important precedent. In 1959 Belafonte's CBS TV special *Tonight with Belafonte* won an Emmy for

Outstanding Performance in a Variety of Musical Program, making him the first black performer to win an Emmy award (Smith 2014, 206). Belafonte's television special was a product of Harbel Productions, which he established in August 1957, "the first, independently black-owned unit in Hollywood" (162). Davis was equally industrious; in the early 1950s he was the first black entertainer to establish his own public-relations office in Hollywood, which helped him hire staff to secure film roles and to manage his relationships with the press (Raymond 2015a, 44).

The underbelly of this newfound black male visibility was heightened public scrutiny, which defined the careers of almost all of these figures, except Mathis. His focus on music, as opposed to any efforts toward a serious film, television, or theatrical career, and his low-key intimate life spared him from embarrassment and bad publicity.

Though Eckstine broke barriers as a romantic singer and was a cross-racial sex symbol, two incidents halted his commercial momentum. In an April 24, 1950, *Life* profile, Eckstine was pictured in front of adoring white female fans, including one pressing her head against his chest, which was still taboo and generated several negative letters (Life 1950, 101–2, 104). In a caption featured beneath the image in the picture and illustrations section of his Eckstine biography, Cary Ginell notes, "The backlash from detractors, mostly from the South, resulted in Eckstine's plans for a career in motion pictures and television being permanently shelved." This taboo behavior was compounded by Eckstine's appearance with French actress Denise Darcel in *Look* magazine in 1951. Belafonte, vocalist Tony Bennett, and jazz pianist Billy Taylor also commented on the impact of the backlash in Ginell's biography (2013, 115–16).

Belafonte's leftist political affiliations and romantic life also generated controversy, as did his early film roles. The anticommunist magazine *Counterattack* published a 1951 story regarding Belafonte's communist political ties (Smith 2014, 86). As his star continued to rise, especially in New York, *Counterattack* published a second Belafonte story in January 1954. Fearing for his career, he wrote a response disavowing his ties to communism officially in a February 1954 article (101). In 1957 *Counterattack* also charged Poitier with spending "considerable time sponsoring, entertaining at, and otherwise supporting communist front causes" based on the company he kept socially, such as actor-activist Paul Robeson, rather than any explicit communist activism (Goudsouzian 2004, 89–90). Before he began shooting *Blackboard Jungle* MGM tried to force him to sign a loyalty oath, but rebellious director Richard Brooks urged him to disregard the demand and shoot the film (102).

Hostility toward miscegenation also factored into the art and personal lives of many of the men. Their identities as gender normative, heterosexual black men with sex appeal generated considerable attention and policing. In 1955–56 rumors about Belafonte's dissolving marriage to his wife, Marguerite, who was black, became gossip fodder (Smith 2014, 129). They divorced in the fall 1956, and he began an interracial relationship with a white and Native American dancer, Julie Robinson (137–38). Belafonte and Robinson married eventually, which generated a series of sensational headlines about him leaving his black wife for a white woman. The controversy compelled Belafonte to write a response piece, "Why I Married Julie," defending his interracial marriage in *Ebony* magazine (Smith 2014, 153–55; Stephens 2014, 129).

In the 1957 film *Island in the Sun*, Belafonte played black labor leader David Boyeur, who is "sexual, militant, and vocal"; it was his breakthrough role (McGill 2005, 66). The controversy over whether Belafonte's character Boyeur would be intimate with the character Mavis Norman, played by white actress Joan Fontaine, was so vast that Fontaine received hate letters and Twentieth Century Fox's studio chief Darryl Zanuck enforced a gag order on Belafonte to not mention Fontaine or her character in press statements regarding the film (65). Though the characters kissed originally at the end of the film, which was a logical narrative progression, Zanuck edited the kiss to avoid controversy (71). Regarding Belafonte's sex-symbol status, McGill argues, "White American audiences valued Belafonte for his sexual provocations, but they also feared him for the political challenges his black male body demanded in the postwar era" (71).[3]

In *Island in the Sun*, he fails to "get the girl," which was also the case in the Belafonte-produced 1959 film, *The World, the Flesh and the Devil*, in which he, as Ralph, does not end up with Sarah, a character played by white actress Inger Stevens. Though Ralph and Sarah are the last remaining humans on earth, the film "works to de-eroticize black male–white female relations," which is driven by Ralph's "resigned acceptance of these internalized social codes and his resistance to Sarah's naïve desire to pretend they do not exist" (Stephens 2014, 150–51). Though Belafonte's peer Sidney Poitier projected a different image, in *Toms, Coons, Mulattoes, Mammies and Bucks: An Interpretive History of Blacks in American Films* Donald Bogle has partially attributed Poitier's success in the 1950s to playing characters who were "nonfunky, almost sexless, and sterile" (Bogle 1997, 176). Biographer Goudsouzian has also observed how "racial taboos precluded him from romantic roles" (Goudsouzian 2004, 3). The combination of his natural cool and willingness to subordinate overt sexuality gave him access to films like his breakthrough in 1950's *No Way Out* as Dr. Luther Brooks. In contrast to stereotypical roles, "Brooks presents no sexual threat. He displays no lust for white women. His demeanor is restrained and genteel" (Goudsouzian 2004, 69). Poitier compromised himself in service of projecting more images of respectable and serious characters, and, like Belafonte, compromising his sexuality was part of the bargain.

Sammy Davis Jr.'s interracial attractions were a well-known fact in the entertainment industry that garnered considerable press and tabloid attention. For example, in March 1955 *Confidential* magazine published a story on Davis, suggesting that he was having an affair with Ava Gardner (Early 2003, 60). Davis generated significant controversy for dating white women. His 1957 romance with actress Kim Novak led Columbia Pictures to threaten her contract and to persuade Davis to end the relationship, which led to a short-lived contract marriage with black dancer Loray White (Raymond 2015b, 46–47). In 1960 he married Swedish actress May Britt, which also generated controversy. According to Gerald Early's *This Is Where I Came In: Black America in the 1960s* (2003), "Davis's marriage to [May] Britt was the most famous interracial marriage in American social history" (49). Though Davis campaigned for John F. Kennedy, the president-elect declined to invite David and Britt to attend the inauguration because of fears their interracial marriage would draw unwanted attention. Kennedy also waffled on inviting Davis to a February 1961 meeting with prominent black entertainers and leaders. Davis and Britt's appearance upset Kennedy, and they ultimately left the meeting because of the tension (Raymond 2015b, 46–47, 71; Haygood 2003, 313).

Even a performer as beloved as Cole generated public controversy. On April 10, 1956, a group of racist white men from the Alabama White Citizens Council attacked Cole and his interracial band during a performance at the Municipal Auditorium in Birmingham, Alabama (Epstein 1999, 251–56). Cole responded with characteristic diplomacy, which angered many blacks who were disheartened by Cole's lack of public involvement with civil rights. The mainstream black press, including Baltimore's *Afro-American* and the *Chicago Defender*, and prominent individuals, such as NAACP chief counsel Thurgood Marshall, all criticized Cole for his distance from the civil rights movement, characterizing him as naïve and even as an "Uncle Tom." Though the pressure to be "political" frustrated him, he became a lifetime member of the NAACP and became more involved in the movement (Smith 2014, 141–42; Epstein 1999, 257–61).

Cole persisted in forging ahead with his career ambitions, hence his decision to launch his 1957 variety series, *The Nat King Cole Show*. Despite his success as a recording artist and the artistic quality of the show, many Southern affiliates refused to air the series because it featured him socializing with white guests, such as Peggy Lee, and the production struggled to secure a national sponsor. These factors ultimately led to Cole's declining to continue with the show (Epstein 1999, 276, 286–88). In a 1958 issue of *Ebony* he addressed the controversy by carefully noting, "It's not the people in the South who create racial problems—it's the people who govern the South. The biggest obsession, it seems, is the mixing of the races. That worries the small-minded man. But the big men are worried about economics" (Cole 1958a, 31).

Contextually, the mid-1950s also witnessed the increasing presence of black celebrities as advocates for civil rights and racial integration, including Belafonte, Poitier, and actors Ossie Davis and Ruby Dee. Dick Gregory, Diahann Carroll, and others joined during the 1960s. Emile Raymond, Thomas Sugrue, and Martha Bondi have written extensively about participants in the movement. Raymond notes that celebrities "did not define the movement or usurp the roles of everyday activists who devoted their lives to the cause," but "their efforts to raise money, publicity, and morale helped develop the infrastructure for the movement and mobilize constituents in its support" (Raymond 2015a, 44). Their involvement had varying consequences on their careers.

Mathis was a peripheral figure in these struggles until the early 1960s, after he "came under fire from participants in the civil rights movement for not doing a benefit show" (Robinson 1965a, 102). He became publicly involved in the summer of 1963, which he explained by noting, "I was simply saying to them 'now I will help you because you have tried to help yourselves.' It took somebody with the integrity and genius of Dr. Martin Luther King to get things going" (102). For example, Mathis was one of several celebrities, including Tony Bennett, Nina Simone, Peter, Paul and Mary, Odetta, Belafonte, and Davis Jr. to attend the Montgomery leg of the Selma-to-Montgomery Pettus Bridge march. He also sang a mini-concert during the event, as did Bennett, Peter Paul, and Mary, and Joan Baez (Raymond 2015b, 190; Belafonte 2011, 302–3).

In the context of other black men who achieved prominence in the postwar era, several important elements buffer Mathis from public scrutiny. Because we can locate Mathis within the movement among black vocalists to break barriers in popular music, as a potent commercial crossover force, and as a discernible "race man" whose politics aligned with the increasingly mainstream politics of the civil rights protest movement, he conforms to standards of black respectability. Further, just as his gender-normative appearance prevented him from being characterized as queer, his lack of overt relationships kept him out of the tabloids, made him a "safe," nonthreatening idol, and enabled him to avoid social taboos such as miscegenation. Having no discernible public intimate life empowered him to convey a certain ambiguity that subtly forced audiences to interpret his sexuality for themselves and decode his persona.

In the Eye of the Beholder: Mathis as Sexually Ambiguous Dandy

Since particular aspects of his life where the public lacked information about Mathis helped him avoid controversy, a question lingers regarding what Mathis actually did convey beyond his vocal style. Mathis created a visual image that reinforced the vagueness of his intimate life and the sexual ambiguity of his music. Infinite possibilities for interpretation inform Mathis's imagery. His status as an idol is as accessible to queer desires as it is for heteronormative ones. For example, one of the most striking photos in the queer historical survey *Becoming Visible* is a black-and-white photo of a black man dressed in a white V-neck blouse and a skirt with a pearl necklace and bouffant wig from the collection of David Hibbert, titled "David and Johnny, 1960s." To the right of him is a poster of Johnny Mathis sitting with his arms crossed above his head—the album cover from his 1961 LP *I'll Buy You a Star*—with a caption below that reads "JOHNNY MATHIS EXCLUSIVELY ON COLUMBIA RECORDS" (McGarry and Wasserman 1998, 79).

This singular image suggests Mathis's possible "idol" status among queer people of the period in a manner that parallels Christopher Nealon's *Foundlings* (2001) of queer sociability and a "secret public" that consumed 1950s physique magazines (101, 102, 110). It is telling that David sat adjacent to a Mathis album cover, as his covers perform a unique sexual function. Several of Mathis's album covers from 1957 to 1966 are illustrations (rather than photos) that depict him as a towering figure with sculpted features resembling pulp-novel imagery and comic-book superheroes. For example, *Heavenly* (1959) and *Johnny* (1963) both feature paintings of Mathis by Ralph Cowan, identified in *Heavenly*'s liner notes as a Norfolk, Virginia–based "personal friend of Johnny's."

On *Heavenly* there is an inset painting, framed in black, of Mathis dressed in a white dress shirt and slacks, barefoot, holding a folded sheet of paper in his left hand. He is standing in the foreground with a swirl of clouds behind him. *Johnny* features a painting of his head; he sports a slick pompadour with a strand of hair touching his forehead, peers outward from a face with subtle accents that highlight his sculpted features.

Several of his Mercury albums (see figure 4.2) also feature paintings of Mathis in various guises. Given Mathis's elusive persona, it is unsurprising that the covers depict him as a malleable figure who can adapt multiple personae. The images include a contemplative Mathis depicted in profile on *This is Love*; a haunting photo of Mathis as a kind of noir-like detective

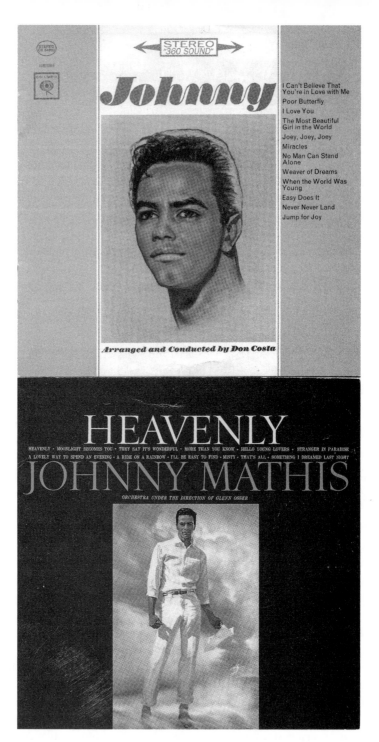

FIGURE 4.1. 1959's *Heavenly* and 1963's *Johnny* depict Mathis in a pulpy visual fashion with a twinge of ambiguous sex appeal (Columbia Records).

FIGURE 4.2. The 1960s Mercury Records LP covers (left) depict Mathis's malleable persona (Mercury Records).

dressed in a white overcoat with an upturned collar in front of a hazy blue fog on 1963's *Tender is the Night*; and Mathis as a conquistador draped in a black bolero jacket in front of three charging horses on *Olé*.

The most consistent visual theme is a presentation of Mathis as a contemporary "dandy"—stylish, elegant, and sexually ambiguous. Mathis's racial identity is also significant in these representations.

The first notable historical "dandy" was George "Beau" Brummell (1778–1840), who emerged during the Regency of the future King George IV. Brummell was born to commoners and launched dandyism in England and France in literature and society with "his meteoric social ascendancy and his theatrical originality" (Garelick 1998, 6). Rhonda Garelick in *Rising Star* (1998) defines "dandyism" as a performance, the performance of a highly stylized, painstakingly constructed self, a solipsistic social icon. Both the early social dandyism of England and the later, more philosophical French incarnations of the movement announced and glorified a self-created, carefully controlled man whose goal was to create an effect, bring about an event, or provoke reaction in others through the suppression of "the natural." Artful manipulation of posture, social skill, manners, conversation, and dress were all accoutrements in the aestheticization of self central to dandyism. (3)

Mathis's covers often have a fantastical element informed by a highly developed sense of sartorial awareness.

For example, *The Wonderful World of Make Believe* is a 1964 album centered on fantasy-oriented songs such as "Shangri-La" and "When You Wish upon a Star" (from *Pinocchio*) (Mathis 1964/2012). On the cover (see figure 4.3), Mathis is dressed in a powder-blue V-neck sweater in front of a sky-blue backdrop posed invitingly with his arms spread open and a gleeful facial expression. The softness of Mathis's features, his laid-back body language, and facial poses convey a tenderness and gentility that signifies a different persona than rebellious and macho archetypes without overtly conveying any singular idea about his sexuality. These sample images could easily be interpreted as sexually benign images, but they arguably sexualize Mathis as a heartthrob.

Though Mathis has a low-key demeanor that aims to avoid the kinds of provocation and controversy Garelick mentions, there is a discernible self-consciousness and intentionality to his stylishness. His navigations of racial, gender, and sexual norms is also integral to this, as discussed by Monica Miller in her analysis of black dandyism, *Black Dandyism and the Styling of Black Diasporic Identity* (2009). Though the dandy is a European construct, Miller argues that, "when racialized as black, the dandy's extravagant or tastefully reserved bodily display signifies well beyond obsessive self-fashioning and play with social hierarchies. The black dandy's style is, from the beginning, always simultaneously personal, cultural, representative of 'the race,' and about representation even as it evaluates norms of racialization, class privileges, gender assignments and the rules of sexuality in ways similar to that of his European dandy brothers" (10–11). In the context of Mathis, the expectation that men conform to generic masculine standards, adhere to ideals of black respectability, and serve as proper "race men" informs the relatively chaste nature of his image. He is usually wearing preppy or formal wear, is never presented in vulgar, lascivious, or lower-class clothing. This is a characteristic he shares with other sexually ambiguous black men of his

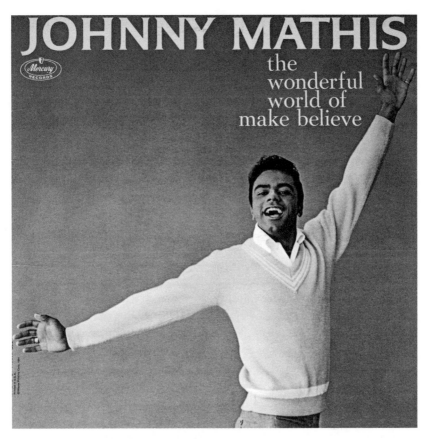

FIGURE 4.3. Johnny Mathis embodies the vulnerable dandy on the cover of 1964's *The Wonderful World of Make Believe* (Mercury Records).

generation, notably cabaret singer Bobby Short, who is also known for his elegant appearance.

Jessica R. Feldman, in *Gender on the Divide* (1993), resists offering a singular definition, but observes the gendered element common to dandyism: "Military in bearing and discipline, the dandy is also as fragile and whimsical as a butterfly. Outwardly cool, he burns inwardly. A man, he pursues an ideal of charm and personal beauty which the dominant culture, against which he poses himself, labels feminine" (3). Garelick also observes how "dandyism attempts to incorporate into the male persona something of the highly social performance usually expected only of women" (Garelick 1998, 6). This feminization can easily be confused with foppery, which Monica Miller challenges by noting, "Anyone can be or can be made to be a fop, but dandies must choose the vocation, must commit to a study of the fashions that define them and an examination of the trends around which they can continually redefine themselves" (Miller 2009, 8). Multiple contextual elements require a nuanced application of Mathis to the dandy archetype. Still, there are notable overlaps with the intentional nature of the dandy these authors describe. His style is an important feature of his persona that allows him to challenge and conform to norms simultaneously, aiding him in signifying to a broad range of audiences and interests. Miller recognizes the intersectional element of the black dandy's performance: "As queer or quare performative beings, black dandies are creatures of invention who continually and characteristically break down limiting identity markers and propose new, more fluid categories within which to constitute themselves" (11). This inventiveness is a navigation of multiple cultures and expectations, informing Miller's reading of black dandies "as a fusion and negotiation of the European dandy's more well-known social semiotics and the inherent bodily and sartorial performativity of the black diasporic cultures created by colonialism, imperialism, and the slave trade" (13).

The gender address of the Mathis covers is fascinating in its sexual ambiguity. He could easily appear to be a crooner idol for female audiences, but the persistent dandy imagery could also be an erotic and cultural signifier to male audiences. Thus, a queer "secret public" could easily idolize Mathis. The images refuse to privilege a singular sexual interpretation and provide viewers with a smorgasbord of motifs to ponder, which reiterates the broad accessibility fundamental to Mathis's public image.

As is the case with many crooners, Mathis's album covers primarily depicted him as a solitary figure. Mathis was exclusively pictured alone on his covers until the 1978 release of the duet album *That's What Friends Are For* with Deniece Williams.

The cover featured a smiling Williams and Mathis with their heads touching, Mathis's right arm straddling Williams's shoulders, his hand cupping her thumb. Though their pose is benign rather than lascivious, and the *Friends* moniker above them suggests a platonic relationship, it is one of the only heterosexually coded corporate images of Mathis. Unlike Tony Bennett, Robert Goulet, Jack Jones, Frank Sinatra, and Andy Williams, Mathis was not married or associated with a longtime romantic partner, nor was he a father. These absences imbued his image with a unique sexual ambiguity. The illusion of sexual availability is a common tactic for pop music idols, and the implication of availability pervades Mathis's image, but there is also no explicit gender address. Audiences could more readily project a sexual

FIGURE 4.4. Mathis was first pictured with a woman on an album cover on his 1978 duets album with Deniece Williams (Columbia Records).

identity onto Mathis's image than his peers because he was unencumbered by public romantic relationships.

Why "Come Out" Again?

Mathis employed a variety of tools to build his career, and mastering the musical and visual language of ambiguity in his persona was the primary outcome. Since he was able to use these tools successfully and make a career out of these navigations while defying conventions, the mention of his sexuality during the 2017 interview might seem superfluous (CBS Sunday Morning

2017). Further, since he technically came out in 1982 (though the magazine
retracted it because it was said off the record) (Petrucelli 1982, 58–60), is
there something about 2017 that makes this information more palatable? I
ask this question since it points to the thorny issue of queer teleology, and
my response is complicated.

This issue at stake is not whether 2017 is more progressive or open than
1982 or 1956 but rather concerns what paths has the singer opened through
his persona that have helped him establish rapport and trust with his audience. They may not necessarily be experts on queer cultures or queer political
movements on a macro level, but on a micro level their individual acceptance
of Mathis means they are willing to negotiate social expectations about social
identity to enjoy his music. This series of negotiations began at the outset of
his career in the mid-1950s, and they continue to color his career.

Based on some of the examples I present in this chapter, I hope it is clear
that telling Mathis's story and those of his queer peers without the social
contexts I explore is incomplete. Their social navigations are inseparable from
their music careers. The diverse ways Mathis challenged heteronormativity
in popular music, which includes but is not limited to his sexual orientation,
is central rather than tangential to understanding his story, especially given
his role as an interpreter of love songs.

As I mentioned earlier, his 2017 televisual "coming out" may have been
genuinely surprising to some fans and viewers. Yet, in looking at his history,
it seems redundant, more an item of fascination for the press than for his
audience. Mathis has always seemed content to project audience fantasies
onto himself, and he has covert ways of conveying elements of his truth
without spelling out their subtexts.

In an unusually forthright 1976 interview with the gay- and lesbian-themed
magazine *The Advocate*, Mathis expressed some sexually provocative, even
risqué perspectives and acknowledged his connection to gay culture without
explicitly stating his sexual identity (Stone 1976, 35–36). For example, he
identified as a regular reader of the magazine—a highly unusual "admission"
for a presumed straight male pop singer in the 1970s—and acknowledged
having a sex life, noting the joy of being able to "seduce to your own music.
I've balled a lot of times to my own music" (35–36). This certainly does not
sound like the public Mathis of the 1950s, who sang love songs but never
discussed relationships. The article invoked Mathis's careful negotiations by
describing him as someone who "wouldn't be caught dead marching in the
Christopher Street parade" but who privately contributed to the L.A. Gay
Community Services Center. Mathis casually referred to his financial con-

tributions as a response to the stigmas attached to venereal diseases during his childhood particularly in an era of cohabitation: "In this day and age we don't need that stigma anymore" (35–36). Even as he openly contributes to a potentially controversial social cause, he is discrete and downplays politics.

Toward the interview's end, when pressed to address "coming out," he refers to it as "very difficult . . . the most difficult thing in the world." He also says, "I wouldn't come out in any publication and say that I was anything, because it would certainly give the impression that I was really *strong, strong, strong* this way or that, and I'm not." Interestingly when asked what would happen if a phalanx of celebrities "came out," he viewed it as "terrible" and "awful": "Everyone knows who's gay. It's almost redundant." This is followed by what the interviewer brackets as a "wicked laugh." The quotation epitomizes an underlying ethos of Mathis's sexual elusiveness that artists may not feel obliged to "come out" if they sense that their audiences are not closeting them. The interview concluded with Mathis dismissing the investment in celebrities "coming out" because of its potential ramifications for an individual's family and friends and the overwhelming singularity gay identity imposes. Mathis noted his pride in his human relationships, his family, and his "contributions to the gay liberation movement," but he was leery of an overt political banner because "it's *all* these things that have to make up your life" (Stone 1976, 35–36; emphasis in the original).

Mathis's comment about being "strong, strong, strong" and his framing of sexual identity as one component of a larger life reflects a natural modesty as well as his ambivalence. Here, I use the term to diffuse the potential perception of him as closeted/self-loathing or as heroic. What I read is a reluctance to adopt the bravado and confidence that makes queer sexual identities seem relatively easy and resolved for political expediency. Though much political progress was in motion during the 1970s, being openly gay (or bisexual)—shifting from a personal recognition to a group identity—continued to be difficult. It is easy to imagine the hesitance to embrace a radical persona and political identity, which would have been obligatory, by someone with Mathis's low-key and presumed "apolitical" persona. I discuss the incongruence of overt politics in the analysis of Liberace's persona in chapter 5.

A 1978 *People* magazine interview conducted on the heels of his popular Deniece Williams duet "Too Much, Too Little, Too Late" was even more revealing of Mathis's romantic cynicism and hinted at a burgeoning openness about his sexuality (Windeler 1978, 67–68). The article noted his charitable contributions to the Los Angeles YMCA and L.A. Health Clinic for Gay People (renamed from the L.A. Gay Community Services Center) as two

Mathis-sponsored charities, about which he commented, "It's where you go to get your VD shots. . . . It's a great thing for young people—not just gays—who are afraid to go to their parents." Pictured below is Mathis playing pool with a muscular, younger white man whom the caption identifies as Wayne Safine, his personal assistant. The juxtaposition of Mathis's charitable giving to gay-iconic spaces and the peculiar photo of him and his assistant could easily tip readers off that Mathis's real life sharply contrasted with his stage persona. Such ironies were elucidated in the article: "'As for romance, I'd rather sing about it,' Mathis says. 'I'm as romantically inclined as anyone, but I've never had a relationship that's lasted longer than a few months. . . . The situation I'm most comfortable in is single and single-minded. Marriage is sharing. I want to do exactly what I want.'" (68).

If the thought of their idol being gay or affiliating with gay culture repelled his core audience, his career momentum would have suffered. Instead, these reports emerged during his commercial rebirth in the late 1970s. His plaintiveness is almost disarming, but the fact that he is so unguarded perhaps speaks to some level of growing personal comfort in discussing his perspective and self-awareness about what was acceptable at the time. I am referring less to the outcomes of overt queer political organizing (for example, "coming out") than the relationship Mathis had with his audience. His music and persona attracted them, and they were not going to abandon him because he mentioned gay culture. Whether they decoded his statement for subtext or not, he remained a viable commercial performer.

Mathis's music appealed to his audiences, and they accepted his persona as an extension of the music. He was sufficiently "different" from other crooners to be interesting, especially considering his place between established singers from the big-band era and younger crooners. Yet he was familiar enough to be comfortable. This liminal positioning also functions as a metaphor for his career. He was sandwiched between black and white social norms, older and younger musical tastes, and gender norms and gender transgressions. Crucially, he conformed to standards of black respectability, which helped him cross over, but as a black man with a very private life who confined himself to one medium, he also stood apart in subtle ways that shielded him from excess scrutiny. While I have emphasized how Mathis's strategic use of tools helped him secure an audience and navigate social politics individually, the import of these negotiations was present for other black performers of his generation and remains useful for other performers.

A "Dandy" Legacy

Bobby Short is a useful point of comparison to Mathis. He was a dandy who specialized in cabaret music, and the largely white Upper Eastside audience was his core audience. His sartorial elegance, sharp wit, and adoring interpretations of American pre-rock standards define his image. Short also had an effete air about his personality, documented on record and video, but he was never overtly perceived as a *pervert* (for example, as a female impersonator) or a social menace.

Like Mathis, he balanced his attraction to white audiences with a sense of grounding in black mainstream culture. He conveyed a respectable image as a dignified performer. Short began recording in the mid-1950s and was part of a generation of black male performers known for singing love songs rather than "ethnic" material. He also immersed himself in black culture socially, affiliating with black cabaret performers like Bricktop and Mabel Mercer, and writer James Baldwin (Short and Mackintosh 1995, 206–8, 210–11). Musically he regularly incorporated songs from composers like Duke Ellington and Andy Razaf into his repertoire. In 1980 Short also co-produced the all-black revue *Black Broadway*, which focused exclusively on featuring black veteran performers from the 1920s and 1930s, such as Eubie Blake and Adelaide Hall (232–34). In addition to recording an album of Razaf songs in 1986, he wrote the foreword to the 1992 *Black and Blue: The Life and Lyrics of Andy Razaf* (Short 1992, xi-xv).

By most accounts, Short's divergence from a heteronormative script, including his affect, his dandyism, and his lack of a romantic partner, led many people to presume he was gay.[4] This "open secret" about his sexuality was not a commercial barrier for Short, who enjoyed an acclaimed performing career from the mid-1950s through the early 2000s. The combination of his bespoke style and witty persona gave him a refined, sophisticated dandy affect that gently challenged stereotypes of black men and provided entrée into what had been a somewhat culturally exclusive performing and recording genre.

Luther Vandross, who was born fifteen years after Mathis and gained fame as a solo vocalist in 1981, is a more contemporary example of the queer black dandy tradition that Mathis represented. Vandross was arguably the most influential black R&B crooner to emerge in the 1980s, and his career has parallels with Mathis. He was known for dressing elegantly (he was frequently photographed wearing suits at his concerts), for singing romantic ballads, and for a polished, refined vocal quality. Like Mathis, he openly idolized female singers who preceded him, including Dionne Warwick, Diana Ross,

Aretha Franklin, and Patti LaBelle. Similarly, he sang love songs, but they were sensual rather than suggestive in content, which endeared him to female audiences and led to his acceptance among many female singers as a fellow *girlfriend*. Vandross had a liminal kind of masculinity: he was neither as virile or as overtly erotic as male R&B singers like Marvin Gaye and Teddy Pendergrass nor as risqué in his gender presentation as performers like Prince and Michael Jackson. The combination of these factors made him unmarked, which left his sexual orientation open to interpretation. This ambiguity fueled considerable speculation about his sexuality, which gave him an air of mystery as well as broad access to different audiences (King 2001, 290–315; Seymour 2004, 195–200, 279–83). Lacking a partner meant he was always available, symbolically to his audience, and they could read whatever they wanted to into his intimate life.

Vandross was "outed" posthumously, as was Short, but these revelations were anticlimactic, since many in their audiences already perceived them as gay yet still enjoyed their music (Weinstein 2005, 60–69). In many ways CBS's interview with Mathis also feels redundant. Mathis's, Short's, and Vandross's ambiguities distinguished them from other performers and made them icons of love songs untouched by the intimate lives of the singers delivering them. Mathis became a premier voice of middle-of-the-road pop among rock-era crooners by hovering under the radar in his music, politics, and personal life. Short, who was considerably less popular than Mathis commercially, was a generational peer who expanded the cultural and gender boundaries of cabaret. Vandross's success demonstrated that R&B audiences could accept sexually ambiguous performers who challenged heteronormativity. Collectively, these black queer musical dandies challenge who was able to sing love songs persuasively in the postwar period and may expand our understanding of how audiences may have experienced these songs. Understanding the personae of the vocalists who delivered these songs transforms what we understand about the songs and their audiences. Ambiguity provided a safe way for Mathis to negotiate a torrent of social expectations. His ability to exist between cultural and musical poles, especially notions of gender, racial, and musical norms, helped him stand out and appeal to multiple audiences. The primary tools I use to frame him—notably, *playing the race card* and *self-neutering*—feel less like calculation than the effects of Mathis's persona, which seems more rooted in showing than telling, informed by both awareness of the social terrain of his time and the knowing style of the black queer dandy.

CHAPTER FIVE

Building an Empire of Illusion

Liberace and the Art of Queering

AUDIENCES DO NOT HAVE to embrace or approve of homosexuality or bisexuality personally to appreciate gestures that challenged traditional masculinity. I hope the previous chapters have illustrated that audiences seem enthralled by these gestures when presented effectively. In Liberace's nearly forty-year career in the national spotlight, he figured out how to appeal to audiences, continually modulating and adjusting his image to speak to the moment. I make this simple point because Liberace's refusal to come out *officially* as gay (he actually claims to have had bisexual experiences) has made him the enemy of many writers who believe he was a selfish closet case. Other writers view him as a hero for surviving the 1950s intact. For the former, he entertained his audiences with gay tropes like camp but never acknowledged his connection to gay culture, even when he was dying of HIV/AIDS—and was thus a coward, a liar, and/or an exploiter. Writers who are more sympathetic have championed him for managing to become successful *despite* living in a homophobic culture.

Both perspectives suffer from flaws common in reflections on LGBTQ history. What I hope the preceding chapters have illustrated is that many queer gestures circulated in 1950s U.S. popular culture well before the late 1960s politicization of sexual identities. Queerness was a central texture of 1950s popular culture, not necessarily a niche element. The commercial success of the figures I have surveyed so far reflect this reality.

Johnnie Ray's early 1950s audience appreciated him for embodying multiple forms of male vulnerability. He stood apart from other male crooners chiefly because he was (initially) fearless about emoting onstage and on record. We have seen how the appeal of vulnerability also informed audiences' responses to vocalist Jimmy Scott. Teenagers embraced Little Richard's visual flair and musical inventiveness. Though he built on R&B's musical conventions, he stood apart from the sobriety of other mainstream black male musicians. These distinctions made him a star regionally and intrigued enough listeners to help him cross over nationally. His irrepressible exuberance has always triumphed even when he has vacillated between secular and gospel music, between queer masculinity and straight-laced religious masculinity. Johnny Mathis's tenor sound, sexual ambiguity, and dandyish style would have seemingly marked him as queer. But he was conventional enough to fit certain expectations of black men of the time and different enough from other crooners to stand apart. His ability to queer gender and racial tropes ultimately propelled him forward. Similar patterns also helped launch the career of cabaret singer Bobby Short and R&B crooner Luther Vandross, who also conveyed a palatable queer dandyism.

Liberace was a master of illusion, but you could not accuse him of being dishonest. His core audience was complicit in making him one of the most famous men to emerge in the postwar era. His wardrobe, humor, showmanship, and musical choices were queer in relation to the conventions of this time, and audiences embraced these differences. If they opposed men who strayed too far away from postwar white masculinist norms, his robust television ratings, album sales, and concert ticket sales would suggest otherwise. They were seduced by the illusions he offered them—he was respite from masculine brutishness; he was a good, loyal son; he was a well-behaved suitor; he was a working-class hero who flaunted his glamour because he understood the economic aspirations of the working class.

The 2013 HBO telefilm *Behind the Candelabra* demonstrates how Liberace (played by Michael Douglas) had developed an ability to skillfully involve his audience. The scene is a 1976 Las Vegas Hilton concert that captures his essence as a performer. Liberace explains the structure of the boogie-woogie break in his show (LaGravenese 2013, 5:05–5:23) and then asks the ladies to shout "Hey" at the end of the passage (5:40–6:00). He asks the men to do the same (6:00–6:09). Immediately after he says to his brother George, "You see George, I told you men come to my concerts," signifying on the long-held joke that only (old) women enjoyed his music, which his audience recognizes and laughs at. He then singles out his mother Frances, who gets her own individual chance to shout "Hey," which the audience applauds heartily (6:32–6:46). It probably felt great to be in on the joke. He drives the act home switching from playing eight beats to the bar to sixteen, which wows the audience further. Liberace asks his protégé and friend "Billy Leatherwood," dressed in a matching glittering tuxedo, to join him onstage for a piano duet. As Billy plays, the scene ends with Liberace's friend "Bob Black" (Scott Bakula)[1] saying to Scott Thorson (Matt Damon), who became Liberace's lover from 1977–1982, "Oh, look—a matched pair of queens," to which an older lady turns and grimaces (8:58–9:02). Scott replies, "It's funny this crowd would like something so gay" (9:05–9:07), to which Black replies, "Oh, they have no idea he's gay" (9:08–9:09).

They may not have known he was gay sexually but they loved his *queerness*—notably, his flamboyant, almost gamine *joie de vivre* (joy of living). More to the point, they willingly embraced his unique version of masculinity. Arguably, they were unaware of, unconcerned about, or simply willing to compartmentalize his homosexuality. It was perfectly acceptable to enjoy the clean and harmless gaiety onstage. There was nothing vulgar, sexual, or suggestive about this act, just *pure, clean fun* fit for all ages. As I discuss later in this chapter, from 1954 to 1959 Liberace frequently appeared in photos with female companions and provided quotes to reporters about his marital status. After he won a libel trial in 1959 protecting his right to be as sexually neutral in his act as he wanted, this behavior disappeared. He never mentioned new female companions or thwarted engagements or having children. This was highly unusual for a public male figure of his generation, but his 1976 audience did not ask these questions.

Whether they knew what he was sexually did not influence who he was to them emotionally and socially. Even when critics attempted to peek behind the illusion and unmask him for being different, his audience insisted on letting him be. They had a mutual agreement: if he adhered to their needs for fabulousness, they adhered to his right to have a private life. What audiences deduced/inferred about his sexual orientation seems less relevant than the ways they processed his initial image and the ways he adjusted it. Liberace inadvertently stood out for his style and affect, which drew negative feedback from critics for his unconventionality. Ironically, he tried and failed to be conventional, much to his audience's relief. After triumphing over a potentially damaging lawsuit, he exaggerated his style and showmanship to new heights.

In this chapter, I begin by briefly describing Liberace's background as a musical prodigy and sissy who fused these elements together as an adolescent. His early roots are essential to understanding his regional and national ascent. I continue by tracing the queering tools he used to become a national act, including a spectacular form of dandyism fully on display on television and in concerts. I illustrate how, as he grew in popularity, critics *enfreaked* him, which led him to *counter-domesticate* himself. In an ironic twist, he responded to a pseudo "outing" from a 1959 newspaper column by self-neutering. Whereas before he was trying to prove he was a "normal" heterosexual, his newest tactic was to demonstrate that he had *no* sexuality in his public persona. Arguably, after he won the lawsuit he entered a new phase, perhaps his most enduring, wherein he *spectacularized* and *enfreaked* his image and reached an apex of sartorial and performative splendor. Toward the end of his life and career in the 1980s he *self-neutered* and *domesticated* himself once again to protect and preserve his image as a wholesome act for his audience.

Wladziu Valentino Liberace as Adolescent Childhood "Proto-freak"

Liberace (born Wladziu Valentino Liberace) was the third child born to working-class parents in Wisconsin. His father, Salvatore, was an Italian immigrant, his mother an American born to Polish parents (Pyron 2000, 9–19). Salvatore was a French horn player who insisted that his three children, George, Angie, and Wladziu, study music. Wladziu, whom the family referred to as Wally, became a piano prodigy and studied privately with a local teacher. Once his skill exceeded hers, at age seven, he studied with Florence Bettray-Kelly at the Wisconsin College of Music. She nurtured his talents until he was twenty years old, encouraging him to compete in piano competitions and perform publicly on radio programs and at various engagements (Pyron 2000, 40; Liberace 1973, 54–55). Liberace was a dedicated student who practiced daily. As a teenager, he translated this passion into entrepreneurship by securing work playing piano locally for the radio station WTMJ on Saturday afternoons, for dance classes, weddings, teas, fashion shows, and other social functions, and even briefly for stag parties and live strippers, unbeknownst to his family (Liberace 1973, 64).

Even before he became famous, his peers treated him as an anomaly for going against gender norms and simultaneously celebrated his talents. This compartmentalization became a defining theme of his career. On a personal level Liberace was a mama's boy growing up. His mother doted on him and taught him domestic feminine skills like cooking. He also loved sewing and designing clothing. The combination of this, with his focus on piano, led children to stigmatize him as a sissy. Despite this stigma, they invited him to play dance music for social events in his school gym. He was also a gifted teen artisan who excelled in drama, painting, typing, home economics, and fashion design. He made silk corsages for classmates, dressed up like Greta Garbo for a school contest, and emceed a high school fashion show in a tongue-in-cheek style (Liberace 1973, 65; Pyron 2000, 53–57). As a teen, he had technical skills and showmanship that created professional opportunities for him and endeared him to his peers, even if he was a sissy. In a sense, the characteristics that made him a kind of proto-freak were also the things that made him appealing.

From Region to Nation: Liberace's Spectacularized Path to Fame

Liberace's initial exuberance and affect attracted audiences for multiple reasons. One primary facet of his appeal was offering an alternative to brutish male norms. Audiences found him charming and warmed up to him instantly. He was an unmarked anomaly, an unintentional "freak" who was more style conscious than most male performers, especially in classical music. He was expressing a kind of showmanship he had cultivated since adolescence. What was intentional was his aspiration to national fame. Liberace consciously *spectacularized* to stand out in the way he approached television (the wink), his wardrobe (white tuxedo), and his musical choices (interpolating pop tunes).

Before launching his national career in the early 1950s, Liberace was developing his penchant for spectacle at a regional level. These tentative gestures, which included renaming himself and tweaking his repertoire to be more populist, laid the foundation for his future success. He eventually established a strong rapport with his audiences, launched a highly successful television variety series, and cemented a legacy of verbal wit and visual flamboyance. I describe his regional pathway to national stardom and explore his role as one of the most prominent queer dandies of the 1950s. His whiteness gave him cultural access to mainstream television and concert audiences. His ingratiating demeanor gave him a nonthreatening appeal that resonated strongly with women. While his audiences adored him, the feminine subtext of his dandy image eventually garnered negative responses for his deviations from postwar male gender norms.

Historians estimate that around 1938 to early 1939 he secured a six-to-seven-month solo engagement at the Wunderbar in Wausau, Wisconsin, under the name of "Walter Buster Keys." A long-standing gig at the Red Room at Milwaukee's Plankton Arcade, where he became a popular staple, followed the Wunderbar. By this time he was very selective about the quality of his piano and experimented with costumes. His weekly salary also grew from $35 to $90 by 1942. Walter was also developing his chops and expanding his repertoire during this time. His most pivotal performance during this phase of his regional career came in spring 1939 at a venue in LaCrosse, Wisconsin, when an audience member requested he play "Three Little Fishes," which he played straight, then as a Bach classical piece. The positive response to this bold move from his audience, as well as wire-service coverage, illuminated his ability to blend his classical and pop interests and win over an audience with his own style (Liberace 1973, 68–69; Thomas 1987, 28; Pyron 2000, 66–67). He was not the first classical musician to do this, but he capitalized on it and made it a concert staple.

The audience's response solidified his performing philosophy, and his shift from classical music to more populist entertainment. As he noted in his 1973 *Liberace: An Autobiography*, "I wanted to give the world *entertainment* that would be new and different to them, to introduce people, who had never been to a piano recital or a symphony concert because they thought it would bore them, to the wonderful works they'd been denying themselves" (Liberace 1973, 69). He perfected a formula of truncating classical songs and interpolating excerpts from popular songs that constituted a preview of classical compositions rather than a full introduction to the works as written. Regardless, this momentary victory inspired him to reshape his career as a populist who offered his acts a bridge to glamour. Liberace figured out "that people want to escape into another kind of world" and that integral to creating rapport with audiences was "to help them do this for a little while, to help them forget work and problems and enjoy, vicariously, a folderol of fun, good music and fancy dress. I give them a little recess from the humdrum" (146). He used this populist appeal to warm up to his audiences and later to draw a boundary between the tastes of critics and the preferences of audiences.

Liberace's ascent toward a national career began in 1941 when he first traveled to New York to seek an East Coast audience beyond midwestern venues. Free to discover new directions in New York, he became a highly peripatetic figure, bouncing between coasts in pursuit of greater fame. In New York he secured some work as an intermission pianist and accompanist for singers and performed in New Jersey as well, but he returned periodically to the Wisconsin area for work (Liberace 1973, 73; Thomas 1987, 30). In 1942 he shortened his name to "Liberace" for simplicity. This is also when he branched out to the West Coast and played clubs in multiple U.S. cities, including Boston, Cleveland, Detroit, Minneapolis, and St. Louis, as well as Montreal and Toronto. The exact date is murky, but in the early 1940s he traveled to Los Angeles and secured some work performing in clubs and bars before returning to New York (Liberace 1973, 134–36; Thomas 1987, 34–36). During his return he played at tony East Side clubs like Le Reuban Bleu, Spivy's, and the Vanguard (Liberace 1973, 77; Thomas 1987, 33). In the early to mid-1940s he also began expanding his act, including integrating his signature candelabra in 1945 and welcoming his brother George to become his manager and musical director (Liberace 1973, 80; Thomas 1987, 42).

Liberace was an emerging "brand" who spent more than a decade developing his repertoire, style, and stage demeanor in nightclubs and supper clubs before becoming a national figure through television in 1952. Darden Asbury Pyron notes 1941 to 1944 as the key period when "[Liberace] abandoned the formal concert stage entirely and remade his career around popular audiences and popular music" (Pyron 2000, 75). Television was the ultimate medium for Liberace's spectacle because it cemented his persona by melding his musical and interpersonal instincts into a contained medium with a repetitive format. After working with a series of managers, he aggressively sought representation from a firm with more resources and vision. He impressed Seymour Heller, of the artistic management team Gabbe, Lutz, and Keller, and secured Heller as his manager (Thomas 1987, 60–62). Heller introduced Liberace to Don Fedderson, the station manager of the Los Angeles television station KLAC-TV. Fedderson persuaded Liberace that television was an ideal medium for building an audience (Liberace 1973, 84–86; Thomas 1987, 62–65). *The Liberace Show* first aired on KLAC-TV in 1951. It instantly achieved high ratings for a local program, garnered Liberace two Emmy Awards, and helped him attract an even larger audience (Liberace 1973, 87; Thomas 1987, 67). *The Liberace Show* was a summer replacement for *The Dinah Shore Show* from July to September 1952 (Thomas 1987, 69). In 1952 Heller also signed Liberace to the Columbia Records label, where he released several popular albums (Liberace 1973, 52–53; Thomas 1987, 83; Pyron 2000, 157).[2] After this show ended its local run, Liberace signed with Guild Films in 1953; the second incarnation of *The Liberace Show*, which ran from 1953–1956, is believed to have been the most popular syndicated program of the time (Liberace 1973, 87; Thomas 1987, 75, 89; Pyron 2000, 156).

Fedderson encouraged him to cater to this element of the audience, which inspired the performer to define his audience through distinguishing "the solid backbone people of America" from "the sophisticated, intellectual element that had a kind of snobbish attitude about all popular entertainment anyway, and so had nothing but sneers for TV" (Pyron 2000, 86). This was a perceptive recommendation because Liberace became an early television pioneer who understood how he could mold television into a format that conveyed his essence to a mass audience. Television allowed Liberace to create a persona that worked within the spatial and emotional confines of the relatively new phenomenon and catered to the national mood. Many Americans experienced class mobility during the postwar period. Their greater awareness as consumers, the more prominent role of women in the household, and mass media's emphasis on safe, family-oriented programming were conditions that gave Liberace's program unique appeal during television's first decade.

His expansion from a regional concert performer and to a national television star relates to the emergence of the variety-show format, which became the most successful genre on American television in the mid- to late 1940s. As David M. Inman argues, "The variety show formula caught on at least partly because it lent itself to the limitations of early television, a medium where everything had to be live and preferably inside a studio. Almost every TV giant of the 1950s—Jackie Gleason, Sid Caesar, Ed Sullivan, Red Skelton, Dinah Shore, Arthur Godfrey—rose to prominence through weekly variety shows" (Inman 2006, 3).

Liberace's embrace of the genre was a logical—if still experimental—step toward expanding his public profile. During the early 1950s several pop vocalists, such as Shore, had fifteen-minute, twice-weekly musical variety shows (Pyron 2000, 264). Hour-long variety shows hosted by singers, however, did not become a significant phenomenon until fall 1955, when *The Perry Como Show* made him "the first singer to successfully headline an hour long show—until that time the role of emcee had been almost exclusively the domain of comedians" (224). Soon Shore, Tennessee Ernie Ford, and Eddie Fisher followed in this path.

On both the local version and the syndicated *Show* Liberace translated his concert persona as a cheerful confidante to the small screen. He has noted how he wanted everyone in his audience to see him as a friend and confidante: "I decided what I had to do was to pretend that the camera was a person and work to it, talk to it as if it were alive and responding to me" (Liberace 1973, 86). This was also the rationale behind his famous wink. By definition, these gestures had the potential power to appeal emotionally to an audience. There is no evidence that it was skewed explicitly toward women, but there are reasonable arguments for why female viewers appreciated his approach. Liberace also professed love for his mother Frances (a fixture on his television show) despite the looming stigma of momism.[3] In one clip from PBS's 2002 retrospective *The Legendary Liberace* he sings "I Want a Girl Just Like the Girl that Married Dear Old Dad" (Liberace 2002, 8:51–10:02) as a tribute to

Frances. Finally, Liberace's humorous send-ups of classical music, featuring interpolations of well-known lullabies, polkas, and other pop music forms, all performed on pianos topped by candelabrum, made audiences feel as if he were exposing them to classical music.

Liberace expanded on the family angle by featuring George, who played violin and conducted its orchestra, as well as acknowledging Frances through singing tributes or greeting her from a remote location. This was also intentional: "I talked to the viewers as if they were my friends, my next door neighbors. We had a kind of over-the-back-fence relationship. I showed them my pets. I talked about my mother and my sister and my brother. My family became everyone's family, sort of" (Liberace 1973, 87). This intimacy potentially grabbed the attention of mothers based on the "peculiar family configuration he defined . . . it was brother and brother, mother and son. Sisters rarely entered in; fathers more rarely still. In essence, then, he described the central relationship between men and women as that of son and mother. In this way, the ideal man was, by definition, the ideal son" (Pyron 2000, 170).

Liberace also played the race card tacitly in highlighting his family. As a white man, he was subject to white normative masculinity standards, but he was exempt from the "race man" pressures black musicians like Little Richard and Mathis faced later in the decade. Whiteness also factored into his wholesome image. He amplified the white working-class family and their aspirations toward middle- and upper-middle-class success that was primarily accessible to white postwar families. Whereas black performers had to fight to desegregate audiences of supper clubs and to stay in hotels in Las Vegas, Liberace's whiteness freed him from these concerns. The outcome of this white wholesomeness was a broad commercial accessibility parallel, in certain ways, to Mathis's nonthreatening "raceless" wholesomeness.

Cecelia Tichi describes the white, middle-class, and domestic biases of early television in *Electronic Hearth* (1991, 6). Television was promoted as a new kind of living room furniture that extended American traditions of familial hearth normally attributed to the domestic fireplace, and this familiarity helped families integrate the new technology into their domestic space as an entertainment ritual (43, 46, 47). This familial element also informed the family-friendly themes of variety programs like *The Liberace Show*. Tichi notes, "From the late 1940s, the TV hearth has also been represented as accommodating the community, since television was often portrayed as a quasi-theatrical experience in the home, with friends and neighbors invited in to view certain programs, perhaps championship boxing or the *Texaco Star Theatre* with Milton Berle" (46). Ultimately, Liberace's targeting of white, middle-class family values was a key ingredient to his success, since "this TV hearth would lose its meaning were the family to be absent from the picture. The human figures say that the new cathode tube hearth brings the family together in a scene of harmony and affection" (50). The family angle always grounded Liberace in the mainstream, which he harnessed to self-neuter and domesticate himself to win his 1959 libel trial.

Liberace's concert style, repertoire, and the intimacy he created on his television show made him the most prominent extant of the dandy tradition. Mathis, who began his career in 1956, was chiefly a dandy in his visual style. His appearance feminized him, but not dramatically so. Nor did this hurt him commercially. Arguably, it helped align him within the tropes of black male respectability because it conveyed polish and refinement. Liberace, as a white man, had more access to certain performing venues and electronic mediums than his black counterparts had, and he expressed his dandyism in a broad variety of venues.

Liberace was highly calculating and intentional in coordinating every aspect of his persona. His highly cultivated visual style, verbal acuity, and self-conscious performativity were characteristics of a postwar dandy and are essential to understand his initial *spectacularization*. First, one of the key characteristics of a dandy Monica L. Miller identifies is "one who studies above everything else to dress elegantly and fashionably" (Miller 2009, 8). Liberace was very meticulous about his appearance, from his hair to his tuxedo, and he enjoyed standing out. He caused a minor controversy at a 1952 concert at the Hollywood Bowl when he performed in white tails instead of black. He wanted to stand apart from the orchestra, and he achieved the effect he wanted: "The white suit did not go unnoticed. . . . I saw the showmanship there is in daring to do something different, in challenging the conventional" (Liberace 1973, 159). A year or so later reviewer Jack Gould referred to him as "the picture of the suave gentleman" on television and noted his hair as being "distinctively barbered and groomed" (Gould 1953, 15). Even when writers intended these remarks as barbs, the point is people *noticed*. The spectacle worked for his audiences. His sense of style surely contributed to his status as an idol for his famous female fan base. As his fame grew, he integrated the style element more overtly. For example, during his 1956 London tour the review noted, "The frequent changes of costume were an integral part of his flamboyance; it was almost a fancy dress show in which silk tails were replaced in turn by a gold lame tux, a jacket covered with a million black glass beads, a silver jacket, etc." (Variety 1956, 63).

During his career, Liberace went through three costumers. They include Sy Devore, who designed the white tails; Ray Acuna, whose designs included tuxedos with heavy doses of sequins and floor-length fur; and Michael Travis, whose famous creations include a sequined chauffeur's uniform and patriotic "hot pants" Liberace premiered in the 1970s (Thomas 1987, 212–15). Prior to 1952 Liberace only performed in "black full-dress tails," but the audience's reception encouraged him to push further, spanning from gold lamé dinner jackets and white dress tails to a progressively elaborate and flamboyant wardrobe. As I will discuss later in the chapter, during the Travis era Liberace wore increasingly extravagant costumes, described in a 1981 souvenir concert book as "created from silk, metallic, and brocaded fabrics, precious and semi-precious jewels and bugle beads; feathers to 24-karat gold embroidery; with furs from blue fox to black shadow mink and sable to chinchilla" (Liberace 1981, n.p.).

Second, Miller notes that dandies are often "beings whose self-presentation identifies them as outrageous—everything from morally bankrupt do-nothing aristocrats, aesthetes in the Byronic or Baudelairean vein, flamboyant sartorial or conversational Wildean wits, to über fey and fashionable sex outlaws" (Miller 2009, 7–8). One of the most remarkable elements of Liberace's performances was his ability to connect with audiences verbally. He was witty, clever, funny, and likable. In a general sense, Liberace was a gregarious storyteller who created intimacy by speaking directly to his audience, discussing his life. Even with sixteen thousand people in attendance at Madison Square Garden in 1954, he "ran the 'concert' as if it were an intimate little soirée between him and his more than 16,000 good and loyal friends. Seated at the piano, he talked idly, almost endlessly about himself and everything he loves and admires" (Plotnik 1954, 1, 10). Similarly, a London reviewer was shocked at how he "breached almost every known rule for an entertainer" by talking, sometimes for twenty minutes between songs, at Royal Albert Hall (Variety 1956, 63). He also introduced his family when they were present at his concerts, adding a layer of intimacy, and told jokes aimed at the expense of critics and even of himself. Doing so affirmed the taste of his audience and showed he did not take himself too seriously.

Related to this skill were the trademarks Liberace developed that bonded him with audiences. He developed a "wink" that is referenced frequently, including in reviews of his syndicated television show (Gould 1953, 15; Taubman 1954a, SM20; Funke 1957, 29). Regarding the wink, Liberace said that he created it to break down the wall between performer and audience, "I looked [television] right in its one big eye just the way I'd look you in the eye if you were sitting talking to me. That's why, when I winked, everyone in the whole television audience could see for themselves that I was winking right at them" (Liberace 1973, 86). Regardless of his intent, it repelled several critics, such as Howard Taubman, who felt the wink "gives you the impression that Liberace is a little amused at all this himself" (Taubman 1954a, SM20). Recalling Liberace's appearance on *The Jack Benny Show*, Taubman concludes that, "the fact that Liberace takes all this kidding good-naturedly is as disarming as his wink" (SM20). What Taubman misses is the self-awareness element and camp inherent in what Liberace is doing. The wink also surfaced in concerts which one critic viewed as part of a predictable routine: "His public loves him and by now he knows exactly what it expects and he gives it without stint. There are those nice cozy winks, those terribly affectionate and roseate smiles." (Funke 1957, 29). He also enjoyed costume changes during his concerts and developed a famous array of sayings that referred to his outrageous clothing and jewelry, including, "I hope you like it, you bought it for me" (Plotnik 1954, 10) and "Go ahead, laugh. You paid for it" (Variety 1955, 60). The wink and the remarks were reliable ways to connect with his audience, which came to expect these lighthearted moments.

Third, the ways Liberace combines visual style and wit, along with his ability to translate these into a broad framework of performing skills, speak to Garelick's argument in *Rising Star* that such "artful manipulation" is the core manifestation of dandyism (Garelick 1998, 3). Based on critical accounts, Liberace was a hardworking people pleaser who used a variety of techniques, visual, verbal, musical, and theatrical, to keep audiences interested. On his 1952 summer replacement show he projected an "ingratiating personality" (Faris 1995, 110). About the 1953 Carnegie Hall concert, critics at *Variety* and the *New York Times* wrote that he "plays the piano, sings and tells stories and jokes in a routine that only lacks some soft-show hoofing to turn it into a one man vaudeville show" and "does everything to please"; his jokes are a "family-humor sort of thing" (Variety 1953, 52; "Liberace Plays" 1953). On his syndicated program circa 1954, there was great attention to detail and staging that a reviewer described as "very wholesome and very gay" (Taubman 1954a, SM40). Though he had an orchestra at the 1954 Madison Square Garden concert, the show was "a fantastic exhibit of one-man showmanship" (Plotnik 1954, 1). At Las Vegas's Riviera, he earned his $50,000 per week salary by offering a full buffet of talents: "He sings, he plays piano, he tap dances, and he pleases" (Variety 1955, 60). During his engagement at Royal Albert Hall, "his act ranged from serious pianistics to downright and uninhibited clowning" (Variety 1956, 63). His 1957 RKO Place Theater show struck the reviewer as "pure vaudeville" (Funke 1957, 29).

These concert reviews are remarkably consistent and credible since the existing audiovisual evidence clearly illustrates that he maintained these techniques for his entire national career. Regardless of his success as a dandy for the 1950s, critics of this period, many of whom were classical-music critics, found him cloying, noted the flaws of his piano playing, and questioned the taste of his audience. His dandy status intrigued his audience but was not benign to certain critics. In the context of the postwar era's standards of masculinity his lack of a heterosexual partner and children, combined with his demeanor, made him unusual. A dandy is always a social outsider to some degree and, as Jessica R. Feldman's *Gender on the Divide* (1993) notes, "pursues an ideal of charm and personal beauty which the dominant culture, against which he poses himself, labels feminine" (Feldman 1993, 3). The tabloids were especially attentive to the feminine signifiers in Liberace's image. They noted the excessive attention he paid to his mother and the lack of a female presence in the life of this newly prominent single-male celebrity. Indeed, one of the threads connecting these three elements of the dandy spectacle is the chaste, almost anodyne nature of the acts, which critics and tabloids seized upon. There was something feminine and asexual about Liberace's wholesome crowd-pleasing, which was anomalous, and thus "queer," for a man of his time.

When the Critics Enfreak, Liberace Counter-domesticates

Liberace's exuberant affect attracted sizable concert and television audiences but also led many people to *enfreak* him by pointing out his anomalies. Music critics and tabloids *enfreaked* Liberace by highlighting his divergences from the postwar masculine norms. Music critics were highly suspicious of a musician upending classical musical convention with interpolated pop songs and folksy humor. There was also ongoing suspicion toward the ubiquitous mama's boy who appealed strongly to female listeners but displayed no conventional heterosexual intimate life. He responded by *domesticating* himself, which included asserting his "normal" heterosexuality via faux stories and press materials and butching up his affect and the décor of one short-lived variant of his television show. The stories about his romances gradually faded, and his retooled show bombed among his core audience. Despite his misgivings about his masculinity, his audience was content with him as a single man and wanted flair over the faux austerity of his television show.

The critical establishment of the 1950s consistently criticized Liberace's piano playing as crowd-pleasing yet bombastic and maladroit by classical standards.[4] Many critics also found his personality cloying and insincere,[5] and there were occasional jabs at his unusual appeal to women.[6] Similar critiques informed responses to Johnnie Ray as well. However, mainstream writers in respectable publications rarely attacked personal elements of Liberace's life, such as the perceived "momism" and his eternal bachelor status. This does not mean critics did not interpret his act as queer privately, but their silence seems to fit the zeitgeist. As long as something unusual remained unspoken, people could tolerate it quietly. Tabloids, however, exercised no restraint in poking holes in the star's asexual dandy persona. Liberace's defiance of the day's masculine codes inspired speculation about his perceived intimate life. Tabloids correlated his effeminacy and asexuality with homosexuality.

If mainstream music critics were only willing to suggest Liberace was a questionable talent with an offbeat style, the tabloids willingly implied that homosexuality was the underbelly of his persona. Liberace was one of the earliest performers 1950s scandal sheets targeted as a sexual transgressor. He was a frequent tabloid subject, appearing in at least twenty-one tabloid stories between 1954 and 1959 and on twenty-four covers through the 1980s, including appearances on *Confidential, Hush-Hush, On the Q.T., Top Secret,* and *Whisper.* The years 1954–1957 are the height of his tabloid coverage. I am careful to avoid overstating the impact of a handful of articles, as we cannot fully assess how they were interpreted. Since they were, however, paralleled by negative reviews of his television show and concert act, the circulation of Liberace jokes, and a rush of calculated efforts to depict him as gender norma- tive (heterosexual), their implications were felt. As their titles indicate, many tabloids operated on the pretense of offer sensational *insider* knowledge. Always a skillful manager of his image, Liberace responded immediately in various forms to assure his public he was *normal*, including staged publicity dates and articles planted in the press. He also attempted a television come- back that backfired. Suing *Confidential* in 1957 and the London's *Daily Mirror* in 1959 effectively silenced public speculation about his sexual orientation.

Liberace's unusual relationship to women was a common tabloid trope. Some articles validated fears that he was not "normal" but reassured readers not to worry. *Sensation's* 1954 article "Liberace and His Women" "portrays Liberace as a man with a normal interest in women who does not want to publicize his romances even though it might quell the sexual preference rumors. Women in his life include Betty White, Selena Walters, and April Stevens" (Faris 1995, 202). Others linked his "momism" and female appeal with his sexual ambiguity. An article by John Cullen in the September 1956 issue of *On the Q.T.* noted, "Bereft of a father's strong support, cut off from masculine companionship of playmates of his own age, reared by a power- ful and perhaps domineering mother—is it a wonder Liberace grew into the curly-haired, dimpled, simpering, lisping advocate of 'momism' that he is today?" The article addressed his audience and image: "Despite the thousands of women who fawn over him, besiege him at public appearances and even follow him across the country, despite the few publicity-stunt 'romances,' Liberace has never been seriously linked with any woman in a romantic way." Finally, the author concludes, "But there can be no doubt that if Liberace wanted romance, he'd just have to let it be known. He doesn't. Not that he doesn't talk about love and marriage (always on an ethereal sexless, non-physical level, of course)" (Cullen 1956, 33–35, 54–56). As these articles remind us, we can discern what a society expects of men based on what its members label as odd and unusual.

Other articles coyly questioned his sexual orientation and his manhood. They used his hobbies, his appearance, Christine Jorgensen's gender reassignment, and well circulated speculation to tease Liberace. A *Private Lives*'s 1955 article titled "Are Liberace's Romances for Real?" asked readers, "Is he is, or is he ain't" (qtd. in Faris 1995, 176). *Rave*'s "Liberace: Don't Call Him Mister," published in 1954, describes Liberace's talents as, "cooking, sewing, and marcelling his hair" and features various hints of homosexuality, including "giving his phone number to a bodybuilder who appeared on the same program as himself" (qtd. in Faris 1995, 206). Several articles also conflated Liberace's queerness with Jorgensen's surgery. In "Why Is Liberace on the Pan?" *Suppressed* writer Michael Davis asserted, "The difference between Liberace, Westinghouse, and Christine Jorgensen is that you can be *sure* if it's Westinghouse." (Davis 1955, 7–9, 55, 56, qtd. in Faris 1995, 186). The tabloid *Exclusive* claimed in its July 1956 issue that Liberace was dating Christine Jorgensen and quoted Jorgensen as saying, "It's not serious. He's nice, but a little strange" (Faris 1995, 189). And *Hush-Hush* capitalized on the seeds planted by William Conner's inflammatory 1956 column (Conner, qtd. in Liberace 1973, 195–96; Thomas 1987, 121–22; and Pyron 2000, 225–26) on Liberace's sexuality in May 1957, asking, "Is Liberace a Man? If not, what? The British are preparing to find the answers to these questions, both of which have bothered Americans for years" (Collins 1957, 8–10, 42, 43, qtd. in Faris 1995, 183).[7]

Tabloid coverage and negative criticism inspired Liberace to counter these attacks through *domesticating* himself. Notably, his management, through a series of highly publicized relationships, amplified the public image of him as a *normal* heterosexual man seeking female companionship. He also changed his television persona. He seemed to believe that appearing more overtly heterosexual and making himself seem more butch would make him more gender normative and palatable.

In 1954 Liberace's personal life shifted from family-related information to his intimate heterosexual relationships, which he overtly presented as public fodder in various ways. Liberace wrote (allegedly) "The Girl I'll Marry" for

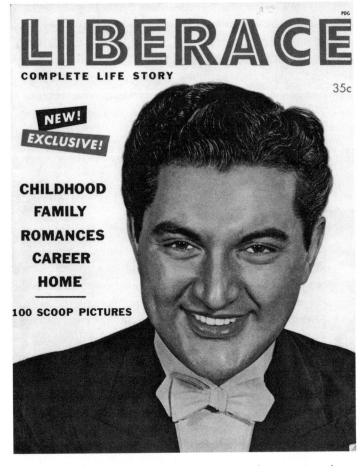

FIGURE 5.1. Cover of the 1954 fan magazine *Liberace: Complete Life Story* detailing Liberace's biography, family background, syndicated TV broadcast stations, and more (*Liberace: Complete Life Story*).

the February 1954 issue of *TV Star Parade*. Faris notes that in the article, he claims to have been engaged three times—to a ballet dancer, a singer, and "a woman of independent means and spirit" (Liberace 1954b, qtd. in Faris 1995, 201; Thomas 1987, 93–94). Liberace biographer Bob Thomas notes, "The article was standard fan-mag stuff that bore little relationship to known fact" (Thomas 1987, 94–95). In 1954, Ideal Publishing Corporation published *Liberace: Complete Life Story*, a seventy-five-page magazine featuring the article " . . . the Girl He'll Marry" on Liberace's ideal wife (Liberace 1954, 38–39).

He knows what he wants in a wife. Here's what it'll take to be . . .

the Girl he'll Marry

FIGURE 5.2. "The Girl He'll Marry," one of many post-1953 articles written to assure audiences that Liberace was a "normal" heterosexual man who intended to marry a woman (*Liberace: Complete Life Story*).

Liberace appeared in fan mags such as the May 1955 issue of *Movie Play*, featuring Liberace and Mamie Van Doren on a date, titled "Mirror, Mirror, on the Wall" (Faris 1995, 229). In September 1955 *Uncensored* published a story by Marvin Parker on Liberace's romance with Sonja Henie, emphasizing their mutual affluence titled "Sonja Henie: All Thi$ and Liberace, Too," (Parker 1955, 40–42, 72–73; Faris 1995, 238). Whether Liberace's management planted the latter or published it for the attention is less salient than its function to assure the public that these figures were interesting people. One of the purported functions of tabloids—besides sales—was to reveal the authentic truth beyond official Hollywood stories created by publicists and managers. As such, it is not surprising that tabloids seized on Liberace's high-profile relationships with Rio and Henie. *Rave*'s August 1955 story, "Whose Torch Melted the Ice Queen?," addressed the Henie-Liberace romance and implied "that this is a phony romance just like the Liberace/Rio romance" (qtd. in Faris 1995, 254). According to Faris, less than a year later, Sylvia Tremaine's "This Month's Candidate for the Pit . . . Liberace: The Ham That Was Overdone," published in the June 1956 issue of *Whisper*, "discusse[d] Liberace's engagement to Joanne Rio as a hoax to build Liberace's masculine stature with the public" (Faris 1995, 251).[8]

Liberace's ultimate assertion that he was entitled to project the image he wanted for his audience came in 1959.[9] Between Conner's publication and the filing of the lawsuit, Liberace's managers encouraged him to return to television, suggesting a 1958 daytime show on ABC targeting housewives. The inversion of Liberace's persona was austerity and sobriety. They tried to make him a grey-flannel-suit-wearing "organization man." Liberace revealed the aesthetic, "the look of austerity": "No candelabra, no fancy clothes, none of the showmanship, that it turned out, was responsible for my first big success" (Liberace 1973, 142). They cut his hair, dressed him in Brooks Brothers suits, and disrupted the show's flow with lots of advertising breaks (93–94). In essence they wanted him to downplay the commercial version of queerness that made him but that was also inspiring backlash. *Variety*'s October 1958 review hinted at the show's unusual tone, commenting, "He seemed to be under the control of some outside force, . . . [including] talking a couple of octaves lower than he is famous for" (qtd. in Faris 1995, 17). The new (butch?) version of the show only lasted for six months (October 1958 through April 1959). The reason was the lack of glamour: his audience *wanted* the flamboyance critics and tabloids were mocking. They wanted the queerness, not the grayness. This broad appeal of his act, in all its glamour and flamboyance, tacitly turned out to be a great weapon in defending himself.

A Winning Strategy: Counter-domesticating and Self-neutering

Liberace's 1959 lawsuit against the *Daily Mirror* altered the trajectory of his career significantly. During the trial he returned to *domesticating* himself by dressing in black, emphasizing the family angle of his show, and intentionally *self-neutering* to disassociate sex and sexuality from his act entirely. Careful observers will note that it is queer for a man living in a heteronormative society to essentially claim the absence of sexuality as a feature of his public identity. Nonetheless, this approach was convincing. Liberace returned to the well of domesticity he honed throughout his career. Though he was anomalous, his folksiness and accessibility signified wholesomeness. Further, his chaste image and lack of overt sexuality, of any kind, made it very difficult to argue that he was trying to court a specific sexual demographic. Just as Mathis's lack of relationships protected him from controversies related to divorce and miscegenation, Liberace's eternal bachelor status shielded him from being branded a pandering pansexual.

Liberace's June 1959 trial against the *Daily Mirror* contributed further to greater reluctance among tabloids to speculate and exploit homosexuality. Despite Liberace's efforts to downplay sex and sexuality in his act, the term "sex" was central to his 1959 victory against the paper. Columnist William Conner, who wrote under "Cassandra," insinuated Liberace was a pansexual gender deviant during the entertainer's visit to London in October 1956. Conner referred to Liberace as "the summit of sex—Masculine, Feminine and Neuter. Everything that He, She and It can ever want," a "fruit-flavored . . . heap of mother love," "the biggest sentimental vomit of all time" who slobbers over his mother and winks at his brother. He also called Liberace "calculating candy-floss," a "slag heap of lilac covered hokum," and said, "There must be something wrong with us that our teenagers longing for sex and our middle-aged matrons fed up with sex alike should fall for such a sugary mountain of jingling claptrap wrapped up in such a preposterous clown" (Conner, qtd. in Liberace 1973, 195–96; Thomas 1987, 122; Pyron 2000, 225–26).[10] "Cassandra" distilled the essence of prior critiques but was most dangerous in emphasizing the neutered yet suggestive aspects of Liberace's performance.

No journalists had described his deliberate use of ambiguous sexuality to appeal to audiences quite so explicitly. The article's language implies sexual gestures that pander to multiple sexual needs and overtly alludes to Liberace's being queer sexually. In his autobiography, Liberace noted how he and his defense team focused on the line about how he was the "summit of sex" because this was a difficult aspect to prove and was a line numerous English papers quoted as a headline, including *The Northern Echo,* published in Darlington, and the *Liverpool Daily Post* (Liberace 1973, 195).

Liberace's lawsuit was as much a business decision as it was about privacy since numerous tabloid appearances and constant harsh criticism made him fear he had weakened his commercial appeal. Indeed, in his autobiography he cited the centrality of a traditional image to his success: "Certainly my manhood had been seriously attacked and with it my freedom . . . freedom from harassment, freedom from embarrassment and, most importantly, freedom to work at my profession" (Liberace 1973, 192). Liberace assumed the public could not overtly perceive him as queer or even mildly lascivious if he wanted to maintain his career, necessitating an overt defense of his masculinity.

Actually, the *lack* of an overt sexual identity in Liberace's concerts was key to his broad appeal and became a major strategy during his defense. Liberace testified in typically self-deprecating fashion that he was not a sex symbol. When his attorney Gilbert Beyfus asked if he gave sexy performances he replied, "I am not aware of it if it exists. I am almost positive that I could hardly refer to myself as a sexy performer. I have tried in all my performances to inject a note of sincerity and wholesomeness because I am fully aware of the fact that my appeal on television and personal performances is aimed directly at the family audience" (Liberace 1973, 208). Though there is a certain irony in a man concerned with appearing to be a traditional man essentially *neutering* himself, which he did throughout the trial, it deflected attention away from the possibility of *deviant* sexuality, making chaste heterosexuality the default sexuality.[11] To build on his claim that he represented "wholesome entertainment not directed to sex appeal," various confidantes attested to Liberace's complete *lack* of sexual appeal on the witness stand (Liberace 1973, 213–19). This was also queer, in that for a normal man, by postwar standards, having no sexuality is also queer. Liberace's victory was for the queerness of his being, not his sexual orientation. The trial valorized the right of performers to be ambiguous, asexual, chaste, which are all queer characteristics in the context of heteronorms, but also signifiers of wholesomeness.

Liberace won by disproving Conner's claim that he was a sexualized performer of any kind; thus, he won by reiterating the validity of his commercial strategy. Though Liberace claimed, "I did not bring this action forward for the sake of money, but principle," this is a partial truth because he filed the suit to protect his career and financial well-being, which entailed defending the right to appear unreadable. Furthermore, his assertion—"If any lesson at all is to be drawn from the whole affair it is that no matter how bad a thing may look, it can turn out to do someone good," which refers to his donating the $22,400 award money to cancer research—is equally distorted. Liberace claims his case "was cited as a surrogate for a long list of celebrities," but the trial legitimated the freedom of popular figures to be as queer and, by association, as elusive about their identities as they choose (Liberace 1973, 233, 236–37; 193).

License to Enfreak and Spectacularize (Part 2)

Once the trial ended, Liberace inverted the external *enfreaking* of his harshest critics and played the freak role with greater flair, ratcheting up his wardrobe and adding new dimensions to his showmanship. Spectacle was always present in Liberace's career, from his experiments with his name to his well-crafted television persona. But his post-trial *spectacularizing*, especially his customized costume designs, exemplify his unspoken revolt against male conventions. Audiences applauded his efforts, and he thrived as a concert performer and TV presence. Most notably, they did not seem to equate his more overt expressions of feminized masculinity—the rococo outfits, his campy humor, and his overt love of feminine crafts like food and fashion—with sexual queerness. He was *fabulous*, to use a vernacular term, and they relished his freedom.

Arguably, his deeper immersion into his "freak" side parallels Little Richard's risqué fashion choices and concert and television talk show antics during his late 1960s through mid-1970s comeback. The more outrageous he was, the more audiences seemed to enjoy his antics. Audiences' openness toward this affective pushing of boundary reflects the liminal space popular-culture personae allow audiences to occupy. Though the fantasy of having access to a musician sexually is a prominent projection, we should also welcome the idea of singers symbolizing other possibilities. For example, the notion of a good son—a male who is polite, witty, and capable of dishing on matters of style, cuisine, and glamour in the company of women—surely factors into Liberace's appeal to certain demographics. Similarly, the idea of a male who is comfortable expressing himself fully and without shame, who embraces masculine and feminine codes and pushes through normative expectations of what is polite, decent, and appropriate, speaks to some of Little Richard's appeal. The fantasies these spectacular "freaks" occupy seem less an outcome of political organizing (the gay political movement was still a niche movement in its infancy in the 1960s through the early 1970s) than embodiments of masculine possibilities that could play out safely onstage, as opposed to in everyday life. Their recordings and television and concert appearances functioned socially as laboratories that exposed their audiences to surprising, and appealing, renditions of masculinity whose contrast with masculine expectations constituted part of the pleasure of consuming their artistry. Like a dirty secret or a guilty pleasure, they gave their audiences something very public they could also relish privately/internally for the safe sense of danger afforded by the unspoken, but recognizable, "queerness" on display.

The period of 1959 through 1963 represented a shift in Liberace's career as one less about perceptions of his sexuality than one of changing cultural tastes. In 1959 he was no longer a television star; as teen pop idols, Motown, and girl groups rose in popularity, his albums were no longer charting and his Riviera contract was over.[12] Liberace spent the 1960s reemphasizing his stature as a concert performer, especially on the West Coast. The 1960s also marked the turning point in his career when he went from tuxedos to sequined jumpsuits and floor-length fur coats.

He actually became even *more* flamboyant after the trial, and his audience embraced this change.

Having enjoyed the previous decade in the commercial spotlight, Liberace was adamant about reminding the public of his stature and viability. One of the primary ways he drew more attention to himself was by amplifying the style component of his show and, in 1965, promoting his twenty-fifth anniversary in show business as an event. His style and affluence grew increasingly more common as topics in reviews and profiles.

A feature on his showbiz anniversary noted the candelabra and "his flashy clothes" as trademarks. Liberace framed his clothing as "something which would make me stand out in the crowd and it kept snowballing" (MacMinn 1965). Liberace fed this association with glamour and excess: in a 1966 profile, Liberace regarded himself as a "curator of Hollywood Glamour" and was troubled by other performers because "they have forgotten that the public expects them to be larger than life, to be myths, not mortals" (Bart 1966, 99). Just a month prior, on January 26, 1966, a *Los Angeles Times* story titled "Liberace Spruces Up for Concerts" notes how he has had to move far beyond the lamé jackets that previously caught the public's attention. He was now wearing $8,000 gem-encrusted coats and $10,000 suits at his concerts, consciously synchronizing his wardrobe with his musical selections (Los Angeles Times 1995). These strategies were lucrative, apparently. According to one 1966 profile, Liberace had just opened an antique salon in Hollywood featuring jewelry from a collection reportedly valued at $1.5 million. The performer also made $800,000 annually from concert tours and television appearances, and he claimed he was attracting more young people to his audience.

You can see how his curatorial glamour philosophy had already taken shape in the early 1960s. In a *New York Times* June 3, 1964, review of a Liberace performance at the Americana Hotel, music critic John S. Wilson referred to Liberace as "the dazzling buffoon, his clothes shrieking with sequins, his teeth agleam, his dimples dimpling. He plays it for easy laughs" (Wilson 1964, 39). He continued noting how Liberace was able to disarm his audience by

LIBERACE

C O N T E N T S

W. M. Cotton, publisher

Muriel Babcock, editorial director

Diana Lurvey, editor

Marie Haller, managing editor

Florence Fletcher,
Lee Hart, associate editors

Ed Rethorn, Jr., art director

Rae Lynn, western editor

Mel Traxel,
Arnold Johnson, staff photographers

Liberace is published by Ideal Publishing Corp., New York, N. Y. Editorial and executive offices, 295 Madison Ave., New York 17, N. Y. Single copy price: 35 cents. (Printed in the U.S.A.) Copyright 1954 by Ideal Publishing Corp. Vol. 1, No. 1.

FIGURE 5.3. A picture of the typical black-tuxedo-with-tails Liberace performed in during the 1940s through the early 1950s (*Liberace: Complete Life Story*).

FIGURE 5.4. Liberace wearing a flamboyant outfit from a 1983 concert (photo by Alan Light/Creative Commons).

appearing "in a jacket glittering with golden sequins, preening himself and throwing down the gauntlet. 'Look me over,' he says. 'I didn't get dressed like this to go unnoticed" (39). Along with playing medleys of classical and popular tunes, Liberace, Wilson noted, allows the "occasional pauses to slip into something more spectacular" (39). Though Liberace's self-deferential humor is not new, it is clear that even before he launched his anniversary, he planned to use fashion as a weapon. It is worth recalling that some of the adjectives Conner used in the "Cassandra" column included digs at his wardrobe: "chromium-plated," "luminous," and "jingling claptrap" (Thomas 1987, 121–22).

There is a queer angle to his increasing luminosity. In *Vested Interests* (1992), Marjorie Garber classifies Liberace's fashionable sensibilities, including his elaborate costumes but also his wearing of makeup, his facelifts, and the wigs he wore to mask his baldness, as examples of "unmarked transvestism." Garber notes, "This is the apparatus of 'woman,' that is to say, the artifactual creation of female impersonation and the drag queen on the one hand, and the youth culture on the other" (359). As I have argued throughout this chapter, part of Liberace's appeal is his ability to push boundaries, including challenging the pretentiousness of classical music and normalizing gender transgressive elements of dandyism, without drawing attention to what he is doing. After all, he is just an "entertainer" (insert wink). A sophisticated sense of self-awareness informs his public presentation. Liberace had an outfit for every occasion, literally and figuratively. Remember, Liberace did not arrive at his trial wearing stage wear, but he did wear a costume: "a conservative blue suit, white shirt, and necktie" (358).

Though Liberace might have blanched at the suggestion from a critic that he was an unmarked "transvestite," he "sometimes told interviewers that he dressed for the stage 'just one step short of drag'" (Thomas 1987, 215). A close reader could interpret this information as a signifier of some level of awareness with queer culture. Garber uses the term "unmasked transvestism" to describe "the possibility that some entertainers who do not overtly claim to be 'female impersonators,' for example, may in fact signal their cross-gender identities onstage, and that this quality of crossing—which is fundamentally related to other kinds of boundary-crossing in their performances—can be more powerful and seductive than explicit 'female impersonation,' which is often designed to confront, scandalize, titillate or shock" (Garber 1992, 354).

In terms of affect, it is useful to note how the queer Quartet employed style differently to define their personae. Johnnie Ray wore plain suits onstage, which conveyed the look of the typical male crooner. His hearing aid was the only visible sign that he was "different." Mathis dressed in a subtle, preppy style that conveyed decorum and worked to draw attention *away* from himself. Muting the body is a component of racial respectability politics. Little Richard has always adapted his style to the occasion. His initial image was a more stylized and exaggerated version of the visual aesthetic of other black R&B performers, including wearing processed hair and dressing in suits. The visual evidence from his initial retreat from the secular world, notably his 1959 gospel album cover, *The King of Gospel Singers: Little Richard* (referenced in chapter 3), reveals a conservative, tailored look with a short, natural haircut, a thin mustache, and a suit. Little Richard's mid-1960s return involved a reversion to his early look, which he exaggerated in the late 1960s and 1970s at concerts and on television. Throughout the late 1970s and 1980s his vacillations between his secular persona and Christian persona entailed differing lengths of hair, levels of makeup, and visual accessories.

Liberace had a different audience than his peers, and balancing explicit and implicit elements was more central to his art. He needed to convey a type of overt glamour that excited and surprised his audience and to provide accompanying gestures to complement his style, but he had to be careful not to delve into drag or anything that one could read as subversive or political. His blurring of genders made a statement without him *making a statement*.

Garber's definition captures the implicit challenges Liberace makes to various musical and gender boundaries and the implicitness so integral to his aesthetic (Garber 1992, 354). Though he never declared the trial to be his gateway to fuller personal expression in a formal sense, in every other sense he more overtly feminized himself after the trial than ever before. First, he expanded the textural range of his wardrobe. His second designer, Ray Acuna, ushered in an era defined by outfits that sought to recreate previous eras, including a George V coronation robe and an outfit modeled on the style of Louis XVI. The Acuna era also included sequins from Spain, rhinestones from Austria, beads and jewels from Los Angeles, and the beginning of Liberace wearing furs. When Acuna retired in 1973, the performer hired Michael Travis, who "took Liberace's costumes to new levels of grandeur and unparalleled extravagance" (Soloman and Jewett 2013, 37). Travis had designed outfits for the Fifth Dimension, The Supremes, and Dionne Warwick, so he had experience with feminine clothing. Examples from Travis's twelve-year reign included a 1975 "Chopin-styled jeweled suit" in honor of the nation's bicentennial: it featured a "jeweled red-and-blue suit topped with an all-white ostrich cape" (36). In 1983 Liberace premiered Travis's Hapsburg Eagle Suit and Cape, a "lavishly appliquéd" gold lamé jacket, a cape with "a double-headed eagle on each shoulder," and matching pants and boots "trimmed with sable fur" (Soloman and Jewett 2013, 38). During his triumphant 1985 concerts at Radio City Music Hall he wore a Fabergé Costume and Cape; he would enter the stage "emerging from a twelve-foot replica of a Fabergé Easter egg" (39).

Second, Liberace created stage gestures that capitalized on his newfound fashion. After the trial, he more overtly integrated costume changes into his shows such that Garber noted, "His performances were more like fashion shows than piano recitals" (Liberace 1973, 358). For his final *coup de grace* he learned to fly onstage. Liberace worked with choreographer Peter Foy (of the English Flying Foys) to fly above the stage at his shows. Mounted on a harness and wearing his signature capes he flew across, joking, "Mary Poppins, eat your heart out!" Garber notes that Foy had also trained "two generations of female Peter Pans" prior to Liberace and viewed this as "a triumph of metonymic transvestism, a middle-aged man imitating a woman who plays a fantasy changeling boy" (359). As biographer Bob Thomas notes, "The flying finale became standard in Liberace's casino appearances" and he wore "an ostrich-feather-cape" to convey the sensation of motion (Thomas 1987, 215–16).

The combination of his newfound immunity to press policing plus the threat of mounting competition led Liberace to complain that his imitators were usurping him: "I really have to exaggerate to look different and to top them" (Thomas 1987, 173). The trial gave him the freedom to push boundaries of fashion and gender to new heights. The transition from wearing a white tuxedo to donning gold lamé jackets and flying across a stage wearing a fur cape is an increasingly queer and seemingly risky transition. However, Liberace had successfully nudged gender boundaries since the early 1950s and witnessed how audiences lost interest in his intimate life, rejected efforts to "masculinize" his established style, and remained loyal to him despite tabloid and mainstream press rumors. Queerness was his brand, not just a flavor of his act, and he let it sparkle on its own.

To match his more elaborate wardrobe and more dynamic stage show, Liberace also planted firmer roots buying properties in California and Nevada and expanding the brand. He epitomized the Las Vegas aesthetic, performing lengthy engagements that ratcheted up the spectacle. Among the twenty-two concert engagements he had during the decade, most were typically two week-month engagements; ten were in the iconic lounge spaces of Lake Tahoe, Las Vegas, and Sparks, Nevada.[13] In a sense, Liberace also translated the "queer" passions that his peers mocked him for as a child—including his love for cooking and fashion—into business assets. Eve Kosofsky Sedgwick notes how queer shame is "integral to and residual in the processes by which identity is formed," not something that can be excised. In Liberace's case, he translated the shame he may have felt initially about his "sissified" hobbies into raw material, "available for the work of metamorphosis, reframing, refiguration, *trans*figuration, affective and symbolic loading and deformation" (Sedgwick 1993, 13). These tools furthered the Liberace star mythology. For example, in addition to opening the interior decor store in 1966, he published *Liberace Cooks! Recipes from his Seven Dining Rooms* (1970) and *Liberace: An Autobiography* (1973) and opened the Liberace Museum and Foundation in Las Vegas in 1975. He continued to employ television to reach broad audiences, which included hosting the 1978 CBS TV special *Leapin' Lizards, It's Liberace!*, a filmed version of his Las Vegas Hilton show. In his final three years he returned to New York, where he performed a series of sold-out Radio City Music Hall concerts acclaimed for their masterful staging.[14]

Liberace's Final Act: Self-Neutering and Counter-Domestication (Part 3)

During Liberace's final years, the two major challenges to Liberace's image were former lover Scott Thorson's 1982 palimony suit against him and the rumors that he was a gay man dying of AIDS. As expected, he addressed these using his old tools of *self-neutering* and *domestication*. First, he framed Thorson as a disgruntled employee rather than a former lover, thus erasing any semblance of an intimate life. The lawsuit attempted to capitalize on the open secret of Liberace's queer sexuality. Once again Liberace self-neutered by denying romantic involvement and protecting himself. The most telling moment of the initial announcement is the way his audience supported him after the lawsuit emerged. After nearly thirty years, they adored him and did not want his reputation sullied.

Second, his managers carefully managed his death, seemingly to protect his image and the audience's impression of him. In the mid-1980s, HIV/AIDS signified pollution, illness, recklessness, and vice at odds with his wholesome image. In the public imagination, homosexuals and drug addicts caught the virus, not "wholesome" entertainers. Even as his health deteriorated, he clung to his image and *self-neutered*. Liberace could not have a virus associated with drug addicts and homosexuals if he was not a drug user and had no sex life. This was also part of his *domestication*; he assumed his audience could not handle anything too far from his established image. Like Ray, he may have underestimated his audience and thought they were more homophobic than they were. They may have been indifferent or even hostile toward queer sexual orientations, but they were voracious consumers of queer dandyism.

Post-Conner Liberace did not have to defend himself against public accusations regarding his sexuality until 1982, when Scott Thorson sued him for palimony. Thorson acknowledged that after Liberace's staff evicted him from his home, he sought to humiliate Liberace because he knew that the entertainer "went to great lengths during his lifetime to conceal his sexual preference from the public" (Thorson and Thorleifson 2013, 200). He and his lawyer sold Thorson's story to the *National Enquirer*, which published the first of two exposés in their November 2, 1982, issue (Thorson 1982, 48–51). Liberace was apparently performing in the Midwest after the story broke; according to friends' accounts, "When he walked out to face the audience they gave him a standing ovation. Either they hadn't believed the things I'd said in the *Enquirer* article or they could forgive Lee anything—including having sex with young men" (Thorson and Thorleifson 2013, 201). Similarly, after Thorson announced his palimony suit, Bob Thomas notes that as Liberace entered the stage at Toronto's O'Keefe Center, "The sounds swept over him like a tidal wave. The cheers and applause were so dense that it felt as if he could lose his balance. The musicians in the pit wondered if they had been struck by a seismic shock. The ovation continued for minute and Liberace stood stage-center basking in it, grateful tears in his eyes" (Thomas 1987, 220). Pyron also commented that audiences "did not seem to care very much about Thorson's charges" and that "they continued to pay to laugh at the showman's antics; he continued to maintain the arduous work schedule he had been following for the preceding forty years" (Pyron 2000, 389).

Liberace began incorporating Thorson onstage in 1977 as his chauffeur, so he was publicly perceived as a part of the act, which, in retrospect, was bold. According to Thorson's biography, Liberace had a pattern of placing male lovers on his payroll, which made it easier to for him to frame their romantic separations as professional splits and protected Liberace from being exposed. The credibility of this notion is disputable in many respects, but Liberace's lawyers successfully depicted Thorson as a disgruntled employee who was fired for substance abuse problems in the press and in court. Liberace offered Thorson a modest settlement in 1986 (Thorson and Thorleifson 2013, 224) and Thorson subsequently struggled with substance abuse and ill-fated associations with criminals that have led him to be incarcerated multiple times.

Even as he was dying, Liberace felt compelled to manage the narrative. His publicist announced that he died of heart failure (Thomas 1987, 272). The Riverside County coroner, however, tested tissue samples and corrected the original statement, announcing that Liberace died of AIDS-related cytomegalovirus pneumonia (275). Though the façade seems pathetic, Thorson alleges that Liberace said to him, "I don't want to be remembered as an old queen who died of AIDS" (Thorson and Thorleifson 2013, 228). Liberace was a queen (dressed as a king and queen), and the public enjoyed that. He was worried about being perceived as gay, not being thought of as a queen, since that was the root of his post-1960s career. Gentlemen did not die of AIDS; homosexuals, hemophiliacs, and drug addicts did. Even toward the end, he tried to manage his image so as not to upset expectations that he and his audience established in true illusory fashion.

Liberace has served as a subject for several biographers, critics, and scholars. The motivation for my critical imperative in writing about the different techniques he employed is to challenge what is sometimes a reductionist discourse about his life and career. By framing the critical axis of his career as a "will he/won't he" question of disclosure, he is defined against the politics of visibility. As I have noted throughout, this pressure overlooks Liberace's navigation of his identity on a personal level, as well as the risk of more overt public affiliations with queer communities. Having a contained social network, such as the group of gay men he met in the 1940s in Wisconsin or among his mostly male staff, was more manageable than coming out and/or affiliating with the political movement. The fact that one of the most famous "queering" men was concerned about audiences remembering him as "an old queen" speaks to a lifetime of awareness regarding the vocabulary that shamed, stigmatized, and essentialized men like him.

Though he was not "out" or involved with the movement, it is telling that he used gay-aware language in private. He knew what he was and how he was perceived, and he clearly wanted to defy and exceed the boundaries of being known for his sexuality. If he had come out overtly, some audiences may have remembered him as an "old queen." Ironically, because he never chose to identify his sexuality publicly, many of his most devoted fans choose to remember him as something else. Reading him in this context affords him some dignity and understanding, which is not always present in contemporary readings of Liberace.

To return to Scott Thorson's opening statement in the HBO telefilm: Thorson, at age eighteen, thought the most notable aspect of Liberace was his (apparent) homosexuality and the perception that Liberace was tricking his audience or somehow deceiving them by not spelling out his sexual orientation. While this narrow perception is understandable, especially coming from a young person as the gay liberation paradigm was slowly infusing mainstream culture, it is more troubling when seasoned critics make what is essentially the same objection.

Ehrenstein's response to Liberace's testimony in the Conner trial that he was not homosexual was that "Liberace was, of course, *lying*." And he qualified this lie, noting, "It goes without saying that Liberace's lie must be seen in its proper context" (Ehrenstein 1998, 118). For him, however, Liberace's status and wealth should have motivated Liberace to come out since Ehrenstein presumes there was less risk: "But there is an enormous difference between a person of average ways and means lying about his or her same-sex affinity in order to keep a job, residence, or family peace, and the lie of a highly paid and well-connected show-business figure who had successfully promoted modest pianistic ability into a career in nightclubs, concert halls, film, and television. Moreover, an overt appeal to the sexual sensibilities of his audience was very much a part of Liberace's act" (118). Kevin Kopelson's *Beethoven's Kiss* describes Liberace's strategy as one in which he deliberately packaged himself "for muffled gay consumption as well as for middlebrow mass consumption." Comparatively, in his view, "post-Stonewall gays who can afford to be out are far less complimentary. They see Liberace as both unliberated and undesirable. They loathe him not because they're homophobic, but because *he's* homophobic. They hate him for having denied his homosexuality, and the fact that he had AIDS, until the day he died—something even Rock Hudson didn't do" (Kopelson 1996, 152). Again, the author privileges certain forms of outness, confined to disclosure, while ignoring the bigger picture of Liberace's career.

Boze Hadleigh's *Sing Out!* calls Liberace's death "the most notable AIDS death in music" and laments Liberace's closetedness: "What made it even more of a headline-grabber was the corpse's unwillingness to come out of the closet" (Hadleigh 1997, 48). He quotes author-lyricist Warren Casey, who also died of AIDS, and opined that Liberace was unforgivable because he "treated his private life as so shameful that even in death he wanted it secret. He could have done so much good, telling the world with dignity that yes, he had AIDS, and so do thousands of good, creative, successful people." Hadleigh concludes with the statement, "The incredible lightness of being Liberace. . . . But enough about a mega-millionaire who died of AIDS yet willed not one cent to combat it or help fellow PWAs" (50). Whether Liberace's identity was totally secret is debatable, given the archive of evidence, but Casey is speaking more to transparency than innuendo.

They also object to Liberace's silence about his sexual identity as a mark of dishonesty and inauthenticity. They discount, overlook, and dismiss an almost unspoken agreement between Liberace and his audience. He gave them quite a lot of himself. As you will recall, he shared his personal story, his family, and his personal passions with this audience, and he refashioned his act to have a more populist appeal.

What his critics have not asked is why his sexual orientation had to be the most salient part of his identity. Arguably, he did more to push boundaries by exiting in a glass closet than he might have if he had taken a more overtly liberated stance. This was not exactly a model available to him in terms of risks or benefits. He had a national career for twenty years before an organized political movement arose around the act of coming out and visibility politics. He also expended a lot of time and resources defending himself in court and would have appeared highly hypocritical.

The techniques he used were part of his aesthetic, and his audience accepted it. Who is being deceived when the essence these critics draw from is happening right in front of his audience? His audience could surely interpret the array of queer signifiers happening in front of them and synthesize those aspects with the social cues about sexuality learned in the culture—if they chose.

Thorson and Liberace's formal critics underestimate his audience. We should not conflate the allure of illusions with lies, assume his audience was ignorant or homophobic, or presume they could not read between the lines. Even if Liberace slept with women, that would not alter the fact that he challenged heteronormative social structures about television, classical music conventions, male fashion, and an individual's right to remain sexually ambiguous.

Discounting Liberace for failing to morph from an entertainer to an activist (the mode through which open gayness was interpreted in during the late 1960s and beyond) is like discounting flirting because it fails to lead to consummation. There are pleasures in the *process* of experiencing Liberace that are going unnoticed. What critics are not seeing and addressing is more of a distortion than Liberace's resistance to disclose his sexuality. Liberace was coy; he was a tease and a flirt whose audience was willfully seduced. His career generates and responds to two questions.

First, should sexual orientation serve as the most salient aspect of a sexually queer person's identity? This notion is especially relevant if we agree with Sedgwick that the most compelling coming-out story is "the coming-out story that doesn't come out" (Sedgwick 1990, 248). Perhaps we could reframe the conversation from one of a flat declarative authenticity to one that appreciates ambiguity and tension and recognizes the joy of secrecy and pleasure of uncertainty.

In a related vein, his career asks how we could shift the terms of authenticity from valorizing politics with a capital "P" toward considering the socially transformative work of popular culture that queers the social environment. The results may be incremental and longitudinal in their impact, as generations of observers internalize Liberace's art, but no less deeply felt. The critical imperative of Heather Love's *Feeling Backward* (2007) and Christopher Nealon's *Foundlings* (2001) to look back at history with some awareness of the space between the person and society is the optimal lens for understanding the profound role of culture as a resistive playground before, and even during, the emergence of LGBTQ politics. This is a key space that continually feeds the grassroots of LGBTQ lives.

The outcomes of a celebrity's techniques tell a story about public tastes and appetites. Liberace's career certainly reveals the seduction of mythology and the utility of the "conspiracy of blindness." (Drewal 1994, 150). Audiences see what they want and hear selectively when they are getting what they want. There is no reason for queer musicians to be exempt from these premises, especially when they are architects of these logics. This dance requires two willing partners, and the intervention many of Liberace's critics want to make is a needless intrusion that seeks him to stomp where the "soft shoe" leaves a more lasting impression.

Conclusion
Disquieting and Exciting: Queering Tools in Popular Music and Queer Becoming

ROCKING THE CLOSET began as a puzzle centered on a question of bewilderment: *How did he do it?* The question reflected my initial awe that the Quartet was able to succeed commercially during what I imagined as an overwhelmingly homophobic and genderphobic era. I thought audiences must have been blind, naïve, and/or dense if they did not see the irony playing out before them. I based my early perception on the assumption that something had to have malfunctioned for audiences to embrace these queer men because this was so dissonant from my own stereotypes about the postwar era. In tracing the careers and gestures of the musicians, I see a gentler, more accommodating relation between performers and audiences. There is something appealing about these outsiders. Within the same decade in which deviants were stigmatized in elaborate forms, such as government purges, queerness became more legible and audiences found it hard to loathe something they were just discovering—*deviance was fun.* This sensibility continues in subsequent generations of male performers. Audiences continually rediscover this element—hence the cycle of mini-crises that seem to emerge every decade when new musicians queer the mainstream. Whether it is a crisis of perversion (Prince, for example) or inscrutability (Ricky Martin, Clay Aiken), the fact that a performer does not fit in remains both disquieting *and* exciting.

Most critical accounts of the Queer Quartet discuss their sexual orientation in terms that usually fall into the category of appraisal or disappointment. The focus on sexual orientation often addresses the intimate, private and illegible elements of the musicians, at the expense of broader, accessible, and eligible ways the figures have queered popular music, popular culture, and the sensibilities of their audiences. These accounts also frequently miss the ambivalence the musicians have about their queerness.

Critical distance affords me and other scholars the opportunities to categorize and theorize about the lives of these public figures. We must remember, however, that they *lived* through the eras I discuss and navigated the social norms. Several palpable risks informed the careers of these musicians in various forms. These include the following: making a living as an African American male entertainer in an era of heightened anxiety about judicial, legislative, and social concerns regarding race; living as a man who was intimate with other men during a time when sexual deviance gained hypervisibility as a national threat; and being an effeminate man whose affect deviated from rigid social expectations that defined manhood through an explicit heteronormative lens. Given these contexts, it is no wonder that their careers required an ongoing series of maneuvers and caused several musicians to question if being "different" was sustainable. These feelings reflect the shame and ambivalence that preceded the late 1960s pride paradigm. We must capture and recognize these experiences and address the ongoing ways shame and ambivalence inform the careers of contemporary cultural figures whose work personae and careers are readable as "queer."

To return to the Quartet: while no reception study can quantify audiences' experiences, I have intentionally focused on popular figures who had radio hits, sold large quantities of albums, and transcended eras, demographics, and, in some cases, mediums. Queer elements pervaded postwar popular culture. Postwar audiences lived in a vividly experimental time, and the new language, attention, and publicity toward queerness was a marker of anxiety *and* curiosity.

It is ironic that an era trying desperately to cement nuclear family structures, clearly defined gender roles, and sociopolitical conformity as the dominant cultural possibility deeply informed subterranean formations that challenged the very notion of norms, and the legacy of these historical tensions continues to shape contemporary social and political discourse. Queer social enclaves, 1950s postwar homophile organizations, the Beats, the civil rights movement, second wave feminist organizing, and other nascent movements owe some of their power to the fervent personal responses everyday people had to oppressive racial, sexual, gender, and class norms. Their robust impact continually challenges notions of postwar America as a monolith, or as a mere extension of a tradition.

During the postwar era, new traditions formed in popular culture that mobilized many of the ingredients for social reform. Both technological developments (the LP, the portable television) and social shifts fostered greater sustained engagement with celebrity personae. Within this shift was an expansive sense of what was entertaining, and whom audiences would value as an entertainer. Effeminate men, black dandies, deaf crooners, and R&B singers wearing makeup and processed hair are not the first images we associate with the 1950s. I hope that my study has shown that these figures were visible in part because postwar audiences were fascinated with gender transgressive performers. The "pansy craze" of 1930s films, Gladys Bentley's Harlem Renaissance–era iconicity, Milton Berle's popularity as a cross-dressing television figure, and other examples all point toward an audience poised for something transformative from popular culture.

In developing and articulating the ways the Quartet employed "queering" tools to develop their personae and careers I see how they endure in subsequent generations of performers. Musicians who employed elements of the queering toolkit have also invited speculation about their sexual orientation because of their gender transgressions. Visual flamboyance, sexual neutrality, dandyism, and effeminacy continue to draw our attention to males who diverge from contemporary gender norms. The playful masculinity of Queen's Freddie Mercury, the understated romanticism of Luther Vandross, the provocative spectacle gender blurring of David Bowie, Prince, and Boy George all reflect a tacit genealogy with the Quartet in various respects. In addition to detecting traces of the patterns I have discussed throughout the book, we can see new tools and techniques emerge that expand the scope of "queer" as a frame for rethinking heteronormativity and the disciplinary effects of social norms. I briefly explore three examples and offer one example of a new queering tool to develop this concluding argument.

Michael Jackson: External Enfreaking, Self-enfreaking, and Playing the Race Card

The biggest pop star of the 1980s was Michael Jackson, and the more he grew in popularity, the more critics externally "enfreaked" him for violating a spate of social rules. Jackson so violated expectations of black masculinity that music critic Nelson George referred to him as "an alarmingly unblack, unmasculine figure" who was also, ironically, "the most popular black man in America" (George 1988, 174). From a historical perspective this should not have been entirely surprising to George, since nonthreatening black men who offered alternate renditions of masculinity from dominant norms were the rule, not the exception, in American popular music. Jackson's commercial ascent during an era that reiterated many tropes of postwar male virility was too daring to go unnoticed. Joseph Vogel catalogs the simultaneous commercial elevation and social degradation of Jackson: "Evangelical leader Jerry Falwell claimed Jackson's 'projection of a femaleness' presented 'a very bad role model for the millions of children who literally idolize' him, and would cause 'wreckage' in their lives" (Vogel 2015, 478). In 1984 Louis Farrakhan of the Nation of Islam also assessed Jackson's image in racial and sexual terms. As Vogel notes, "[Farrakhan] warned that the image Jackson and other black androgynous artists like him projected was 'ruin[ing] young men and mak[ing] your young women have nothing to look up to as a real man'" and that his "female-acting, sissified-acting expression is not wholesome for our young boys, nor our young girls" (480). The enfreaking of Jackson escalated to a point where, in September 1984, Jackson's manager read a press release stating Jackson's intention to marry and have a family in response to press comments regarding his effeminate appearance and sexual speculation (Marsh 1985, 106–17).

A variety of critics and scholars have approached his "queering" of conventions from a more strategic angle. For example, Margo Jefferson sees Jackson as an heir apparent to Little Richard in many regards: "I am not saying that Michael Jackson is gay. I am saying that he draws on gay culture—its signs and codes—but pretends that he doesn't and that we shouldn't notice" (Jefferson 2006, 103–4). Susan Fast reads Jackson's performance in the 1983 video "Beat It," where he tries to locate peace between warring gangs, as a queer performance. Notably, "He is outside of their performance of conventional masculinity, both in terms of the narrative and, of course, by virtue of his androgynous looks," which evoke the "soft masculinity of early adolescence," and his "dancing body" (Fast 2012, 283). Fast cites multiple examples of video performances wherein Jackson "used sensuous dance routines to counter conflict or violence" modeled after "Beat It," including videos for "Bad" (1987) and "Black or White" (1991) (284). She also surveys other moments in which his voice inhabits that of a female victim in "Smooth Criminal" ("Jackson slipping into drag as the music reaches a climactic point," 292) and where his voice is virtually indistinguishable from a female vocal register ("I Just Can't Stop Loving You" [1988], sung with Siedah Garrett) to illustrate examples of gender blurring (293). When we consider the conservative gender norms of the 1980s, Jackson's commercial triumph is quite impressive, as were his challenges to racial and sexual tropes.

Tragically, the critical responses to his image and personal life overwhelmed his career to the point of overshadowing his talents and contributions and turned him into a spectacle. Jackson followed the military jacket, diamond-studded glove, and high-water pants and loafers of the *Thriller* era with a more stylized appearance on the 1987 cover of *Bad*. As Jefferson describes, "The lipstick grows brighter. The features look even more chiseled. All this atop black leather gear for *Bad* album cover. The ebony sheen of the jacket matches the ebony sheen of the hair" (Jefferson 2006, 95). Jefferson notes the way Jackson's increasingly lightened skin color and feminized appearance contributed to the spectacle that surrounded him. By the early 1990s "his face was chalk-white, a fact that registered with the same shock a sex-change operation might provoke. He was even wearing eyeliner and lipstick and sporting beauty-shop hairdos. At first people talked more about the whitening than about the femme-ing" (80). What was important was that people were talking, but the conversation descended into madness.

The inverse of his signature "soft masculinity" and queering was the audience's inability to recognize Jackson as an adult rather than a perpetual man-child. Audiences reacted very negatively, for example, to Jackson's expression of violent outbursts and crotch grabbing in the original version of his controversial 1991 video for "Black or White" which was recut (Knopper 2015, 194–97). Things descended further when the Los Angeles police department raided Jackson's Neverland Ranch in August 1993 in search of clues after a father filed a lawsuit on his child's behalf alleging inappropriate sexual behavior (212). This was the beginning of a series of lawsuits and settlements alleging similar charges and a period of heightened scrutiny of Jackson's sexuality, racial identity, and marital status—and beyond—that persisted until his death from painkillers on June 25, 2009 (341). In Jackson's career, "queering" is a discernible technique, but "pride" and other celebratory terms do not quite fit. While we can articulate the ways the public embraced certain challenges to racial and sexual norms, these responses were not entirely reliable. At a certain interval, Jackson's boundary crossing made him vulnerable to heightened cultural scrutiny and led to widespread stigma and excoriation beyond anything the Quartet experienced in the 1950s. Decades of civil rights organizing and cultural shifts have pushed our consciousness, but racial and sexual anxieties still color the popular imagination.

Prince: Self-enfreaking, External Enfreakment, Spectacularizing, and Playing the Race Card

Prince, whose death I referenced in the introduction, is an example of a heterosexual male who employed multiple "queering" tools to queer a host of masculine conventions, especially those associated with the black male, post-funk R&B tradition. After his initial bow as a conventional funk and

R&B singer, he *spectacularized* his image and *self-enfreaked*. Many critics noticed his blurring of gender boundaries, his references to risqué sexuality, and his divergences from R&B into rock music. The result was a budding popularity that reached its apex with the 1984 *Purple Rain* soundtrack. Before this milestone, he had already begun to stand apart from other R&B musicians of his generation, and it solidified him as a "crossover" performer in R&B, pop, and rock music.

On the cover of his debut album, *Prince*, his hair is straightened and blown out in a bouffant feather style common among African American women during the 1970s. His thick eyebrows, longing gaze, and unclothed bodice also convey a vulnerability and effeminacy very different from most male R&B singers of the time. On his 1980 *Dirty Mind* album, he also conveys an ambiguous vulnerability. He poses in the center, shirtless and in black bikini underwear, wearing a shortened but still feminine straightened hairstyle that gently drapes his face. On the back cover he lies on a bed; he wears black leggings that span from his thighs to his boots. This album also features the song "Uptown," the lyrics of which echo speculation about his racial identity and about his sexuality, indicating a knowingness about his ambiguity. Like David Bowie, Prince trafficked in elements of freakishness and spectacle and was chameleonic in image and sound.

Fans of early 1980s rock music were openly hostile to his androgynous style. For example, during his opening sets for the Rolling Stones' 1981 West Coast tour, "the suggestions of androgyny in his fluid body movements and flamboyantly minimal stage costume" may have drawn from Mick Jagger's early image and performing style, "but the almost entirely white Stones audience apparently failed to make the connection. They pelted Prince with fruit and bottles, causing him to cut his sets short" (Palmer 1981). Touré describes his early 1980s visual aesthetic: "In his work in the early 1980s, Prince was playing with gender norms, shocking people with the audacity of his androgyny in a time when many musicians were toying with it. He was wearing heels and eyeliner and earrings and thongs and stockings and blouses that were wide open to the navel, showing his curly, masculine chest hair, practically cross-dressing in public while singing in a falsetto" (Touré 2013, 78).

Despite the hostility he faced occasionally, Prince was strategic about queering his image and testing the bounds of acceptability. Dez Dickerson, who played guitar with Prince from 1979 to 1983, explained to Touré, "It's Prince's marketing genius and his desire to shock and play with taboos that led him to tease people into thinking he could be gay. He was courting controversy as a business tactic. . . . [a]s a marketing tactic. So Prince didn't back away from suggestions of homosexuality. It was almost like a martial arts move where you use your opponent's momentum against him. . . . This is the most drivenly heterosexual man I've ever known. But he was intrigued by using all of it. People like Bowie had used that as a branding tool, and Prince seized on that and used it as well as anybody'" (Touré 2013, 78). Stan Hawkins and Sarah Niblock's *Prince: The Making of a Pop Music Phenomenon* (2011) also highlights the intentionality behind Prince's provocations and their symbolic impact: "Lyrics, gestures and mannerisms were theatricalized humorously in tandem with the sound and stylistic referents he turned to. The spectacle of Prince's posturing was important in challenging traditional representations of gender, as he demonstrated the phenomenon of parodying the construction of masculinity" (41).

His divergences helped him build an audience and caught the attention of critics. Nelson George noted Prince's sexual and racial transgressions: "No black performer since Little Richard had toyed with the heterosexual sensibilities of black America so brazenly" (George 1988, 174). As he crossed over in the mid-1980s, through *Purple Rain*, one critic noted how his image became "less campy, less outrageously ambisexual than before," in part because "he's toned down his old costume of bikini underpants and lace gloves" (Kakutani 1984). He may have toned things down but he remained a maven of queer style.

In the 1990s, for example, his style changed, but as Rhonda K. Garelick in *Rising Star* notes, he adapted a modern dandy look that reiterated traces of ambiguity. She describes his 1995 *Esquire* magazine cover, where he is, "Dressed in an all-red suit and high-collared shirt designed by Gianni Versace, Prince leans on a crystal, bejeweled walking stick, his fingers covered with heavy rings" as a conscious homage to dandyism (Garelick 1998, 155). She ties his look to his overall persona, noting, "Prince's performance, like the dandy's, must be continuous and apparently seamless; there can be no 'backstage Prince' and no photographs taken when he is not in full costume and makeup. These trappings normally include silk shirts with Byronic ruffles, chiffon scarves, skin-tight leather pants that expose derriere cleavage, heavy black eyeliner, and, most recently, the penciled word 'slave' on one cheek" (155). Even his female protégés have mirrored the highly stylized and vain tendencies of dandies: "All have been fashioned into female versions of the star. All have been . . . given one-word stagenames (Appollonia, Vanity, Mayte); all have been dressed in costumes matching Prince's; and all have been known publicly as his lovers" (158). Hawkins and Niblock also locate the dynamism of Prince's visual style within the dandy tradition. In terms of interpretations, they argue that "the nature of Prince's queering permits his straightness to sidestep the direct questions of sexual preference. In common with the legacy of British pop artists, Prince has successfully negotiated the movement between queer and straight, exhibiting the sensational possibilities of sexual identity on his terms" (Hawkins and Niblock 2011, 48). In many ways, he is a precursor to Justin Timberlake, discussed below, whose "queering works on a sliding scale" (48).

Like Jackson, Prince also died tragically and unexpectedly. Historically speaking, his queering efforts were controversial to an extent, but his use of the tools mostly gave him access to the commercial mainstream before he transitioned into other visual styles. Clearly, the queering tools were not exclusive to sexually queer men. In terms of his early 1980s persona Prince was more overtly queer—experimental, daring, provocative—than sexually queer men like George Michael and Vandross, and therefore upset norms on a different scale.[1]

Clay Aiken: Self-neutering and Self-domestication

A recent example of a somewhat "neutered" and "domesticated singer" is Clay Aiken, the 2003 *American Idol* runner-up. Aiken specialized in chaste middle-of-the road love songs and never mentioned a relationship or lover during his initial fame. Visually and verbally, he framed himself as a bland schoolteacher, and even when he received a makeover, he was dressed in bland, sexually neutral clothing. As I noted in a previous analysis of Aiken, his February 2003 *American Idol* audition photo "features him wearing a white striped shirt and baggy jeans. Though he wears a sleek suit and make-up, and sports more sculpted hair in his May 2003 finale photos, his image has never been overtly sexual" (Stephens 2015, 148). Blandness *was* his image. He evoked the asexual ideal son/gentleman type seen in Liberace and Mathis for a contemporary audience.

In an astute review of his 2003 debut album *Measure of a Man*, music critic David Browne noted: "As listeners are told several times on his painstakingly assembled debut, *American Idol* runner-up Clay Aiken is an ordinary guy, a nobody." Some of the examples he cites include "his earnest, emotive voice," an "antiseptic" production style where "the tunes add up to an aisle of greeting cards, each set unerringly to glistening pianos, swelling choruses, and every other Lite FM cliché," and the fact that "he and his handlers also avoid anything remotely audacious or saucy." Unlike other singers in his age range, such as Christina Aguilera and Justin Timberlake, there are "no racy photo shoots or hints of hip-hop for him." For Browne, "Aiken likes being average, going with the flow. The product of an increasingly homogenized culture, he's our first focus-group pop star" (Browne 2003).

Though many people presumed or insinuated Aiken was gay, the review was published in 2003, five years before Aiken came out as gay in *People* (Caplan 2008, 72–78). What was "queer" about Aiken was the intentional effort to downplay any trace of personality or discernible sexuality, which Browne subtly critiques. As a then-"closeted" singer, it probably felt easier for Aiken to market himself as average, ordinary, and edgeless to assure that he did not offend anyone with his potentially troublesome sexuality. In actuality, his gentle masculinity and virtual sexuality were the root of his appeal. Aiken's debut was a multiplatinum seller, as was his follow-up holiday album. As adult contemporary music declined in popularity, Aiken was able to translate his undefined image into other media, including performing on Broadway in *Spamalot* and recording crooner pop (Stephens 2015, 152–53).

* * *

New queering tools that have emerged since the 1950s reflect changing social norms. For example, corporations became increasingly aware of gays and lesbians as consumers in the late 1970s, especially gay white men (Chasin 2002, 29–56). This awareness inspired targeted promotion through LGBT media, as well as what Alexandra Chasin refers to as "gay window" or "gay vague" ads "in which the use of in-group language, gesture, and symbol, and the ambiguity of same-sex social groupings or pictures of individuals, are codes for gay or lesbian identity or activity" (140).

This heightened level of consumer awareness also informs pop-music marketing. Stan Hawkins refers to heterosexually identified Justin Timberlake as a "straight-queer pop idol" (Hawkins 2007, 197). He describes his ability to court straight and queer fans via "gender travel through straight-play" that "emphasizes the restrictions of masculinity while clinging to them" (197). Hawkins emphasizes how the clever framing of Timberlake's body, and his falsetto voice, referred to as "camped-up mannerisms," "a cute boyish look," and a "highly coded voice," have made him a queer tease without relinquishing his straight-male status (198). His ability to dwell on these borders speaks to social changes, such as the increased commercialization of muscular male bodies in the 1980s and the emergence of metrosexual men (for example, British soccer player David Beckham), whom he also terms "stylistic straight-queers" (203, 207). As genres subdivide, technology evolves, and markets expand, more strategies for queering gender norms in popular music will continue to emerge.

Framing the Queer Quartet as queer historical heroes, pioneers, and/or innovators is tempting when we consider the elaborate, sophisticated, and often successful way they used the tools to secure a spot in the mainstream and evade certain forms of social scrutiny. One could also retroactively frame them as radicals whose "queering" stripped yet another layer from the oppression of social norms. But we must remember that some envy of normalcy informs even the most radical project, and this is too tidy a reading. As Matt Brim has observed, "Even as queer theory embraces and privileges radical emancipatory futural projects, it binds itself to normativity not simply because norms create the boundaries through which queerness breaks but, rather, because that rupture is never a clean break" (Brim 2014, 4). When scholars champion radicalism over pride and identity politics, we can easily overlook how ambivalence, shame, and other negative emotions inflect the artifacts and figures we study. Their stories are complicated, and our readings must be commensurate.

I appreciate the historical and theoretical projects of gay and lesbian historical recovery approaches, and the often radical aims of queer readings. However, I remain most interested in the *effect* rather than the intentions of the "inarticulate, unconscious" gestures I have outlined (Nealon 2001, 18). I also want to continue thinking about the import of the tools beyond the Quartet and the era. The tools clearly challenged masculine expectations of the immediate postwar era and have continued to shape the techniques of other musicians beyond the 1950s. An excellent example is McCracken's discussion of how the TV series *Glee* and the singing competition shows *American Idol* and *The Voice* represent a twenty-first-century "paradigmatic shift" in mainstream U.S. popular culture toward not only "*exposing*," but "*critiquing* and *disrupting*" masculinist norms in popular music. Notably, there is a greater presence of, "audience desires for long-suppressed queer voices pushing against their cultural gatekeepers" in characters featured on the series and some of the contestants who have excelled in the competitions (McCracken 2015, 321).

Equally compelling are the ways audiences responded to these elements in the art and personae of musicians. These responses suggest postwar audiences were very willing *accomplices* and demonstrates the ongoing relevance of popular culture as a fertile site for examining slippages and divergences from postwar social norms. The emergence of these figures and their tools during the postwar period, when queer people were discovering their own eligibility, also represents a space between individual and social queerness that offers great ongoing critical promise as well. In this project I focus on mainstream pop, but there were (and are) certainly queer gestures among musicians in more commercially obscure fields, such as jazz.[2] The struggle between discovering queerness as an individual and potentially coexisting in a community organized around desire might operate differently for queer female musicians of the era. For example, Laura Nyro and Dusty Springfield were women who challenged expectations of female musicians in the 1960s and who began their careers several years before Stonewall and gay liberation. Their assertive and involved approach in producing their music queered a host of gendered expectations in the music industry and led to speculation that they were queer which imbued them with reputations for being "difficult."[3] The overt blurring of gender binaries in the artistry of musicians like the cabaret duo Kiki & Herb and Anonhi (formerly known as Antony Hagerty, leader of Antony and the Johnsons) also offers spaces for critical discussion of the tools they have used to build and sustain audiences.

I hope the preceding list points toward other ways to adapt and apply the queering tools. I want to end my discussion by returning to Butler's argument that coming out is not a finite process. This is important because who we are and what we want is frequently in process. Since the postwar era, a range of queer political affiliations, identity categories, and codes have emerged. Based on the visibility and discernibility of these elements, it has become increasingly difficult to determine what elements of queer being are "commonsense" and what is obscure. Coming out has become a recognizable metaphor for disclosure, for example, but the way communities re-appropriated the slur "queer" and the increased visibility of people who identify as agender, asexual, and intersex appear to be ongoing concepts for the public to embrace. Queerness, understood as a relation between norms and margins, changes as norms change. The relational nature of the term means that queerness as a practice, and as an identity, is always a process of becoming. Examining the lives of the Quartet and those who followed them reveals this dynamism. I am compelled by James Baldwin's observation in 1961 about the value of combating the received nature of identities and the norms they enforce: "Now, in order to survive this, you have to really dig down into yourself and re-create yourself, really, according to no image which yet exists in America. You have to impose, in fact—this may sound very strange—you have to *decide* who you are, and force the world to deal with you, not with its *idea* of you" (Terkel 1989, 5–6).

Notes

Introduction

1. In Stan Hawkins and Sarah Niblock's 2011 *Prince: The Making of a Pop Music Phenomenon*, they note that "monogamy, gender fixity, adherence to religious doctrines and being defined by ethnicity . . . were being promoted heavily during the neo-conservative Reagan/Thatcher period" (97).

2. Vicki Eaklor (2001) describes gay and lesbian history as the historical interplay of relative success and failure (286) and gains and losses (288) rather than settling for the "progressive 'grand narrative' of the U.S." that has filtered into gay and lesbian history and politics (290).

3. For more information on sexuality, see Liberace, *The Wonderful, Private World of Liberace* (1986), in which he elaborated on a story first published in Karl Fleming and Anne Taylor Fleming's 1975 book, *The First Time*, that when he was sixteen years old, a blues singer "took advantage" of him on a ride home from a gig (40). Darden Asbury Pyron also discusses the incident in *Liberace: An American Boy* (2000, 70). As relayed to Liberace's former lover Scott Thorson, he lost his virginity to a man who came to watch him perform at the Wunderbar in Wisconsin circa 1939. The man was supposedly a muscular prospect for the Green Bay Packers. In addition to their intimate relationship, the man introduced Liberace to a network of other gay men throughout Wisconsin (Thorson 2013, 17, 19; Pyron 2000, 71–72). On Johnnie Ray see Jonny Whiteside's *Cry: The Johnnie Ray Story* (1994). Whiteside describes Ray and Kilgallen's affair in great detail throughout the biography (232–300, 318–27, 332–49). Little Richard was married to Ernestine Campbell for a brief period (White 1984, 105–6). On Johnny Mathis see (Petrucelli 1982, 58–60; Gavin 1993, sec. 2, 36).

4. Brittney C. Cooper's 2017 *Beyond Respectability: The Intellectual Thought of Race Women* critiques the gender politics of black respectability politics and the overlooked intellectual contributions of black female intellectuals, otherwise known as race women.

5. Even as black men achieve high levels of notoriety and success, they continue to struggle with a kind of racialized closeting. Maurice O. Wallace's *Constructing the Black Masculine* (2002) has described as "an obscured interiority defined by a particular and paralyzing discursive exteriority of equivocation" (113). It is notable that Wallace's conception of closeting is in reference to *black men* in the American public imaginary of multiple sexual orientations, not just black *queer* men. The result of this equivocation is a suppressed presentation of subjectivity that fulfills an observation in John W. Blassingame's *The Slave Community: Plantation Life in the Antebellum South* (1972) that "few [black] men are able to tell the *whole* truth about themselves. Some things are either too painful to recall or reveal to others" (228).

6. See the chapter by Keith M. Harris, "'Stand Up, Boy!': Sidney Poitier, 'Boy' and Filmic Black Masculinity" (Harris 2006, 39–62). Ian Gregory Strachan also describes the way this shifts in Poitier's career, noting how "in his post-1967 films, we see him shed the cloak of noble neuter and present himself as a man of passion and desire. A man uninterested in the moral education, recognition, or affirmation of whites; a man pursuing his own ends largely on his own terms" (Strachan 2015, 168).

7. Cary Ginell describes the negative backlash Eckstine received after he was photographed in the May 15, 1950, issue of *Life* magazine surrounded by adoring white female teenage fans (Ginell 2013, 115–17).

8. My discussion of Rock Hudson draws from Mercer 2015; Klinger 1994; Hofler 2005; Hudson and Davidson 1986; and Oppenheimer and Vitek 1986. Tab Hunter sources include Hunter and Muller 2005; and Ehrenstein 1998.

9. My discussion of Montgomery Clift draws on Cohan 1997; Girelli 2013; and Lawrence 2010. For Anthony Perkins see Winecoff 1996/2006.

10. Adrienne Rich initially explored this concept in 1980 to capture the systemic dominance of heterosexuality and sexism in gender relations. See an updated version in Rich 1993 (227–54).

11. Etymologically, "the very word 'Freak' is an abbreviation for 'freak of nature,' a translation of the Latin *lusus naturae*" (Fiedler 1978, 19). According to Michael M. Chemers, "'Freak' enters common usage in reference to a particular type of performance of human abnormality in the late eighteenth or early nineteenth century, co-emergent with the scientific classification craze" (Chemers 2008, 6). Traditionally, freak referred to "human beings with physical, mental, and behavioral anomalies" (Bogdan 2008, viii). In addition to the disabled people commonly exhibited at freak shows were non-Western people and people who feigned physical and mental abnormalities to qualify for the business. Others included novelty acts "whose talents were unusual but not the product of any condition with which they were born" (viii), with 1840 to 1940 being a period of the sideshow's greatest popularity (ix).

In terms of gender, hermaphrodites have emerged as a specific type of gendered body within freak discourse. Leslie Fiedler's *Freaks* describes how the ways certain bodies challenge binaries inform the designation of freak, noting, "To be sure, no actual Freak threatens all of these limits at once. Dwarfs and Giants, for instance, challenge primarily our sense of scale, Hermaphrodites our conviction that the world neatly divides into two sexes, and so on" (Fiedler 1978, 24). Rosemarie Garland Thomson's *Extraordinary Bodies* (1997) makes a similar observation: "Hence, the most wondrous freaks—such a conjoined twins (one person or two?) or mentally disabled Africans (human or ape?) or hermaphrodites (men or women?)—represented the knottiest scientific dilemmas" (77–78).

After "freak show" exhibitions faded in popularity after 1940, the term's meaning morphed. For example, Chemers notes how it became a post-1940 English slang term referring to "anything that appears in contrast to expectations as in a 'freak hailstorm,' a 'freak allergic reaction,' or a person whose behavior is bizarre or unconventional (as in 'an acid freak') or obsessive (as in a 'computer freak')" (Chemers 2008, 7). During the late 1970s and early 1980s the term was recast with "an undoubtedly positive and erotic spin: 'Le Freak, C'est Chic' (sung by Chic on their 1978 album *C'est Chic*) and 'Superfreak' (on Rick James's 1981 *Street Songs*) are but two examples, and this tradition persists" into the twenty-first century (7).

Chapter 1. Visibly Hidden

1. Lesbian pulp novels were usually original works that peaked commercially from the mid-1940s to the mid-1960s (Stryker 2001, 12). Comparatively, "gay-male themed paperbacks were generally made up of reprints of previously published novels from established, respected houses" and included a number of mainstream novels, such as Gore Vidal's *The City and the Pillar*, that "were quickly issued in inexpensive paperback editions that sported predictable pulp images and cover copy" (Bronski 2011, 4). Though many "legitimate" novels with gay male themes were reprinted as pulps, "it is reasonable to assume no gay male titles sold the tremendous quantities attained by the most successful of the lesbian pulps." In terms of sales, "there was no burgeoning market for gay male novels in the 1950s because they apparently had little crossover appeal for a substantial heterosexual readership. The titillating nature of lesbian sexuality seemed to outweigh any potential threat it might present to the social order" (4).

A sample of critical discussions regarding the narrative patterns and reception of lesbian pulps and gay male pulps includes the following: Stryker 2001; Bergman 1999, 26–41; McGarry and Wasserman 1998, 112–14; Nealon 2001, 141–75; and Bronski 2003.

2. Gay and lesbian histories frequently reference the following articles that address homosexual motifs in theater: Kauffmann 1966a and 1966b; Taubman 1961 and 1963. In a 2007 letter to the *New York Times*, Kauffmann responds to Thomas Mallon's review of Michael Sherry's *Gay Artists in Modern American Culture* (2007) by correcting Mallon's interpretation of his writings on homosexuality and theater: "[P]lease permit me to point out two matters regarding my own articles. (There were two such articles, on Jan. 23 and Feb. 6, 1966, both available in my collection "Persons of the Drama.") First, the phrase 'insidious influence' or any comparable phrase does not appear in my articles. Second, my intent was precisely the reverse of the one given above. I at-

tacked a society that prevented gay playwrights from treating their lives frankly and then complained about disguises in gay writers' plays." See Kauffmann 2007.

3. For example, "Is There Hope for Homosexuals?" was a cover headline on the August 7, 1952, issue of *Jet* magazine. Some samples stories I reviewed for content include the following: "Can Science Eliminate the Third Sex?" *Jet*, January 22, 1953, 46–50; "Women Who Pass for Men," *Jet*, January 28, 1954, 22–24; "Are Homosexuals Becoming Respectable?" *Jet*, April 15, 1954, 26–28.

4. Capote (1924–1984), who was diminutive and effete, confided to biographer John Brinnin that at age fifteen he decided "to be so obviously who I am and what I am that anyone who so much as asked the question would look like a fool" (Brinnin 1986, 6). What was obvious is that he was an effeminate homosexual, and he embraced his queer sexuality as part of his essence, not something hidden or incidental. As Tison Pugh notes in *Truman Capote: A Literary Life at the Movies* (2014), "Capote's celebrity persona as an author and socialite allowed him relative candor concerning his homosexuality, whereas the homophobia of Hollywood stardom prohibited [Montgomery] Clift from enjoying such freedoms" (27). Pugh also addresses how the critical establishment often used homophobic rhetoric to attack Capote's work early in his career. However, Capote got the last laugh, translating his queerness into an entertaining persona he performed regularly on television shows and in film roles (6, 31–42).

Poet Allen Ginsberg (1926–1997) also performed queerness quite publicly in his personae and his writing. It has always been unclear what exactly inspired the controversial epic poem *Howl and Other Poems* (1956), but queerness was a definite theme. As Jonah Raskin's *American Scream* points out, Ginsberg continually added to "the mythology of the poem" throughout his career, claiming it was about self-deception, art, his mother, the military-industrial complex, among others (Raskin 2004, xix–xx). In 1974 he claimed it was a "coming out of the closet" as well as "an acknowledgement of the basic reality of homosexual joy" (313). Regardless of *Howl*'s origins, its role in making Ginsberg an influential artist and a notable public figure is indisputable. When Ginsberg arrived at Columbia University in 1943, he was a virgin who had wrestled with homosexuality personally. His access to other queer men in the private college setting and the burgeoning queer life of Greenwich Village helped him explore homosexuality in adulthood with a variety of partners, including poets such as Lucien Carr and Neal Cassady. He also explored sex with women unsuccessfully (57, 105). Ginsberg struggled with mental health issues, seeing a psychoanalyst in the mid-1940s, and was hesitant about following the path of Walt Whitman, "putting himself out as a 'queer' in print and in the flesh" (110).

Ginsberg gradually summoned the courage to explore "anal sex, oral sex, and what middle-class Americans in 1955 would sure have called promiscuous sex" in *Howl*, and its reception helped revolutionize American poetry by "making it more personal, more confessional, and more akin to the performing arts" (Raskin 2004, xx). After Ginsberg premiered *Howl* at 3119 Filmore Street in San Francisco as part of the pivotal "6 Poets at 6 Gallery" reading, which also featured Lawrence Ferlinghetti,

Philip Lamantia, Michael McClure, Gary Snyder, Philip Whalen and launched the Beats as a poetic movement (16), he gained enough momentum for it to be published and widely distributed. In 1957 San Francisco's Police Department seized the book on an obscenity charge against publisher Ferlinghetti that was ultimately dismissed in 1957 (222–23). The attention *Howl* garnered made Ginsberg one of the most public openly queer people; and a closet door, which was barely closed, flew off the hinges. Alongside sexuality, Ginsberg employed his voice for the remainder of his life espousing progressive political perspectives (see Brinnin 1986; and Raskin 2004).

Chapter 2. A Freak Deferred

1. Greek American bandleader Johnny Otis (born John Veliotes [1921–2012]) was a pioneer in the development of R&B music who led the Rhythm and Blues Caravan from 1950–1954. Otis was a champion of black artists and discovered "Little" Esther Phillips, Mel Walker, and The Coasters, among other acts. He was also active in the civil rights movement in the 1960s (George-Warren and Romanowski 2001, 78). See also his autobiography, *Listen to the Lambs* (Otis 1968/2009).

2. I declined to discuss Jimmy Scott at greater length because my study focuses on commercially mainstream performers to illustrate the pervasive nature of queering in pop culture, and Scott was mostly a cult singer who had only one commercial hit during his career. His career is fascinating, and the following resources illuminate his story further: Ritz 2002; Keepnews 2014; PBS 2004 (compact disc).

3. Jonny Whiteside describes Johnnie Ray and Dorothy Kilgallen's affair throughout *Cry* (Whiteside 1994, 232–300, 318–27, 332–49).

4. In addition to the two *Confidential* stories and the *Lowdown* story, seven tabloid stories targeted Johnnie Ray from December 1955 to September 1957: see Mason 1955, 48; On the Q.T. 1956, 36; Coates 1956, 42; Tip Off 1956, 12; Header 1957, 28; Hunter 1957, 10; and Inside 1957, 18 (referenced in Whiteside 1994, 264).

5. Ray has not been forgotten entirely. From a historical perspective, contemporary vocalists like Ian Dury, a polio survivor who grew up listening to and adoring Ray, and (non-deaf) British singer Morrissey, who periodically wore a hearing aid as an homage to Ray in the 1980s, have cited Ray as an influence (McKay 2013, 137). His name also surfaces in song lyrics occasionally (for example, "Come On, Eileen" 1982), and some have suggested him as an early progenitor of "emo-ness" (McKay 2013, 135), alluding to the "emo" genre that includes singers like 1960s pop vocalist Scott Walker and bands like Jimmy Eats World, Dashboard Confessional, and My Chemical Romance.

Chapter 3. Spectacular Vacillations

1. In 1951 Penniman met pianist and vocalist Esquerita, who was also a flamboyant, stylish queer black man. Esquerita (born Eskew Reeder Jr.) is a cult figure who later recorded rock 'n' roll and R&B sides for Capitol Records from 1958 to 1959 and

multiple labels during the 1960s (White 1984, 29; Simels 86; Esquerita 1958, album). He helped Little Richard develop his piano technique further. Regarding Esquerita, David Kirby suggests there were multiple lessons Little Richard learned from Esquerita beyond his claims. He notes: "As a gay, black, flamboyant, gospel-trained and immensely talented singer, songwriter and pianist, Esquerita is the template on which the Architect of rock 'n' roll drew his own image. And as an itinerate shape-shifter who changed his name when he had to and flirted with greatness but also crime, poverty and catastrophic disease Esquerita is the gold standard of what Greil Marcus calls the Old, Weird America" and that "Esquerita provided Little Richard with more than eye-popping visual imagery. The earliest Little Richard recordings show none of the flair that would make him famous, and even his first New Orleans session for Specialty Records has a generic r 'n' b sound to it—up to a point" (Kirby 2009, 41, 42). On the life and career of Billy Wright see Houndblog (2009) and KingCake (2013).

2. The chitlin' circuit was a network of theaters and clubs throughout the United States that served black audiences and operated as training grounds for up-and-coming black performers during the Jim Crow era and well into the late 1960s. Alumni include Louis Armstrong, Gladys Knight and the Pips, and the Jackson 5. Though northern venues like the Regal in Chicago and the Apollo Theatre in New York are among the best-known chitlin'-circuit venues, there were also major venues in the South attracting promising acts (Marsh 1985, 33–34; Knopper 2015, 24).

Chapter 4. Fine and Dandy

1. I address Nelson George's discussion of Michael Jackson's and Prince's black masculinity in *The Death of Rhythm and Blues* (1988, 174) in more detail in the conclusion of this book. Critic Dave Marsh discusses the controversies surrounding Jackson's sexuality and a bizarre September 5, 1984, Los Angeles press conference where Jackson's manager read a press release stating Jackson's intention to marry and have a family in response to press comments regarding his effeminate appearance and sexual speculation in *Trapped: Michael Jackson and the Crossover Dream* (Marsh 1985, 106–17). Craig Seymour's biography on Vandross, *Luther: The Life and Longing of Luther Vandross* (2004), features several passages, noting AIDS-related and gay rumors, as well as Vandross's unwillingness to verbalize his sexual orientation (195–200, 279–83).

2. For example, a 1961 *Variety* magazine concert review detected his plaintive, multisexual appeal when it noted, "He is a singer with a gimmick. He just sings." The author continued by framing him as "a romantic with a style which gets to the females and doesn't antagonize the males" (66). Mathis has also commented on his intentional emphasis on the purity of music over overt performative stylization. As he notes in the liner notes booklet of *The Music of Johnny Mathis*, "I was always adamant about the fact that I was not an entertainer, I was a singer" and admired the way singers like Cole, Eckstine, and Vaughan "would always stand there; nothing would get in the way of the music" (Mathis 1993, 37).

3. Michelle Ann Stephens argues that the film *Island in the Sun* (Hayes 1957) employs national anxieties about Caribbean independence to thwart the budding romance between the characters. She notes, "David's renunciation of Mavis serves a nationalist politics that extends across the Caribbean archipelago, the film thereby providing, in his voice, a new ideological rationale against miscegenation more suited to decolonizing times" (Stephens 2014, 139). The film attempts to proffer mere individual character differences ("her racism, his will to power") as the reason they never explore romance. Stephens challenges this, arguing that "a social taboo against miscegenation that still stands as the overarching logic of the film" is the barrier (139).

4. Writer Michael Henry Adams was a friend of Short's and claimed the singer once commented, "I have a living to make! I can't afford to march in the Gay-Pride Parade" (Adams 2011).

Chapter 5. Building an Empire of Illusion

1. The character's name is Bob Street, a dancer-choreographer who introduced Thorson to Liberace in 1976 (Pyron 2000, 332–33).

2. Liberace was commercially popular during the pre-rock era, when instrumental pop music, including big band music, film scores, pop orchestral music, and classical concertos were commercially mainstream. His 1952 rendition of "September Song" reached #27 on the pop singles chart (Whitburn 1973b, 33). Five of his LPs were commercial hits from 1952 to 1954, including: *Liberace at the Piano* (1952), #1; *Liberace By Candlelight* (1953), #6; *Concertos for You* (1954), #7; *An Evening with Liberace* (1954), #10; and *Sincerely, Liberace* (1954), #11 (Whitburn 1973a, 86). See Whitburn 1973a and 1973b.

3. Liberace was a solitary child perceived as effeminate. Liberace's sister has recalled, "The kids would pass by and hear him practicing. They'd yell all kinds of names at him. They called him a sissy because he preferred the piano to baseball and football" (Pyron 2000, 24). In his autobiography Liberace notes his mix of "masculine" and "feminine" hobbies: "While the boys I played with made model cars and model airplanes, I liked to make things out of fabrics I found lying around" (Liberace 1973, 59). Van den Oever (2012) provides a thorough analysis of the history and evolution of postwar hysteria over "momism."

4. "At the keyboard, Liberace is an artist of pure schmaltz" and "there are plenty of arpeggios and other musical furbelows to spotlight his skill. His audience digs him the most when he plays the fastest, and Liberace does everything to please" (Variety 1953, 52). The reviewer describes his technique as comprising "good fingers and prodigious skill at faking 'brilliant' runs up and down the keyboard. He has two styles of playing—fast, loud and energetic: and slow, with sentimentally exaggerated retards and accelerandos. It is a type of piano playing that is frequently heard in cocktail lounges, and is very pleasant to go with cocktails" (15). Howard Taubman notes the "slackness of rhythms, wrong tempos, distorted phrasing, an excess of prettification

and sentimentality, a failure to stick to what the composer has written" (Taubman 1954b, SM44). Another disparages his playing for using "all the available tricks, as loud as possible, as soft as possible, and as sentimental as possible," referring to the act as "almost all showmanship topped by whipped cream and cherries" (Funke 1957, 29).

5. Regarding his 1952 TV persona, one reviewer noted he was "on the schmaltzy side" and "a little too saccharine," (Faris 1995, 110). Regarding his syndicated show, another warned it "may be too cloying for some tastes" (111). Another suggested, "Alas, it is then that Liberace speaks and smiles and all the painstaking pursuit of mood tends to go slightly awry." (Gould 1953, 15). Taubman went further by noting the gap between "the square" critic who can readily point out the pianist's serious technical flaws and "the people who claim that Liberace has discovered great, new audiences and that its exposure to what he is doing will prepare them for the next step up the ladder of musical cultivation." Notably, he questions Liberace's role as a bridge between pop and classical music and suggests, "Sound tastes grow best out of the finest standards. Tastes based on denatured music end in debasement of an art" (Taubman 1954a). Finally, he places Liberace's success in the context of mid-1950s mass culture: "He is a product of the superficiality, sentimentality, and uneasy nostalgia of our times. . . . Let the long-hairs rave; they're squares, all of them."

6. Regarding Carnegie Hall, *Variety* noted, "Liberace is undoubtedly a new kind of matinee idol for middle-aged bobbysoxers. He's an attractive looker with grey-streaked hair and seems to have an uncomplicated, amiable personality. He smiles as if he means it through his whole performance and gives out with those intimate comments and touches for immediate audience rapport" (Variety 1953, 52). A reviewer of Madison Square Garden referred to "music, which again was that unique admixture of class and the corn the whole Liberace phenomenon represents" (Plotnik 1954, 10). Lewis Funke described Liberace's act as "a double dose of saccharine and honey," mocked him for "the air of being oh so grateful for the privilege of entertaining those wonderful people, indeed the overflowing attitude for just being alive," and concluded that "everything is subject to the showmanship, every effect is calculated" (Funke 1957, 29).

7. Faris quotes excerpts from "Liberace and His Women," *Sensation*, August 1954, 58–62; and John Cullen, "Mama's Boy in Curls," *On the Q.T.*, September 1956, 33–35, 54–56. Faris also quotes from the following: "Are Liberace's Romances for Real?" *Private Lives*, March 1955, 24–28; "Liberace: Don't Call Him Mister," *Rave*, August 1954, 4–13; "The Exclusive on Liberace and Christine," *Exclusive*, July 1956, 28–29; Jay Collins, "Is Liberace a Man?" *Hush-Hush*, May 1957, 8–10, 42, 43; and Michael Davis, "Why is Liberace on the Pan?" *Suppressed*, January 1955, 7–9, 55, 56.

8. See "The Girl I'll Marry," *TV Star Parade*, February 1954, 46, 47, 68, 69; "Mirror, Mirror, on the Wall," *Movie Play*, May 1955, 43; and Parker 1955, 40–42, 72, 73.

9. *Confidential*'s July 1957 article, "Why Liberace's Theme Song Should Be . . . 'Mad about the Boy,'" accused Liberace of predatory homosexual behavior, claiming he attempted, "to make beautiful music with a handsome but highly reluctant young publicity man" during concert stops in Akron, Ohio, Los Angeles, and Dallas, Texas"

(Streete 1957, 16–21, 59, 60). Liberace sued in response to *Confidential*'s article in 1957 and won $40,000 because he proved he was not in Dallas during the incident, not because he disproved the supposed encounter (Faris 1995, 249; Ehrenstein 1998, 100). The case received limited publicity (Liberace was not present for the hearing) and had no discernible impact on his career, compared with the 1959 lawsuit.

10. The article's text is reproduced numerous places, including Liberace 1973, 195–96; and Pyron 2000, 225–26.

11. Liberace said to the defense's lawyer Gardiner, "I have never considered myself a sex-appeal artist" (Pyron 2000, 203) He also said, "I consider sex appeal as something possessed by Marilyn Monroe or Brigitte Bardot. I certainly do not put myself in their class!" (205).

12. Reebee Garofalo's *Rockin' Out: Popular Music in the USA* (2005) discusses these genres in detail, including teen idols (132–40), surf pop (145–49), girl groups (153–58), and Motown (158–62).

13. Faris's "Personal Appearances" chapter in her 1995 *Liberace: A Bio-Bibliography* is a mostly comprehensive listing of Liberace's concerts from 1951 to 1987. For his 1960s concerts, see 67–76, and for his 1970s concerts, see 76–80.

14. *Liberace Interiors and Objets d'Art* (Thomas 1987, 174–75); *Liberace Cooks!* (1970) (Pyron 2000, 364–65); *Liberace: An Autobiography* (1973, 367–68); Liberace Foundation and Museum (363–64); *Leapin' Lizards, It's Liberace!* (1973) (Thomas 1987, 202); Discussions of Liberace's 1984–1986 Radio City Music Hall engagements can be found in Pyron 2000 (380–87) and Thomas 1987 (239–45).

Conclusion

1. Peraino links Jackson and Prince to black gay disco vocalist Sylvester, famous for his falsetto, who she argues "foreshadowed an increase in the number of effeminate men (some of whom were African-American) in dance and pop music of the 1980s." Among those she mentions are "top-selling straight-acting stars in this camp, such as Michael Jackson and especially Prince, whose early albums feature his Sylvester-like falsetto and who used disco's sexual glamour to push the boundaries of pop from soulful crooning to orgasmic cries" (Peraino 2005, 193).

2. Major jazz magazines have published several articles on gender and sexuality in jazz. See, for example, Gavin 2001 and Murph 2010. David Hajdu discusses gay composer, pianist, and arranger Billy Strayhorn's navigations of the gender and sexual climate of his era in *Lush Life: A Biography of Billy Strayhorn* (1996). Contemporary musicians vibraphonist Gary Burton and pianist Fred Hersch discuss gender norms in jazz and their experiences as gay men in their respective autobiographies (see Burton 2013 and Hersch 2017). Other queer-identified contemporary jazz musicians include Patricia Barber, Andy Bey, Theo Bleckmann, Terri Lynne Carrington, Dena De Rose, Dave Koz, Allison Miller, and Ian Shaw.

3. Two biographies discuss these issues in depth, including Kort 2002 and Valentine and Wickham 2001.

References

ABC. 1970. "Little Richard—The Dick Cavett Show 1970: Lucille-Lawdy Miss Clawdy." https://www.youtube.com/watch?v=WPAnpvISiu4.

Adams, Michael Henry. 2011. "Queers in the Mirror: A Brief History of Old-Fashioned Gay Marriage in New York, Part II." *Huffington Post*, May 25, 2011. http://www.huff ingtonpost.com/michael-henry-adams/queers-in-the-mirror-a-br_b_227473.html.

Ali, Abdul. "In Nineteen Eighty-Four." In *Trouble Sleeping*, 35–36. Kalamazoo, Mich.: New Issues.

Auslander, Philip. 2006. *Performing Glam Rock: Gender and Theatricality in Popular Music*. Ann Arbor: University of Michigan Press.

Baldwin, James. 1985. "Here Be Dragons." In *The Price of the Ticket: Collected Nonfiction 1948–1985*, 677–90. New York: St. Martin's.

Bart, Peter. 1966. "Liberace: 'So There I Am at My Piano in the Louvre. . . .'" *New York Times*, February 13, 1966.

Belafonte, Harry. With Michael Shnayerson. 2011. *My Song: A Memoir of Art, Race, and Defiance*. New York: Knopf.

Bentley, Gladys. 1952. "I Am a Woman Again." *Ebony*, August 1952, 92–98.

Bergman, David. 1993. "Introduction." In *Camp Grounds: Style and Homosexuality*, 3–10. Amherst: University of Massachusetts Press.

———. 1999. "The Cultural Work of Sixties Gay Pulp Fiction." In *The Queer Sixties*, edited by Patricia Juliana-Smith, 26–41. New York: Routledge.

Bérubé, Allan. 1990. *Coming Out under Fire: The History of Gay Men and Women in World War Two*. New York: Free Press.

Billboard. 1951. "The Ray Story: $90 to $1,750." *Billboard*, October 6, 1951, 1, 45.

Bogdan, Robert. 2008. *Freak Show: Presenting Human Oddities for Amusement and Profit*. Chicago: University of Chicago Press.

Bogle, Donald. 1997. *Toms, Coons, Mulattoes, Mammies and Bucks: An Interpretive History of Blacks in American Films*. New York: Continuum.

Bradby, Barbara. 1995. "Lesbians and Popular Music: Does It Matter Who Is Singing?" In *Popular Music: Style and Identity*, edited by Will Straw, Stacey Johnson, Rebecca Sullivan, and Paul Friedlander, with Gary Kennedy, 33–44. Montreal: Centre for Research on Canadian Cultural Industries and Institutions.

Breines, Wini. 1992. *Young, White, and Miserable: Growing Up Female in the Fifties*. Boston: Beacon.

Brett, Phillip. 1994. "Musicality, Essentialism, and the Closet." In *Queering the Pitch: The New Gay and Lesbian Musicology*, edited by Philip Brett, Elizabeth Wood, and Gary C. Thomas, 9–26. New York: Routledge.

Brim, Matt. 2014. *James Baldwin and the Queer Imagination*. Ann Arbor: University of Michigan Press.

Brinnin, John. 1986. *Truman Capote: Dear Heart, Old Buddy*. New York: Delacorte.

Bronski, Michael, ed. 2003. *Pulp Friction: Uncovering the Golden Age of Gay Male Pulps*. New York: St. Martin's.

———. 2011. *A Queer History of the United States*. Boston: Beacon.

Browne, David. 2003. Review of *Measure of a Man*, by Clay Aiken. *Entertainment Weekly*, October 24. http://ew.com/article/2003/10/24/measure-man.

Burton, Gary. 2013. *Learning to Listen: The Jazz Journey of Gary Burton; An Autobiography*. Boston: Berklee.

Butler, Judith. 1993. "Imitation and Gender Insubordination." In *The Lesbian and Gay Studies Reader*, edited by Henry Abelove, Michèle Aina Barale, and David M. Halperin, 307–20. New York: Routledge.

Buzzell, Matthew. 2004. *Jimmy Scott: If Only You Knew*. DVD. Directed by Matthew Buzzell. San Francisco: Rhino.

Canby, Vincent. 1973. "Screen: Music of the '50s: Let the Good Times Roll Is Rock Revival." *New York Times*, May 26, 1973.

Caplan, David. 2008. "No More Secrets." *People*, October 6, 2008, 72–78.

Carby, Hazel. 1998. *Race Men*. Cambridge, Mass.: Harvard University Press.

CBS Sunday Morning. 2017a. "Web Extra: Johnny Mathis on Coming Out." https://www.youtube.com/watch?v=IEavdhe__k8.

CBS Sunday Morning. 2017b. "The Legendary Johnny Mathis." Interview with Nancy Giles. https://www.youtube.com/watch?v=8MLhOyUuNf8.

Chasin, Alexandra. 2002. *Selling Out: The Gay and Lesbian Movement Goes to Market*. New York: St. Martin's.

Chauncey, George. 1994. *Gay New York: Gender, Urban Culture, and the Making of the Gay Male World 1890–1940*. New York: Basic.

Chemers, Michael M. 2008. *Staging Stigma: A Critical Examination of the American Freak Show*. New York: Palgrave Macmillan.

Christgau, Robert. 1998. *Grown Up All Wrong: 75 Great Rock and Pop Artists from Vaudeville to Techno*. Cambridge, Mass.: Harvard University Press.

Coates, Paul. 1956. "Why Johnnie Ray Has to Get Half Stiff Every Night." *Anything Goes*, May 1956, 42.

Cohan, Steven. 1997. *Masked Men: Masculinity and the Movies in the Fifties*. Bloomington: Indiana University Press.

Cole, Nat King. 1953. "Are Second Marriages Better?" *Ebony*, March 1953, 82–87.

———. 1958a. "Why I Quit My TV Show." *Ebony*, February 1958, 29–34.

———. 1958b. "St. Louis Blues." *Ebony*, May 1958, 27–32.

Collins, Jay. 1957. "Is Liberace a Man?" *Hush-Hush*, May 1957, 8–10, 42, 43.

Conerly, Gregory. 2001. "Swishing and Swaggering: Homosexuality in Black Magazines during the 1950s." In *The Greatest Taboo: Homosexuality in Black Communities*, edited by Delroy Constantine-Simms, 384–94. Los Angeles: Alyson.

Coontz, Stephanie. 2000. *The Way We Never Were: American Families and the Nostalgia Trap*. New York: Basic.

Cooper, Brittney C. 2017. *Beyond Respectability: The Intellectual Thought of Race Women*. Urbana: University of Illinois Press.

Corber, Robert J., and Stephen Valocchi. 2003. "Introduction." In *Queer Studies: An Interdisciplinary Reader*, edited by Robert J. Corber and Stephen Valocchi, 1–17. Malden, Mass.: Blackwell.

Craig, Maxine. 1997. "The Decline and Fall of the Conk; or, How to Read a Process." *Fashion Theory* 1 (4): 399–420.

Crosley, Hillary. 2013. "Is There Room for a Race Man Today." *Root*, August 19, 2013. http://www.theroot.com/is-there-room-for-a-race-man-today-1790897782.

Cullen, John. 1956. "Mama's Boy in Curls." *On the Q.T.*, September 1956, 33–35, 54–56.

Cummings, Tony. 1975. "Roots, Forerunners, and Originators." In *The Soul Book*, edited by Ian Hoare, 1–31. London: Methuen.

Davis, Michael. 1955. "Why Is Liberace on the Pan?" *Suppressed*, January 1955, 7–9, 55, 56.

D'Emilio, John. 1998. *Sexual Politics, Sexual Communities: The Making of a Homosexual Minority in the United States 1940–1970*. Chicago: University of Chicago Press.

D'Emilio, John, and Estelle B. Freedman. 1988. *Intimate Matters: A History of Sexuality in America*. New York: Harper and Row.

Del Mar, David Peterson. 2011. *The American Family: From Obligation to Freedom*. New York: Palgrave Macmillan.

Desjardins, Mary. 2001. "Systematizing Scandal: Confidential Magazine, Stardom, and the State of California." In *Headline Hollywood: A Century of Film Scandal*, edited by Adrienne L. McLean and David Cook, 206–31. New Brunswick, N.J.: Rutgers University Press.

Devega, Chauncey. 2016. "Prince Was the Weirdo We Needed: On Race, Masculinity and the Indelible Legacy of a Musical Icon." *Salon.com*, April 22, 2016. http://www.salon.com/2016/04/22/prince_was_the_weirdo_we_needed_on_race_masculinity_the_indelible_legacy_of_a_musical_icon.

Doty, Robert C. 1962. "Growth of Overt Homosexuality in City Provokes Wide Concern." *New York Times*, December 17, 1962.

Dove, Ian. 1973. "Little Richard et al. Give Garden Fans More 1950's Rock." *New York Times*, March 4, 1973.

———. 1975. "Royalty in Court for Week of Rock." *New York Times*, October 20, 1975.

Drewal, Margaret Thompson. 1994. "The Camp Trace in Corporate America: Liberace and the Rockettes at Radio City Music Hall." In *The Politics and Poetics of Camp*, edited by Moe Meyer, 149–81. London: Routledge.

Dudley, Francis. 1955. "Knock, Knock! Who's There? . . . Why Did Johnny Ray Try to Break Down Paul Douglas' Door?" *Confidential*, November 22–23, 1955, 46.

Eaklor, Vicki. 2001. "Where Are We Now, Where Are We Going, and Who Gets to Say?" In *Modern American Queer History*, edited by Allida M. Black, 285–99. Philadelphia: Temple University Press.

Early, Gerald. 2003. *This Is Where I Came In: Black America in the 1960s*. Lincoln: University of Nebraska Press.

Ebony. 1957. "Boy with the Golden Voice: Young Johnny Mathis Sings Way to $100,000-a-year Success." *Ebony*, December 1957, 28, 30, 32.

Eckstine, Billy. 1952a. "Celebrities Flock to Eckstine Party." *Ebony*, March 1952, 27–31.

———. 1952b. "Mr. B. Finds His Dreamhouse." *Ebony*, October 1952, 15–22.

Ehrenreich, Barbara. 1983. *The Hearts of Men: American Dreams and the Flight From Commitment*. New York: Anchor.

Ehrenstein, David. 1998. *Open Secret: Gay Hollywood 1928–1998*. New York: Morrow.

Elgrably, Jordan, and George Plimpton. 1989. "The Art of Fiction LXXVIII." In *Conversations with James Baldwin*, edited by Fred L. Standley and Louis H. Pratt, 232–54. Jackson: University Press of Mississippi.

Ephron, Phoebe, and Henry Ephron. 1954. *There's No Business Like Show Business*. DVD. Directed by Walter Lang. 2002. Los Angeles: 20th Century Fox.

Epstein, Daniel Mark. 1999. *Nat King Cole*. Boston: Northeastern University Press.

Erlewine, Stephen Thomas. 2017. "Little Richard Sings the Gospel." *Allmusic.com*. All Music Guide. http://www.allmusic.com/album/little-richard-sings-the-gospel-mw0000587770.

Evans, Sara. 2001. "Sources of the Second Wave: The Rebirth of Feminism." In *Long Time Gone: Sixties America Then and Now*, edited by Alexander Bloom, 189–208. New York: Oxford University Press.

Exclusive. 1956. "The Exclusive on Liberace and Christine." *Exclusive*, July 1956, 28–29.

Faderman, Lilian. 1991. *Odd Girls and Twilight Lovers: A History of Lesbian Life in Twentieth-Century America*. New York: Penguin.

Faris, Jocelyn. 1995. *Liberace: A Bio-Bibliography*. Westport, Conn.: Greenwood, 1995.

Fast, Susan. 2012. "Michael Jackson's Queer Musical Belongings." *Popular Music and Society* 35 (2): 281–300.

Feldman, Jessica R. 1993. *Gender on the Divide: The Dandy in Modernist Literature*. Ithaca, N.Y.: Cornell University Press.

Fiedler, Leslie. 1978. *Freaks: Myths and Images of the Secret Self*. New York: Simon and Schuster.

Field, Douglas. 2011. *James Baldwin*. Devon, U.K.: Northcote.

———. 2015. *All Those Strangers: The Art and Lives of James Baldwin*. New York: Oxford University Press.

Fleming, Karl, and Anne Taylor Fleming. 1975. *The First Time*. New York: Simon and Schuster.

Floyd, Samuel A., Jr. 1995. *The Power of Black Music: Interpreting its History from Africa to the United States*. New York: Oxford University Press.

Foner, Eric. 1998. *The Story of American Freedom*. New York: Norton.

FOX. 1986. "Little Richard Great Gosh A' mighty." *The Late Show Starring Joan Rivers*. https://www.youtube.com/watch?v=OkLhRNff5YM).

———. 2000. "Emotional Little Richard Interview on the Donnie and Marie Osmond Show." Posted by DavEvans066, https://www.youtube.com/watch?v=PgjCSY41L7Y.

François, Anne-Lise. 1995. "Fakin' It/Makin' It: Falsetto's Bid for Transcendence in 1970s Disco Highs." *Perspectives of New Music* 33 (1/2): 442–57.

Frazier, E. Franklin. 1965. *The Black Bourgeoisie: The Rise of a New Middle Class*. New York: Free Press/Macmillan.

Friedwald, Will. 2010. *A Biographical Guide to the Great Jazz and Pop Singers*. New York: Pantheon.

Frith, Simon. 1996. *Performing Rites: On the Value of Popular Music*. Cambridge, Mass.: Harvard University Press.

Funke, Lewis. 1957. "The Theatre: Liberace: Smiling Pianist Heads Bill at the Palace." *New York Times*, April 22, 1957.

Gaines, Kevin K. 1996. "Introduction." In *Uplifting the Race: Black Leadership, Politics, and Culture in the Twentieth Century*, 1–17. Chapel Hill: University of North Carolina Press.

Garber, Marjorie. 1992. *Vested Interests: Cross-dressing and Cultural Anxiety*. New York: Routledge.

Garelick, Rhonda K. 1998. *Rising Star: Dandyism, Gender, and Performance in the Fin de Siècle*. Princeton, N.J.: Princeton University Press.

Garofalo, Reebee. 2005. *Rockin' Out: Popular Music in the USA*. 3rd ed. Upper Saddle River, N.J.: Pearson/Prentice Hall.

Gavin, James. 1993. "A Timeless Reminder of Back Seats in '57 Buicks." *New York Times*, December 19, 1993.

———. 2001. "Homophobia in Jazz." *Jazztimes.com*, December 1, 2001. https://jazztimes.com/features/homophobia-in-jazz.

George, Nelson. 1988. *The Death of Rhythm and Blues*. New York: Plume.

George-Warren, Holly, and Patricia Romanowski. 2001. "Johnny Otis." In *The Rolling Stone Encyclopedia of Rock and Roll*, edited by Holly George-Warren and Patricia Romanowski, 78. 5th ed. New York: Fireside.

Gill, Andy. 2004. "Ten Questions for Little Richard." In *Rip It Up: The Black Experience in Rock 'n' Roll*, edited by Kandia Crazy Horse, 1–4. New York: Palgrave Macmillan.

Gill, John. 1995. *Queer Noises: Male and Female Homosexuality in Twentieth Century Music*. Minneapolis: University of Minnesota Press.

Gillett, Charlie. 1996. *The Sound of the City: The Rise of Rock and Roll*. 2nd ed. New York: Da Capo.

Ginell, Cary. 2013. *Mr. B: The Music and Life of Billy Eckstine*. Milwaukee: Leonard.

Girelli, Elisabetta. 2013. *Montgomery Clift, Queer Star*. Detroit: Wayne State University Press.

Goodman, Ezra. 1961. *The Fifty-Year Decline and Fall of Hollywood.* New York: Simon and Schuster.

Gordon, Robert, Tom Graves, and Morgan Neville. 2015. *Best of Enemies: Buckley vs. Vidal.* Directed by Robert Gordon and Morgan Neville. DVD. 2015. New York: Magnolia Home Entertainment.

Goudsouzian, Adam. 2004. *Sidney Poitier: Man, Actor, Icon.* Durham, N.C.: University of North Carolina Press.

Gould, Jack. 1953. "Television in Review." *New York Times,* August 14, 1953.

Gracyk, Theodore. 2001. *I Wanna Be Me: Rock Music and The Politics of Identity.* Philadelphia: Temple University Press.

Guild, Hazel. 1957. "Johnnie Ray on Presley: Giving Record Industry Greatest Shot-in-the Arm." *Variety,* August 21, 1957, 49.

Guralnick, Peter. 2005. *Dream Boogie: The Triumph of Sam Cooke.* New York: Little, Brown.

Hadleigh, Boze. 1997. *Sing Out! Gays and Lesbians in the Music World.* New York: Barricade.

Hajdu, David. 1996. *Lush Life: A Biography of Billy Strayhorn.* New York: North Point.

Hamilton, Marybeth. 1998. "Sexual Politics and African-American Music; or, Placing Little Richard in History." *History Workshop Journal* no. 46, 160–76.

Harris, Keith M. 2006. *Boys, Boyz, Bois: An Ethics of Black Masculinity in Film and Popular Media.* New York: Routledge.

Hawkins, Stan. 2007. "[Un]Justified: Gestures of Straight-Talk in Justin Timberlake's Songs." In *Oh Boy! Masculinities and Popular Music,* edited by Freya Jarman-Ivens, 197–212. New York: Routledge.

Hawkins, Stan, and Sarah Niblock. 2011. *Prince: The Making of a Pop Music Phenomenon.* Surrey, U.K.: Ashgate.

Hayes, Alfred. 1957. *Island in the Sun.* Directed by Robert Rossen. DVD. 2006. Los Angeles: 20th Century Fox.

Haygood, Wil. 2003. *In Black and White: The Life of Sammy Davis Jr.* New York: Knopf.

Hayward, Philip. 1999. *Widening the Horizon: Exoticism in Post-War Popular Music.* Bloomington, Ind.: Libbey.

Header, Gilbert. 1957. "When Marlon Brando and Johnnie Ray Flipped for That Paris Playgirl." *Uncensored,* July 1957, 28.

Heckman, Don. 1972. "Little Richard and Lloyd Price Star in a Revival of '50's Rock." *New York Times,* June 4, 1972.

Heilbut, Anthony. 2012. *The Fan Who Knew Too Much: Aretha Franklin, the Rise of the Soap Opera, Children of the Gospel Church, and Other Meditations.* New York: Knopf.

Herr, Cheryl. 2009. "Roll-Over-Beethoven: Johnnie Ray in Context." *Popular Music* 28 (3): 323–40.

Hersch, Fred. 2017. *Good Things Happen Slowly: A Life In and Out of Jazz.* New York: Crown Archetype.

Hevey, David. 1992. *The Creatures Time Forgot: Photography and Disability Imagery.* London: Routledge.

Higginbotham, Evelyn Brooks. 1993. *Righteous Discontent: The Women's Movement in the Black Baptist Church, 1880–1920*. Cambridge, Mass.: Harvard University Press.

Hirshman, Linda. 2012. *Victory: The Triumphant Gay Revolution*. New York: HarperCollins.

Hofler, Robert. 2005. *The Man Who Invented Rock Hudson: The Pretty Boys and Dirty Deals of Henry Willson*. New York: Carroll and Graf.

"The Homosexual in America." 1966. *Time*, January 21, 1966, 40–41.

Houndblog. 2009. "Billy Wright." *Houndblog*, June 15, 2009. http://thehoundblog .blogspot.com/2009/06/billy-wright.html.

Hubbs, Nadine. 2004. *The Queer Composition of America's Sound: Gay Modernists, American Music, and National Identity*. Berkeley: University of California Press.

Hudson, Rock, and Sara Davidson. 1986. *Rock Hudson: His Story*. New York: Morrow.

Hunter, Calvin. 1957. "What Happened When Johnnie Ray Was Noel Coward's House Guest." *Top Secret*, August, 10 1957.

Hunter, Tab, with Eddie Muller. 2005. *Tab Hunter Confidential: The Making of a Movie Star*. Chapel Hill, N.C.: Algonquin.

Inman, David M. 2006. *Television Variety Shows: Histories and Episode Guides to 57 Programs*. Jefferson, N.C.: McFarland.

Inside. 1957. "Tears, Fears and Too Many Beers." *Inside*, November 1957, 18.

Jahn, Mike. 1969. "Little Richard Rouses Crowd at Central Park Rock Concert." *New York Times*, August 7, 1969.

———. 1970. "Rock Revival Show of '50's Fills Garden With 20,000 Fans." *New York Times*, November 1, 1970.

Jefferson, Margo. 2006. *On Michael Jackson*. New York: Pantheon.

Jet. 1953. "Can Science Eliminate the Third Sex?" *Jet*, January 22, 1953, 46–50.

———. 1954a. "Women Who Pass for Men." *Jet*, January 28, 1954, 22–24.

———. 1954b. "Are Homosexuals Becoming Respectable?" *Jet*, April 15, 1954, 26–28.

Johnson, David K. 2004. *The Lavender Scare: The Cold War Persecution of Gays and Lesbians in the Federal Government*. Chicago: University of Chicago Press.

Julien, Isaac, and Kobena Mercer. 1991. "True Confessions: A Discourse on Images of Black Male Sexuality." In *Brother to Brother: New Writings by Black Gay Men*, edited by Essex Hemphill, 167–73. Conceived by Joseph Beam. Boston: Alyson.

Kakutani, Michiko. 1984. "Why These Pop Singers Have Risen to Stardom." *New York Times*, September 2, 1984.

Kauffmann, Stanley. 1966a. "Homosexual Drama and Its Disguises." *New York Times*, January 23, 1966.

———. 1966b. "On the Acceptability of the Homosexual." *New York Times*, February 6, 1966.

———. 2007. "Gay Playwrights." *New York Times*, November 25, 2007. https://www .nytimes.com/2007/11/25/books/review/Letters-t-2.html.

Keepnews, Peter. 2014. "Jimmy Scott, 88, Singer Whose Star Rose Late, Dies." *New York Times*, June 14, 2014.

Kent, Robert E. 1956. *Don't Knock the Rock*. DVD. Directed by Fred F. Sears. 2007. New York: Sony.

Kerby, Bill, and Daniel Tiplitz. 2000. *Little Richard*. Directed by Robert Townsend. Los Angeles: NBC.

Kimmel, Michael. 1996. *Manhood in America: A Cultural History*. New York: Free Press.

———. 2012. *Manhood in America: A Cultural History*. 3rd ed. New York: Oxford University Press.

King, Jason. 2001. "Any Love: Silence, Theft, and Rumor in the Work of Luther Vandross." In *The Greatest Taboo: Homosexuality in Black Communities*, edited by Delroy Constantine-Simms, 290–315. Los Angeles: Alyson.

KingCake. 2013. "Billy Wright—The Complete Billy Wright—WAY before His Time!" *Chitlins, Catfish and Deep Southern Soul*, June 6, 2013. http://deepsouthernsoul .blogspot.com/2013/06/billy-wright-complete-billy-wright-way.html.

Kinsey, Alfred C., Wardell Pomeroy, and Clyde E. Martin. 1948. *Sexual Behavior in the Human Male*. Philadelphia: Saunders.

Kirby, David. 2009. *Little Richard: The Birth of Rock 'n' Roll*. New York: Continuum.

Kirk, Kris. 1999. *A Boy Called Mary: Kris Kirk's Greatest Hits*. Edited by Richard Smith. Brighton: Millivres.

Klinger, Barbara. 1994. *Melodrama and Meaning: History, Culture and the Films of Douglas Sirk*. Bloomington: Indiana University Press.

Knadler, Stephen. 2002. *Fugitive Race: Minority Writers Resisting Whiteness*. Jackson: University Press of Mississippi.

Knopper, Steve. 2015. *MJ: The Genius of Michael Jackson*. New York: Scribner.

Koestenbaum, Wayne. 1993. *The Queen's Throat: Opera, Homosexuality, and the Mystery of Desire*. New York: Vintage.

Kopelson, Kevin. 1996. *Beethoven's Kiss: Pianism, Perversion, and the Mastery of Desire*. Stanford, Calif.: Stanford University Press.

Kort, Michelle. 2002. *Soul Picnic: The Music and Passion of Laura Nyro*. New York: Dunne/St. Martin's.

Kristeva, Julia. 1982. *Powers of Horror*. New York: Columbia University Press.

LaGravenese, Richard. 2013. *Behind the Candelabra*. DVD. Directed by Steven Soderbergh. New York: HBO.

Lait, Jack, and Lee Mortimer. 1948. *New York: Confidential! The Big City after Dark*. New York: Dell.

———. 1950. *Chicago Confidential: The Lowdown on the Big Town*. New York: Crown.

———. 1951. *Washington Confidential: The Lowdown on the Big Town*. New York: Crown.

———. 1952. *U.S.A. Confidential*. New York: Crown.

Lauterbach, Preston. 2011. *The Chitlin' Circuit and the Road to Rock 'n' Roll*. New York: Norton, 2011.

Lawrence, Amy. 2010. *The Passion of Montgomery Clift*. Berkeley: University of California Press.

Leeming, David. 1994. *James Baldwin: A Biography*. New York: Knopf.

Liberace. 1954a. *Liberace: Complete Life Story*. New York: Ideal.

———. 1954b. "The Girl I'll Marry." *TV Star Parade*, February 1954, 46, 47, 68, 69.

———. 1970. *Liberace Cooks! Recipes from His Seven Dining Rooms*. New York: Doubleday.

———. 1973. *Liberace: An Autobiography*. London: Allen.

———. 1978. *Leapin' Lizards, It's Liberace!* Directed by Tony Chamoli. DVD. 2012. Phoenix: 101 Distribution.

———. 1981. *The Liberace Show*. A show program, London Palladium. London: Scoop.

———. 1986. *The Wonderful, Private World of Liberace*. New York: Harper and Row.

———. 2002. *The Legendary Liberace*. Directed by JoAnn Young and Jim Scalem. VHS. Orland Park, Ill.: MPI Home Video.

"Liberace Plays; Tells Jokes, Too." 1953. *New York Times*, September 26, 1953.

Life. 1950. "Mr. B." *Life*, April 24, 1950, 101–2, 104.

Life. 1952. "Johnnie Ray Sings and Sobs His Way to a Quick Fortune." *Life*, March 24, 1952, 99–102.

Lipsitz, George. 1990. *Time Passages: Collective Memory and American Popular Culture*. Minneapolis: University of Minnesota Press.

Little Richard, and Tanya Tucker. 1994. "Little Richard & Tanya Tucker—Somethin' Else." Posted by RememberEddieCochran. https://www.youtube.com/watch?v=7swbqJUdR9g.

Los Angeles Times. 1966. "Liberace Spruces Up for Concerts." *Los Angeles Times*, January 26, 1966.

Loughery, John. 1998. *The Other Side of Silence: Men's Lives and Gay Identities; A Twentieth-Century History*. New York: Holt.

Love, Heather. 2007. *Feeling Backward: Loss and the Politics of Queer History*. Cambridge, Mass.: Harvard University Press.

MacMinn, Aleene. 1965. "25 Candles Mark Return of Liberace." *Los Angeles Times*, March 28, 1965.

Mallon, Thomas. 2007. "The Homintern." *New York Times*, November 11, 2007. http://www.nytimes.com/2007/11/11/books/review/Mallon-t.html.

Marsh, Dave. 1985. *Trapped: Michael Jackson and the Crossover Dream*. Toronto: Bantam.

Martin, Joe. 1952a. "Case History II: Many Fingers Dip into Ray Pie; Few Get Cuts." *Billboard*, July 12, 1952, 19, 45.

———. 1952b. "Case History III: Many Ventures Keep Ray's Coffers Filled." *Billboard*, July 19, 1952, 18, 21.

———. 1952c. "Case History IV: Ray Credits those Who Helped Him Up." *Billboard*, July 16, 1952, 16, 19.

Martin, Linda, and Kerry Segrave. 1993. *Anti-Rock: The Opposition to Rock 'n' Roll*. New York: Da Capo.

Mason, Bert. 1955. "Why the Babes Still Cry for Johnnie Ray." *Uncensored*, December 1955, 48.

May, Elaine Tyler. 1999. *Homeward Bound: American Families in the Cold War Era*. 2nd ed. New York, Basic.

Mazursky, Paul, and Leon Capetanos. 1986. *Down and Out in Beverly Hills*. DVD. Directed by Paul Mazursky. 2002. Los Angeles: Buena Vista.

MCA Records. 1994. "Little Richard and Tanya Tucker-Somethin' Else." https://www.youtube.com/watch?v=7swbqJUdR9g.

MCA Soundtracks. 1986. "Little Richard—Great Gosh A'mighty." https://www.youtube.com/watch?v=SoEB4Ppsg4Q.

McClary, Susan. 2013. "Soprano Masculinities." In *Masculinity in Opera: Gender, History, and New Musicology*, edited by Philip Purvis, 33–50. New York: Routledge.

McCracken, Allison. 2015. *Real Men Don't Sing: Crooning in American Culture*. Durham, N.C.: Duke University Press.

McGarry, Molly, and Fred Wasserman, eds. 1998. *Becoming Visible: An Illustrated History of Lesbian and Gay Life in Twentieth-Century America*. New York: Penguin.

McGee, David. 1992. "Little Richard." In *Rolling Stone Album Guide*, edited by Anthony Decurtis and James Henke, 428–29. New York: Random House.

McGill, Lisa Diane. 2005. *Constructing Black Selves: Caribbean American Narratives and the Second Generation*. New York: New York University Press.

McKay, George. 2013. *Shakin' All Over: Popular Music and Disability*. Ann Arbor: University of Michigan Press.

Mercer, John. 2015. *Rock Hudson*. London: BFI.

Miller, D. A. 1988. *The Novel and the Police*. Berkeley: University of California Press.

———. 1998. *Place for Us: Essay on the Broadway Musical*. Cambridge, Mass.: Harvard University Press.

Miller, James. 1999. *Flowers in the Dustbin: The Rise of Rock and Roll, 1947–1977*. New York: Simon and Schuster.

Miller, Monica L. 2009. *Slaves to Fashion: Black Dandyism and the Styling of Black Diasporic Identity*. Durham, N.C.: Duke University Press.

Mitchell, Carmen. 2001. "Creations of Fantasies/Constructions of Identities: The Oppositional Lives of Gladys Bentley." In *The Greatest Taboo: Homosexuality in Black Communities*, edited by Delroy Constantine-Simms, 211–25. Los Angeles: Alyson.

Morris, James R. 1984. *American Popular Song: Six Decades of Songwriters and Singers*. Washington, D.C.: Smithsonian Institution Press.

Morris, Wesley. 2016. Interview with Ari Shapiro. *All Things Considered*. "On the Men Who Rattled Pop's Gender Rules—And What It Means to Lose Them Now." *National Public Radio*, December 30, 2016. http://www.npr.org/2016/12/30/507575982/on-the-men-who-rattled-pops-gender-rules-and-what-it-means-to-lose-them-now.

Murph, John. 2010. "Rhapsody in Rainbow: Jazz and the Queer Aesthetic." *Jazztimes.com*, December 1, 2010. https://jazztimes.com/features/rhapsody-in-rainbow-jazz-and-the-queer-aesthetic.

NBC. 1982. "Little Richard on *Late Night [with David Letterman]*, May 4, 1982." Posted by Don Giller. https://www.youtube.com/watch?v=bqxbyZDoFnk (accessed May 27, 2017).

Neal, Mark Anthony. 1999. *What the Music Said: Black Popular Music and Black Public Culture*. New York: Routledge.

———. 2007. "Race Man: Does Denzel Always Have to Represent." *Washington Post*, December 23, 2007.

Nealon, Christopher. 2001. *Foundlings: Lesbian and Gay Historical Emotion before Stonewall*. Durham, N.C.: Duke University Press.

Newsweek. 1969. "Policing the Third Sex." *Newsweek*, October 27, 1969, 76, 89.

New York Times. 1968. "Little Richard Draws Crowd in Central Park." *New York Times*, August 19, 1968, 44.

On the QT. 1956. "Why Johnnie Ray Likes to Go in Drag." *On the Q.T.*, January 1956, 36.

Oppenheimer, Jerry, and Jack Vitek. 1986. *Idol: Rock Hudson The True Story of an American Film Hero*. New York: Villard.

Otis, Johnny. 1968/2009. *Listen to the Lambs*. 1968. Minneapolis: University of Minnesota Press.

Palmer, Robert. 1981. "Is Prince Leading Music to a True Biracism?" *New York Times*, December 2, 1981.

———. 1995. *Rock & Roll: An Unruly History*. New York: Harmony.

Parini, Jay. 2015. *Empire of Self: A Life of Gore Vidal*. New York: Doubleday.

Parker, Marvin. 1955. "Sonja Henie: All This and Liberace, Too." *Uncensored*, September 1955, 40–42, 72–73.

Patton, Cindy. 1994. "Foreword." In *Lavender Culture*, edited by Karla Jay and Allen Young, ix–xxviii. New edition. New York: New York University Press.

Pennabaker, D. A. 1969. *Keep on Rockin'*. Directed by P. A. Pennabaker. DVD. 1998. Long Beach, Calif.: Geneon.

Peraino, Judith. 2005. *Listening to the Sirens: Musical Technologies of Queer Identity from Homer to Hedwig*. Berkeley: University of California Press.

Petrucelli, Alan. 1982. "Celebrity Q&A." *Us Weekly*, June 22, 1982, 58–60.

Phelan, Shane. 2001. *Sexual Strangers: Gays, Lesbians, and Dilemmas of Citizenship*. Philadelphia: Temple University Press.

Plotnik, Gene. 1954. "Liberace Keys Pack Madison Square Garden." *Billboard*, June 5, 1954, 1, 10.

Private Lives. 1955. "Are Liberace's Romances for Real?" *Private Lives*, March 1955, 24–28.

Pugh, Tison. 2014. *Truman Capote: A Literary Life at the Movies*. Athens: University of Georgia Press.

Pyron, Darden Asbury. 2000. *Liberace: An American Boy*. Chicago: University of Chicago Press.

Raskin, Jonah. 2004. *American Scream: Allen Ginsberg's Howl and the Making of the Beat Generation*. Berkeley: University of California Press.

Rave. 1954. "Liberace: Don't Call Him Mister." *Rave*, August 1954, 4–13.

———. 1955. "Whose Torch Melted the Ice Queen?" *Rave*, August 8, 1955, 28–31.

Ravens, Simon. 2014. *The Supernatural Voice: A History of High Male Singing*. Woodbridge, Suffolk: The Boydell Press.

Ray, Johnnie. 1953. "Negroes Taught Me to Sing: Famous 'Cry' Crooner Tells What Blues Taught Him." *Ebony*, March 3, 1953, 48, 53.

Raymond, Emilie. 2015a. "Sammy Davis Jr.: Public Image and Politics." *Cultural History* 4 (1): 42–63.

———. 2015b. *Stars for Freedom: Hollywood, Black Celebrities and the Civil Rights Movement*. Seattle: University of Washington Press.

Reilly, Peter. 1981. Review of *Johnny Mathis: The First 25 Years—The Silver Anniversary Album*. *Stereo Review*, October 1981, 72.

Renee, Lauren. 1974. "Johnny Mathis: 'I Always Sang For My Father.'" *Encore*, June 1974, 30–32.

Rich, Adrienne. 1993. "Compulsory Heterosexuality and Lesbian Existence." In *The Lesbian and Gay Studies Reader*, edited by Henry Abelove, Michèle Aina Barale, and David M. Halperin, 227–54. New York: Routledge.

Richardson, Niall. 2010. *Transgressive Bodies: Representations in Film and Popular Culture*. Surrey, U.K.: Ashgate.

Ritz, David. 2002. *Faith in Time: The Life of Jimmy Scott*. New York: Da Capo.

Roberts, Clifford. 1955. *The Complete Life of Johnnie Ray*. New York: Pocket Magazines.

Robinson, Louie. 1965a. "Johnny Mathis: Millionaire With Problems." *Ebony*, March 1965, 99–104.

———. 1965b. "Nat King Cole: Death Stills Voice of World-Famed Master Balladeer at Age 45." *Ebony*, April 1965, 123–34.

———. 1976. "Johnny Mathis: His Own Man Now; Popular Vocalist Learns to Manage His Own Affairs." *Ebony*, March 1976, 44–52.

Rockwell, John. 1987. "Tracing Little Richard to the Source." *New York Times*, February 1, 1987.

Rosenberg, Alyssa. 2016. "Mourning Prince and David Bowie, Who Showed There's No One Right Way to Be a Man." *Washington Post*, April 21, 2016. https://www.washingtonpost.com/news/act-four/wp/2016/04/21/mourning-prince-and-david-bowie-who-showed-theres-no-one-right-way-to-be-a-man/?utm_term=.f874b0f5e7f5.

Ross, Marlon. 2000. "Some Glances at the Black Fag: Race, Same-Sex Desire, and Cultural Belonging." In *African-American Literary Theory: A Reader*, edited by Winston Napier, 498–522. New York: New York University Press.

———. 2004. *Manning the Race: Reforming Black Men in the Jim Crow Era*. New York: New York University Press.

———. 2005. "Beyond the Closet as Raceless Paradigm." In *Black Queer Studies: A Critical Anthology*, edited by E. Patrick Johnson and Mae G. Henderson, 161–89. Durham, N.C.: Duke University Press.

Royster, Francesa T. 2013. *Sounding Like a No-No: Queer Sounds and Eccentric Acts in the Post-Soul Era*. Ann Arbor: University of Michigan Press.

Russo, Vito. 1987. *The Celluloid Closet: Homosexuality in the Movies*. Rev. ed. New York: Harper and Row.

Sanneh, Kelefa. 2007. "The Rap against Rockism." In *The Rock History Reader*, edited by Theo Cateforis, 351–54. New York: Routledge.

Schott, Webster. 1967. "Civil Rights and the Homosexual: A 4-Million Minority Asks for Equal Rights." *New York Times Magazine,* November 12, 1967, 44–72.

Schweighofer, Katherine. 2016. "Rethinking the Closet: Queer Life in Rural Geographies." In *Queering the Countryside: New Frontiers in Rural Queer Studies,* edited by Mary L. Gray, Colin R. Johnson, and Brian J. Gilley, 223–43. New York: New York University Press.

Scott, Henry E. 2010. *Shocking Story: The Rise and Fall of Confidential, "America's Most Scandalous Magazine."* New York: Pantheon.

Sedgwick, Eve Kosofsky. 1990. *Epistemology of the Closet.* Berkeley: University of California Press.

———. 1993. "Queer Performativity: Henry James's *The Art of the Novel.*" *Gay and Lesbian Quarterly* 1 (1): 1–16.

Selvin, Joel, and Kevin Burke. 1999. "Little Richard." In *Musichound Rock: The Essential Album Guide,* edited by Gary Graff and Daniel Durchholz, 677–78. Detroit: Visible Ink.

Sensation. 1954. "Liberace and His Women." *Sensation,* August 1954, 58–62.

Seymour, Craig. 2004. *Luther: The Life and Longing of Luther Vandross.* New York: HarperCollins.

Sherry, Michael. 2007. *Gay Artists in Modern American Culture: An Imagined Conspiracy.* Chapel Hill: University of North Carolina Press.

Shindler, Merrill. 1978. "Mathis: Too Little Just in Time." *Us Weekly,* July 11, 1978, 69, 71.

Short, Bobby. 1992. Foreword to *Black and Blue: The Life and Lyrics of Andy Razaf,* by Barry Singer, xi–xv. New York: Schirmer.

Short, Bobby, with Robert Mackintosh. 1995. *Bobby Short: The Life and Times of a Saloon Singer.* New York: Clarkson Potter.

Shumway, David R. 1997. "Watching Elvis: The Male Rock Star as Object of the Gaze." In *The Other Fifties: Interrogating Midcentury American Icons,* edited by Joel Foreman, 124–43. Urbana: University of Illinois Press.

Smith, Judith E. 2014. *Becoming Belafonte: Black Artist, Public Radical.* Austin: University of Texas Press.

Smith, R. J. 2012. *The One: The Life and Music of James Brown.* New York: Gotham.

Smyth, Ron, Greg Jacobs, and Henry Rogers. 2003. "Male Voices and Perceived Sexual Orientation: An Experimental and Theoretical Approach." *Language in Society* 32 (3): 329–50.

Soloman, Connie Furr, and Jan Jewett. 2013. "Liberace Extravaganza!" *Theatre Design and Technology* 49, no. 1 (Winter): 34–43.

Starr, Larry, and Christopher Waterman. 2003. *American Popular Music: From Minstrelsy to MTV.* New York: Oxford University Press.

Stephens, Michelle Ann. 2014. *Skin Acts: Psychoanalysis, and the Black Male Performer.* Durham, N.C.: Duke University Press.

Stephens, Vincent. 2005. "Queering the Textures of Rock and Roll History." PhD diss. University of Maryland.

———. 2015. "Open Secrecy: Self-presentation by Queer Male Musicians." In *Masquerade: Essays on Tradition and Innovation Worldwide*, edited by Deborah Bell, 145–55. Jefferson, N.C.: McFarland.

Stone, Christopher. 1976. "Interview: Johnny Mathis." *Advocate*, February 25, 1976, 35–36.

Strachan, Ian Gregory. 2015. "A Blues for Tom: Sidney Poitier's Filmic Sexual Identities." In *Poitier Revisited: Reconsidering a Black Icon in the Obama Age*, edited by Ian Gregory Strachan and Mia Mask, 163–87. New York: Bloomsbury.

Street, Andrew P. 2016. "Bowie, Prince, and George Michael: We've Lost the Icons Who Dared to Do Manhood Differently." *Stuff.Co.NZ*, December 27. http://www.stuff.co.nz/life-style/life/87963808/bowie-prince-george-michael-weve-lost-the-icons-who-dared-to-do-manhood-differently.

Streete, Horton. 1957. "Why Liberace's Theme Song Should Be . . . 'Mad about the Boy.'" *Confidential*, July 1957, 16–21, 59, 60.

Stryker, Susan. 2001. *Queer Pulp: Perverted Passions from the Golden Age of the Paperback*. San Francisco: Chronicle.

Sylvester, Robert. 1952. "Million-Dollar Teardrop." *Saturday Evening Post*, July 26, 1952, 30, 112, 114.

Szatmary, David. 2004. *Rockin' in Time: A Social History of Rock-and-Roll*. 5th ed. Upper Saddle River, N.J.: Pearson/Prentice Hall.

Tashlin, Frank, and Herbert Baker. 1956. *The Girl Can't Help It*. DVD. Directed by Frank Tashlin. 2006. Los Angeles: 20th Century Fox.

Taubman, Howard. 1952. "Cry with Johnnie Ray: His Success May Depend on More than Singing." *New York Times*, April 27, 1952.

———. 1954a. "A Square Looks at a Hotshot." *New York Times*, March 14, 1954.

———. 1954b. "Crooners, Groaners, Shouters and Bleeders." *New York Times Magazine*, November 21, 1954, 26–27, 54–56.

———. 1961. "Not What It Seems." *New York Times*, November 5, 1961.

———. 1963. "Modern Primer." *New York Times*, April 28, 1963.

Taylor, Diana. 2003. *The Archive and The Repertoire: Performing Cultural Memory in the Americas*. Durham, N.C.: Duke University Press.

Terkel, Studs. 1989. "An Interview with James Baldwin." In *Conversations with James Baldwin*, edited by Fred L. Stanley and Louis H. Pratt, 2–23. Jackson: University of Mississippi Press.

Thomas, Bob. 1987. *Liberace: The True Story*. New York: St. Martin's.

Thomas, Kendall. 1998. "'Ain't Nothin' Like the Real Thing': Black Masculinity, Gay Sexuality, and the Jargon of Authenticity." In *The House that Race Built*, edited by Wahneema Lubiano, 116–35. New York: Vintage.

Thomson, Rosemarie Garland. 1997. *Extraordinary Bodies: Figuring Physical Disability in American Culture and Literature*. New York: Columbia University Press.

Thorson, Scott. 1982. "Liberace Bombshell—Boyfriend Tells All about Their Six-Year Romance." *National Enquirer*, November 2, 1982, 48–51.

Thorson, Scott, with Alex Thorleifson. 1998/2013. *Behind the Candelabra: My Life with Liberace*. Old Saybrook, Conn.: Tantor Media, 2013.

Tichi, Cecelia. 1991. *Electronic Hearth: Creating an American Television Culture*. New York: Oxford University Press.

Time. 1963. "Races: Freedom—Now." *Time*, May 17, 1963, 26–30.

Tip Off. 1956. "Why the Roman Rave Kicked Out Johnnie Ray." *Tip Off*, October 1956, 12.

Touré. 2013. *I Would Die 4 U: Why Prince Became an Icon*. New York: Atria.

Tremaine, Sylvia. 1956. "This Month's Candidate for the Pit . . . Liberace: The Ham That Was Overdone." *Whisper*, June 1956, 26, 27, 52, 63, 65.

TV Guide. 1954. "When Will Liberace Marry?" *TV Guide*, September 18, 1954.

Valentine, Penny, and Vicki Wickham. 2001. *Dancing with Demons: The Authorized Biography of Dusty Springfield*. New York: St. Martin's.

Van den Oever, Roel. 2012. *Mama's Boy: Momism and Homophobia in Postwar American Culture*. New York: Palgrave Macmillan.

Variety. 1952. Review of Liberace Concert at Ciro's. *Variety*, January 30, 1952, 52.

———. 1953. "Liberace, Mid-age Bobby-Sox Idol; Mops Up on Pops Concert Route." *Variety*, September 30, 1953, 52.

———. 1955. Review of Liberace Concert at The Riviera. *Variety*, April 27, 1955, 60.

———. 1956. Review of Liberace Concert at Royal Festival Hall. *Variety*, October 10, 1956, 63.

———. 1958. Review of *The Liberace Show*. *Variety*, October 15, 1958.

———. 1961. Review of Johnny Mathis Concert at the Latin Casino. *Variety*, March 8, 1961, 66.

Vidal, Gore. 1948. *The City and the Pillar*. New York: Dutton.

———. 1993. *United States: Essays 1952–1992*. New York: Random House.

———. 1995. *Palimpsest: A Memoir*. New York: Random House.

Vogel, Joseph. 2015. "Freaks in the Reagan Era: James Baldwin, the New Pop Cinema, and the American Ideal of Manhood." *Journal of Popular Culture* 48 (3): 464–86.

Vogel, Shane. 2009. *The Scene of Harlem Cabaret: Race, Sexuality, Performance*. Chicago: University of Chicago Press.

Wallace, Maurice O. 2002. *Constructing the Black Masculine: Identity and Ideality in African American Men's Literature and Culture, 1775–1995*. Durham, N.C.: Duke University Press.

Ward, Brian. 1998. *Just My Soul Responding: Rhythm and Blues, Black Consciousness, and Race Relations*. Berkeley: University of California Press.

Watrous, Peter. 1992. "Back to Basics, Little Richard Is Happy at Last." *New York Times*, December 8, 1992.

Weinstein, Steve. 2005. "The Secret Gay Life of Luther Vandross." *Out*, April 2006, 60–69.

Welch, Paul. 1964. "The 'Gay' World Takes to the City Streets." *Life*, June 26, 1964, 68–74.

Whitburn, Joel. 1973a. *Joel Whitburn's Top LPs 1945–1972*. Menomonee Falls, Wisc.: Record Research.

———. 1973b. *Joel Whitburn's Top Pop Records 1940–1955*. Menomonee Falls, Wisc.: Record Research.

———. 1973c. *Joel Whitburn's Top Rhythm and Blues Records 1949–1971*. Menomonee Falls, Wisc.: Record Research.

———. 2002. *Top Adult Contemporary, 1961–2001*. Menomonee Falls, Wisc.: Record Research.

———. 2006. *The Billboard Albums*. 6th ed. Menomonee Falls, Wisc.: Record Research.

———. 2007. *Top Pop Singles 1955–2006*. Menomonee Falls, Wisc.: Record Research.

———. 2010. *Hot R&B Songs, 1942–2010*. 6th ed. Menomonee Falls, Wisc.: Record Research.

White, Charles. 1984. *The Life and Times of Little Richard: The Quasar of Rock*. New York: Harmony.

Whiteside, Jonny. 1994. *Cry: The Johnnie Ray Story*. New York: Barricade.

Williams, Jay. 1953. "Is It True What They Say about Johnnie Ray?" *Confidential*, April 1953, 37–39, 63–64.

Williams, Rhonda. 1998. "Living at the Crossroads: Explorations in Race, Nationality, Sexuality and Gender." In *The House that Race Built*, edited by Wahneema Lubiano, 136–56. New York: Vintage.

Wilson, James F. 2010. *Bulldaggers, Pansies, and Chocolate Babies: Performance, Race, and Sexuality in the Harlem Renaissance*. Ann Arbor: University of Michigan Press.

Wilson, John S. 1964. "Two Minstrels Blend Mirth and Music: Liberace Builds Show on Self-Mockery." *New York Times*, June 3, 1964, 39.

Wilson, Sloan. 1956. *The Man in the Gray Flannel Suit*. London: Cassell.

Windeler, Robert. 1978. "Happy." *People*, October 23, 1978, 67–68.

Winecoff, Charles. 1996/2006. *Anthony Perkins: Split Image*. New York: Advocate.

Wise, Sue. 1990. "Sexing Elvis." In *On Record: Rock, Pop, and the Written Word*, edited by Simon Frith and Andrew Goodwin, 390–97. New York: Pantheon.

Young, Allen. 1978/1994. "No Longer the Court Jesters." In *Lavender Culture*, edited by Karla Jay and Allen Young, 23–47. New York: New York University Press, 1994.

Zittlau, Andrea. 2012. "Enfreakment and German Medical Collections." In *Exploring the Cultural History of Continental European Freak Shows*, edited by Anna Kérchy and Andrea Zittlau, 150–68. Newcastle upon Tyne, U.K.: Cambridge Scholars.

Discography

Aiken, Clay. 2003. *Measure of a Man*. November 1. Los Angeles: RCA (compact disc).

Coltrane, John, and Johnny Hartman. 1963. *John Coltrane and Johnny Hartman*. March 7. Santa Monica, Calif.: Impulse Records (compact disc).

Esquerita. 1990. *Esquerita! Rockin' the Joint*. Los Angeles: Capitol Records (compact disc).

Jackson, Michael. 1982. *Thriller*. December 25. Los Angeles: Epic Records/CBS (compact disc).

———. 1987. *Bad*. September 26. Los Angeles: Epic Records/CBS (compact disc).

———. 1991. "Black or White." November 23. Los Angeles: Epic Records/CBS (single).

Liberace. 1952. *Liberace at the Piano*. September 12. New York: Columbia Records (LP).

———. 1953. *Liberace By Candlelight*. July 11. New York: Columbia Records (LP).

———. 1954a. *Concertos for You*. January 23. New York: Columbia Records (LP).

———. 1954b. *An Evening with Liberace*. February 6. New York: Columbia Records (LP).

———. 1954c. *Sincerely, Liberace*. July 24. New York: Columbia Records (LP).

Little Richard. 1956a. "Tutti Frutti." January 14. New Orleans: Specialty (single).

———. 1956b. "Long Tall Sally." April 7. New Orleans: Specialty (single).

———. 1956c. "Rip It Up." July 7. New Orleans: Specialty (single).

———. 1958. "Good Golly, Miss Molly." February 10. New Orleans: Specialty (single).

———. 1959. *The King of Gospel Singers: Little Richard*. New York: Mercury Records (LP).

———. 1963. *Little Richard Sings the Gospel*. Los Angeles: MCA Special Products (compact disc).

———. 1970a. "Freedom Blues." May 23. Los Angeles: Reprise Records (single).

———. 1970b. *The Rill Thing*. August. Los Angeles: Reprise Records (LP).

———. 1986a. "Great Gosh A'mighty! (It's a Matter of Time)." March 8. Los Angeles: MCA (single).

———. 1986b. *Lifetime Friend.* Los Angeles: WEA Records (LP).

———. 1989. *It's Real.* New York: Polygram Records (compact disc).

———. 1996. "I Feel Pretty." *The Songs of Westside Story.* February 17. Los Angeles: RCA Victor (compact disc).

Little Richard and Tanya Tucker. 1994. "Somethin' Else." *Rhythm, Country and Blues.* March 19. Los Angeles: MCA (compact disc).

Mathis, Johnny. 1956. *Johnny Mathis: A New Sound in Popular Song.* July 16. New York: Columbia Records (compact disc).

———. 1958. *Johnny's Greatest Hits.* April 14. New York: Columbia Records (compact disc).

———. 1959. *Heavenly.* April 14. New York: Columbia Records (compact disc).

———. 1963. *Johnny.* August 24. New York: Columbia Records (compact disc).

———. 1964/2012. *The Wonderful World of Make Believe.* July 25. Los Angeles: Mercury Records (compact disc; reissued in 2012).

———. 1981. *The First 25 Years—The Silver Anniversary Album.* July 25. New York: Columbia Records (compact disc).

———. 1993. "Misty." *The Music of Johnny Mathis: A Personal Collection.* October 5. New York: Columbia/Legacy (compact disc).

Mathis, Johnny, with Deniece Williams. 1978. *That's What Friends Are For.* July 29. New York: Columbia Records.

Prince. 1979. *Prince.* November 17. Los Angeles: Warner Bros. Records (compact disc).

———. 1980. *Dirty Mind.* November 8. Los Angeles: Warner Bros. Records (compact disc).

———. 1984. *Purple Rain.* July 14. Los Angeles: Warner Bros. Records (compact disc).

Ray, Johnnie. 1951. "Cry." October 1951. New York: Columbia Records, Okeh Records (single).

———. 1991. *Johnnie Ray: 16 Most Requested Songs.* September 3. New York: Columbia Records.

———. 1997. *High Drama: The Real Johnnie Ray.* October 21. New York: Columbia Records (compact disc).

———. 1999. *'Til Morning* (1958)/*A Sinner Am I* (1959). June 7. London: Sony Music UK (compact disc).

———. 2002a. *The Big Beat* (1957)/*I Cry for You* (1955). March 19. New York: Sony Music Entertainment Inc/Collectables Records (compact disc).

———. 2002b. *Johnnie Ray* (1952)/*On the Trail* (1959). March 19. New York: Sony Music Entertainment Inc/Collectables Records (compact disc).

———. 2003. *Hysteria! The Singles Collection.* London: Sony Music UK (compact disc).

Index

VINCENT L. STEPHENS is the director of the Popel Shaw Center for Race & Ethnicity and a contributing faculty member in music at Dickinson College. He is a coeditor of *Postracial America? An Interdisciplinary Study.*

NEW PERSPECTIVES ON GENDER IN MUSIC

The University of Illinois Press
is a founding member of the
Association of University Presses.

———————————————

Composed in 10.5/13 Adobe Minion Pro
with Futura display
by Jim Proefrock
at the University of Illinois Press
Cover designed by Jim Proefrock
Cover image by Edi Welshons

University of Illinois Press
1325 South Oak Street
Champaign, IL 61820-6903
www.press.uillinois.edu